The Food and Drink
of Seattle

Big City Food Biographies Series

Series Editor
Ken Albala, University of the Pacific, kalbala@pacific.edu

Food helps define the cultural identity of cities in much the same way as the distinctive architecture and famous personalities. Great cities have one-of-a-kind food cultures, offering the essence of the multitudes who have immigrated there and shaped foodways through time. The **Big City Food Biographies** series focuses on those metropolises celebrated as culinary destinations, with their iconic dishes, ethnic neighborhoods, markets, restaurants, and chefs. Guidebooks to cities abound, but these are real biographies that will satisfy readers' desire to know the full food culture of a city. Each narrative volume, devoted to a different city, explains the history, the natural resources, and the people that make that city's food culture unique. Each biography also looks at the markets, historic restaurants, signature dishes, and great cookbooks that are part of the city's gastronomic make-up.

Books in the Series

New Orleans: A Food Biography, by Elizabeth M. Williams

San Francisco: A Food Biography, by Erica J. Peters

New York City: A Food Biography, by Andrew F. Smith

Portland: A Food Biography, by Heather Arndt Anderson

Chicago: A Food Biography, by Daniel R. Block and Howard B. Rosing

Kansas City: A Food Biography, by Andrea L. Broomfield

Rio de Janeiro: A Food Biography, by Marcia Zoladz

Madrid: A Culinary History, by Maria Paz Moreno

The Food and Drink of Sydney: A History, by Heather Hunwick

A History of the Food of Paris: From Roast Mammoth to Steak Frites, by Jim Chevallier

The Food and Drink of Seattle: From Wild Salmon to Craft Beer, by Judith H. Dern, with Deborah Ashin

The Food and Drink
of Seattle

From Wild Salmon to Craft Beer

Judith H. Dern
with
Deborah Ashin

ROWMAN & LITTLEFIELD
Lanham • Boulder • New York • London

Published by Rowman & Littlefield
A wholly owned subsidiary of The Rowman & Littlefield Publishing Group, Inc.
4501 Forbes Boulevard, Suite 200, Lanham, Maryland 20706
www.rowman.com

Unit A, Whitacre Mews, 26-34 Stannary Street, London SE11 4AB

British Library Cataloguing in Publication Information Available

Library of Congress Cataloging-in-Publication Data
Names: Dern, Judith H., author. | Ashin, Deborah, contributor.
Title: The food and drink of Seattle : from wild salmon to craft beer /
    Judith H. Dern with contributions by Deborah Ashin.
Description: Lanham : Rowman & Littlefield, [2018] | Series: Big city food
    biographies series | Includes bibliographical references and index.
Identifiers: LCCN 2017059801 (print) | LCCN 2018003236 (ebook) |
    ISBN 9781442259775 (electronic) | ISBN 9781442259768 (cloth : alk. paper)
Subjects: LCSH: Cooking—Washington—Seattle Region—History. | Cooking,
    American—Pacific Northwest style.
Classification: LCC TX360.U63 (ebook) | LCC TX360.U63 S43 2018 (print) |
    DDC 641.59797772—dc23
LC record available at https://lccn.loc.gov/2017059801

∞™ The paper used in this publication meets the minimum requirements of American National Standard for Information Sciences—Permanence of Paper for Printed Library Materials, ANSI/NISO Z39.48-1992.

Printed in the United States of America

Contents

Big City Food Biographies— Series Foreword

Cities are rather like living organisms. There are nerve centers, circulatory systems, structures that hold them together, and of course conduits through which food enters and waste leaves the city. Each city also has its own unique personality, based mostly on the people who live there but also on the physical layout, the habits of interaction, and the places where people meet to eat and drink. More than any other factor, it seems that food is used to define the identity of so many cities. Simply say any of the following words and a particular place immediately leaps to mind: bagel, cheesesteak, muffuletta, "chowda," and cioppino. Natives, of course, have many more associations—their favorite restaurants and markets, bakeries and donut shops, pizza parlors, and hot dog stands. Even the restaurants seem to have their own unique vibe wherever you go. Some cities boast great steakhouses or barbecue pits; others, their ethnic enclaves and more elusive specialties like Frito pie in Santa Fe, Cincinnati chili, and the Chicago deep dish pizza. Tourists might find snippets of information about such hidden gems in guidebooks; the inveterate flaneur naturally seeks them out personally. For the rest of us, this is practically unchartered territory.

These urban food biographies are meant to be not guidebooks but rather real biographies, explaining the urban infrastructure, the natural resources that make each city unique, and most importantly the history, people, and neighborhoods. Each volume is meant to introduce you to the city or reacquaint you with an old friend in ways you may never have considered. Each biography also looks at the historic restaurants, signature dishes, and great cookbooks that reflect each city's unique gastronomic makeup.

These food biographies also come at a crucial juncture in our culinary history as a people. Not only do chain restaurants and fast food threaten the existence of our gastronomic heritage, but also we are increasingly mobile as a people, losing our deep connections to place and the cooking that happens in cities over the generations with a rooted population. Moreover, signature dishes associated with individual cities become popularized and bastardized and are often in danger of becoming caricatures of themselves. Ersatz versions of so many classics, catering to the lowest common denominator of taste, are now available throughout the country. Our gastronomic sensibilities are in danger of becoming entirely homogenized. The intent here is not, however, to simply stop the clock or make museum pieces of regional cuisines. Cooking must and will evolve, but understanding the history of each city's food will help us make better choices, will make us more discerning customers, and perhaps will make us more respectful of the wonderful variety that exists across our great nation.

Ken Albala
University of the Pacific
Series Editor

Preface

What will you eat when you move to Seattle? My friends in San Francisco kept asking this question before I moved north in 1994. We shared a fascination with food in all its forms, loved to cook and host dinner parties, appreciating these occasions for their conviviality (and terrific food!), and were earning our livings as professionals in the food world. Add to this that San Francisco and the Bay Area in the 1980s and 1990s were vibrant hotbeds cultivating an American food revolution led by restaurateurs and chefs such as Alice Waters, Jeremiah Tower, Mark Miller, Deborah Madison, Barbara Tropp, Judy Rogers, and others. Based on the farm-to-table awakening, local was a keystone of the concept. Primarily chef-driven in the early days, new restaurants were exploding to demonstrate the deliciousness of the idea. (Personal food history factoid: I ate at the French Laundry *before* Chef Thomas Keller arrived, and it was memorable even then.) Needless to say, for a passionate food person I was in the right place at the right time.

The farm-to-table movement linked to my own food awareness from growing up in rural upstate New York across from a dairy farm and having a father who planted a large backyard garden every spring. I knew when tomatoes were truly ripe, learned to shell peas quickly, and picked blackberries in the brush beyond the lawn surrounding my family's new house. The cows walked up and down in the pasture across the road twice a day. Baking brownies and pies made people happy.

As things turned out, Dahlia Lounge and blackberries were my first connection to Seattle's local food potential. My move north happened after flying in and out of SeaTac Airport on a sunny day en route to Copenhagen, when the light on the water and surrounding islands and mountains reminded me of my year living in Scandinavia. I was also ready for a change of surroundings, and Seattle seemed to offer everything—even though I knew no one there. But was there any reason not to move? I couldn't come up with one. I had visited the city five times before finally moving, and each time it proved more intriguing. There was lunch at Lowell's in Pike Place Market, the fish and chips even more delicious served with a stunning view of the Olympics, and a classic diner-style brunch at Twin T-Ps before it caught fire. Who wouldn't be smitten with the fun, funky parts of Seattle's food scene? Meeting a new friend for lunch at Dahlia Lounge, which was justly earning accolades for Chef Tom Douglas, introduced me to one chef's cooking style celebrating Seattle's local ingredients. The farm-to-table movement had come north and was earning attention here, too.

Finally arriving in the warmth of early August, I camped out with the welcoming aunt of my California cousin's husband, Jeanne Bien, on the west side of Mercer Island. While exploring my new surroundings, I discovered the blackberries. A jungle of vines grew up and down the road near her home, and the berries were huge and sweet. Perfect for Christmas present jam-making! Aunt Jeanne was generous in letting me use her kitchen for my project. She also introduced me to Copper River salmon the next spring when we met in downtown Seattle at the Metropolitan Grill. One taste, and I was smitten forever. I had no idea salmon could taste so blissfully wonderful.

Of course, there was Pike Place Market with all its food glories to discover. For a food person arriving in Seattle, the only word to use for the market is "awesome." Eventually, living in a tiny rental house on the west side of Queen Anne made zipping downtown by bus or car to tour the market an easy excursion. It was also the first place I took curious Bay Area friends when they came to visit. I heard the word "awesome" a lot.

Add my involvement with Seattle's Nordic community, and another food culture came to life to renew my Scandinavian connections. Swedish pancake breakfasts, salmon dinners, open-face sandwiches, Carlsberg beer readily available in local grocery stores, IKEA opening down the road in 1995, and the Norwegian American Chamber of Commerce's festive Julbord at the Seattle Golf Club all exposed me to living food traditions that I hadn't experienced in San Francisco. As a volunteer at the Nordic Museum's summer Viking Days event, I finally mastered making *æbleskiver*, round doughy balls sometimes called the Danish version of doughnuts, in seasoned cast iron skillets. Life in the Pacific Northwest was decidedly sweet. It became even sweeter when I had a reason to cut back on my independent writing assignments and accepted a position at Allrecipes.com in 2007.

When Deborah Ashin, a fellow food-writing friend, called me in 2015 and proposed working together on a book delving into Seattle's culinary history, in its many dimensions, I had to say yes. How could I not after living in the midst of Seattle's own food revolution and discovering the bounty of local foods from nearby farms at Pike Place Market and the Ballard and Magnolia farmers' markets and the frigid and abundant waters of Alaska—after driving to the Skagit Valley in tulip and apple seasons, discovering IPAs and aquavit in Ballard, and annually picking blackberries at my secret spot on Mercer Island? This city's food scene has flourished in the past two decades as locals and newcomers alike discover and celebrate the abundance and accessibility of local ingredients—so many from fields, farms, and the sea so nearby.

Deborah laid the groundwork for this book's birth by writing an enthusiastic, thorough proposal and having it accepted by the publisher before I came on board. I owe her a huge thank-you for that effort because I know it didn't happen overnight. Alas, Deborah encountered other life events that pulled her away from collaborating on the book, but I sensed that she was hovering over my shoulder as I typed.

I also must thank several persons key to my completing this project. Two were literally looking over my shoulder after I typed: my splendid, alert editors and proofreaders, Robin DeCook and Joely Johnson—I couldn't have finished the manuscript without your support and enthusiasm. My gratitude list also includes Tyrel Stendahl for his assistance with the photos you see throughout the book. On the publisher's side, executive editor Suzanne Staszak-Silva proved supportive, patient, and firm as needed, with a dose of humor in her efforts to encourage me onward. Everyone, please hear my applause!

That's a clue for me to confess that pulling the final text together for this book was challenging. The issue: Where to stop? There are so many stories to explore and share about Seattle's delicious food history. Uncovering one story nugget typically led to six others. I knew that I didn't have room to include everything and everyone. The process underscored again for me that Seattle is a place blessed with indigenous food abundance. Add creative and caring chefs, food product entrepreneurs, restaurateurs, and inventors joined through a sense of community and sharing, and it's a very fine time to be shopping, cooking, and eating in Seattle. Food means a lot here, and with so many newcomers arriving lately, those of us who have experienced its bounty over the years will affirm its significant contribution to our Pacific Northwest lifestyle. I trust the stories collected in this book will expand your knowledge and show you the way.

Judith H. Dern
Seattle, Washington
September 2017

Acknowledgments

No book is ever a solo undertaking. The people listed here generously shared their knowledge and perspectives to enrich the vibrant story of Seattle's culinary history, and I thank them all.

Ken Albala
Laura Almaas
Allan Aquila
Paula Becker
Taylor Bowie
David Brewster
Maxine "Max" Chan
Douglas Chin
Rebekah Denn
Stuart Eskenazi
Charles and Rose Ann Finkel
Robert Fisher
Leonard Garfield
Rahul Gupta
Christine Keff
Mari-Ann Kind Jackson
Elizabeth King George
Warren King George
Richard Kinssies
Lisa Kransler

Kristy Leissle, PhD
Nancy Leson
Priscilla Long
Tony Magnano
Maria McCaffery
Jeffrey Perkins, PhD
Fred Poyner IV
Kai Raymond
Beverly Rengert
Braiden Rex-Johnson
Louie Richmond
Stuart Rose
Norma Rosenthal
Jon Rowley
Jessica A. Rubenacker
Kurt Stream
Jacqueline Williams
Tamara Wilson
Mikala Woodward

Special thanks are also due to the following organizations:

The Burke Museum of Natural History and Culture
Hibulb Cultural Center and Natural History Preserve
HistoryLink
Museum of History and Industry (MOHAI)
The Nordic Museum
Rainier Valley Historical Society
Seattle Public Library Special Collections
University of Washington Library, Special Collections
Washington State Jewish Historical Society
Washington State Wine Commission
Wing Luke Museum of the Asian Pacific American Experience

Introduction

To eat in and around Seattle, which I did recently and recommend heartily, isn't merely to eat well. It is to experience something that even many larger, more gastronomically celebrated cities and regions can't offer, not to this degree: a profound and exhilarating sense of place. I'm hard-pressed to think of another corner or patch of the United States where the locavore sensibilities of the moment are on such florid (and often sweetly funny) display, or where they pay richer dividends, at least if you're a lover of fish.

—Frank Bruni, *New York Times*, 2011

Seattle's culinary heritage begins with Native Americans from the Coast Salish tribes who foraged forests, fields, and the sea to pick wild blackberries, smoke freshly caught salmon on cedar planks, and dig clams and geoducks at low tide. Today, these culinary traditions are still followed within the Native American community. Given their established practicality and delicious results, many of these food customs have been discovered and adopted among Seattle's home cooks, restaurateurs, and world-class chefs who value the region's locally sourced ingredients to prepare Seattle's interpretation of Pacific Northwest cuisine.

Any exploration of Seattle's culinary history in an attempt to define what might be considered "Pacific Northwest cuisine" must start with the region's geography and geology. This beginning guarantees a fascinating journey across pristine lakes, into the sea, down rivers, and occasionally across rugged mountains. The city's early boomtown history revolved around logging, fishing, mining, and canning, all industries that took advantage of the region's remarkable natural resources. Given the surroundings of their new landscape and climate, pioneers who moved to the Pacific Northwest were also adventurous and resilient.

As Seattle grew from a wild frontier settlement into a major twentieth-century hub for transportation and commerce, the region's enviable location and entrepreneurial spirit inspired the masterminds behind the launches of major corporations such as Boeing, Nordstrom, Starbucks, Microsoft, Amazon, REI, and Costco. The robust (for the most part) business presence of these companies and their employee base helped shape Seattle's culinary character by stimulating diverse attitudes toward food, restaurants, and cultural traditions, whether from the Midwest, Scandinavia, the Mediterranean, or the Middle East.

By making connections between Seattle's natural resources, its past and present residents, historical events, a rich influx of immigrants, and larger cultural trends, this book aims to explore the how and why behind the city's fascinating culinary heritage. Within the context of US history and Washington's statehood in 1889, Seattle's culinary timeline is relatively short. However, its recent and rapid development—and recognition—as a significant culinary destination is impressive. Investigating what people in the Emerald City (a nickname alluding to Seattle's lush year-round greenness) cooked and ate throughout its history not only connects us to the past but also illuminates today's culinary traditions, and may also predict what will be on our plates tomorrow.

Because Seattle's culinary history and food traditions extend beyond the official municipal borders, the following definitions will provide context for the city's placement among its Pacific Northwest neighbors (particularly Oregon and Alaska) and define the different regions of Washington State. To give a contemporary geographical context to Seattle's location in the Pacific Northwest, the following descriptions may be referenced to identify areas connected with significant historic or contemporary food-related activities.

Salish Sea: The inland fresh and saltwater sea and its integrated ecosystem between the coast of Washington and British Columbia.

Puget Sound: The coastal region including Seattle that begins in Olympia (the state capital) and stretches west and northward to the Canadian border to include the verdant Olympic Peninsula and the San Juan Islands, where farms have historically contributed to Seattle's dinner tables.

Greater Seattle: The metropolitan area comprised of King County, Snohomish County, and Pierce County, all surrounding the city.

The Eastside: Both a business and population center in its own right, consisting of the Bellevue, Redmond, and Mercer Island communities on the eastern shore of Lake Washington and connected to Seattle via the I-90 and the S-520 floating bridges.

Woodinville Wine Country: Northeast of downtown Seattle and once rural, today it's a suburb of Bellevue and a destination with tasting rooms to explore wineries that may be based in Eastern Washington.

Eastern Washington: On the other side of the Cascade Mountains, this mostly rural region is Washington State's agricultural paradise, thanks to irrigation, climate, and soil conditions within Yakima, Spokane, the Tri-Cities area, and Ellensburg as population centers.

Skagit Valley: North of Seattle and centered around Mount Vernon and La Conner, the fertile Skagit County continues to be one of the largest and most diverse agricultural communities west of the Cascade mountain range.

With these parameters established, it makes sense that the challenge of defining Seattle cuisine typically ends up centered on these adjectives: seasonal, local, fresh, and creative. When local culinary professionals and food enthusiasts are asked to name ingredients used in cooking the Pacific Northwest way, it's almost guaranteed that salmon, oysters, clams, blackberries, and mushrooms will be mentioned first. What may distinguish Seattle's interpretation of dishes using these ingredients are the quirky and creative personalities behind the stoves. Welcome to a journey through Seattle's colorful history to discover the city's distinct culinary heritage.

Seattle Timeline

NATIVE PEOPLES BEFORE EUROPEAN CONTACT

- 15,000 years before present (BP): Glacial ice covers Puget Sound lowland areas, including Seattle
- 11,000 BP: The last glacier (Vashon) begins its retreat from the Puget Sound area
- 8,000 BP: Humans begin inhabiting the region, living in areas above the mouth of the Fraser River and on the lower Columbia River
- 2,000 BP: Native people live along the shores of Puget Sound, subsisting on salmon, shellfish, and native plants and berries

EUROPEAN AND AMERICAN EXPLORERS

- 1776: The United States Declaration of Independence is signed in Philadelphia, Pennsylvania
- 1778: British captain James Cook, while searching for the Northwest Passage, locates Cape Flattery at the mouth of the Columbia River
- 1792: British captain George Vancouver sights Mt. Rainier and surveys Puget Sound
- 1805: The Lewis and Clark Expedition arrives at the mouth of the Columbia River and camps at Fort Clatsop

- 1833: The British-based Hudson's Bay Company establishes a trading site at Fort Nisqually above the Nisqually River, the first non-native settlement in the Puget Sound region
- 1841: U.S. exploring expedition led by Lieutenant Charles Wilkes enters Puget Sound and names Elliott Bay
- 1846: The Oregon Treaty permanently establishes the 48th parallel as the boundary between the United States and British North America
- 1848: Oregon Territory designated by US Congress
- 1848: California Gold Rush

EARLY SEATTLE SETTLERS

- 1851: Arthur Denny lands with family and friends at Alki Point
- 1851: Charles Terry opens the first retail store on Alki Point
- 1853: City of Seattle established and named for Chief Sealth, a leader of the Suquamish and Duwamish tribes
- 1853: President Fillmore establishes the Washington Territory
- 1853: City of Olympia named provisional capital of Washington Territory
- 1854: Chief Sealth gives his famous speech, but it is not transcribed until 1887
- 1855: Henry Yesler's cook and mess house opens
- 1855–1856: Indian War conflict between Washington settlers and native people over land; June 26, 1856, Battle of Seattle
- 1858: Manuel Lopes arrives in Seattle, the city's first black resident
- 1861: University of Washington holds first classes
- 1862: President Lincoln signs the Homestead Act
- 1863: Congress approves Idaho Territory
- 1865: The Civil War ends
- 1865: Seattle officially incorporated by the Washington Territorial Legislature
- 1867: The Occidental Hotel, with upscale dining room, opens in Pioneer Square
- 1873: Seattle and Walla Walla Railroad is organized
- 1874: Gas street lamps are installed for the first time
- 1875: Pacific Coast Steamship begins services between Seattle and San Francisco
- 1878: Seattle Malting and Brewing (later Rainier Brewery) established
- 1880: Seattle receives its official city charter
- 1882: Chinese Exclusion Act passed by Congress, prohibiting Chinese from entering the United States and denying residence to those already here
- 1882: First trans-Pacific steamship departs from Seattle, opening the gateway to the Pacific Rim
- 1883: Northern Pacific Railroad line completed to Tacoma

- 1888: Rainier Club is established
- 1889: The Great Fire destroys downtown Seattle (June); Washington becomes the forty-second state
- 1890: Ballard is incorporated as an independent city

A GROWING CITY

- 1891: Seattle Public Library opens
- 1893: Maison Riche, first high-end restaurant, opens in Pioneer Square
- 1893: Great Northern Railway completed, from St. Paul to Seattle
- 1893: Columbia is incorporated as an independent city
- 1893: Rainier Beer first kegged by the Seattle Brewing & Malting Company
- 1896: Nippon Yusen Kaisha steamship line arrives in Seattle, providing Chinese businesses with ingredients such as dried ducks, roots, herbs, smoked meats, and tea
- 1897–1899: Klondike Gold Rush; miners pass through Seattle on their way to Alaska
- 1898: Seattle begins regrade of downtown hills to expand the business district
- 1899: First cans of Carnation evaporated milk processed in Kent
- 1899: Tilingit totem pole erected in Pioneer Square
- 1900: Seattle Business Directory lists 92 restaurants
- 1902: First Sephardic Jews arrive
- 1904: Georgetown is incorporated as an independent city
- 1904: Maneki Restaurant, Seattle's first Japanese restaurant, opens (and still operates today)
- 1906: King Street Train Station opens in Pioneer Square
- 1906: The Mountaineers Club forms
- 1907: Pike Place Public Market opens
- 1907: Ballard, Columbia, Ravenna, Southeast Seattle, South Park, and West Seattle are annexed into the City of Seattle
- 1908: Alaska Club and Arctic Club merge, joining Seattle and Alaska businessmen
- 1909: Alaska-Pacific-Yukon Exposition opens on what is now the site of UW
- 1909: Chicago, Milwaukee and St. Paul railroad begins operating
- 1910: Women in Washington State are granted the right to vote; the state is the fifth in the nation to enfranchise women
- 1910: Georgetown annexed by Seattle
- 1911: Port of Seattle established
- 1913: Auto ferry service begins on Lake Washington
- 1914: Smith Tower is built
- 1914: Fishermen's Terminal opens on Salmon Bay

WORLD WAR I

- 1916: Prohibition begins in Washington State, and continues until its repeal in 1932
- 1916: First Boeing-built airplane takes off from Lake Union
- 1917: United States enters World War I
- 1917: Hiram Chittenden Locks open, connecting Lake Union and Lake Washington with Puget Sound
- 1918: Frederick & Nelson Department Store opens with tea room and restaurants
- 1919: Seattle General Strike
- 1920: National Prohibition goes into effect and continues until its repeal in 1933

BOOM AND BUST

- 1924: Immigrant Act of 1924 severely restricts the immigration of Italians and Eastern European Jews and bans Asian immigrants
- 1924: Olympic Hotel opens with the Georgian Room restaurant
- 1926: US Naval Air Station established at Sand Point on Lake Washington
- 1928: The Uwajimaya grocery store founded
- 1929: Stock market crashes
- 1933: Unemployment in Washington reaches 30 percent; formation of the Cannery Workers' and Farm Laborers' Union with Virgil Duyungan, a Filipino cannery worker, as the first president
- 1934: Steele Liquor Act signed, establishing the Washington State Liquor Control Board
- 1934: Chateau Ste. Michelle is founded
- 1938: Ivar Haglund opens a fish and chips stand at Pier 54 (now Ivar's Fish Bar), the first of his seafood eatery empire

WAR AGAIN

- 1939: Germany invades Poland, starting World War II in Europe
- 1939: REI (Recreational Equipment Incorporated) co-op opens
- 1940: Trader Vic's opens first franchise (initially called the Outrigger) inside Seattle's Westin Hotel (closes in 1991)
- 1940: First floating bridge in the world (now I-90) connects Seattle, Mercer Island, and the Eastside

- 1942: More than 12,000 US citizens of Japanese ancestry living in the Puget Sound region are transported to what is now Puyallup Fairgrounds, and then to internment camps across the West Coast, closing local farms and restaurants

POSTWAR GROWTH

- 1947: SeaTac Airport opens and airline service from Seattle to Far East begins
- 1948: Voters pass a statewide initiative allowing restaurants to serve hard liquor by the glass
- 1950: Northgate Mall opens (earliest suburban shopping mall in the United States), and restaurateur Walter Clark opens first restaurant in a mall
- 1953: Canlis opens, first four-star restaurant to showcase Pacific NW cuisine
- 1953: El Gaucho opens
- 1954: Dick's Drive-In opens in Wallingford
- 1956: Rosallini's Four-10 opens, serving as one of the first places for power/ political dining
- 1962: Space Needle opens, and Seattle hosts the Century 21 World's Fair
- 1963: Evergreen Point Floating Bridge (SR520) opens
- 1964: Puget Sound Mycological Society founded
- 1970: Seattle's unemployment rate reaches 14 percent, including massive Boeing layoffs
- 1971: Starbucks opens first café and voters save Pike Place Market, stopping an eight-year "urban development" effort to replace it with offices, hotels, and parking garages
- 1971: Bumbershoot music festival launches on Labor Day weekend
- 1972: Nikko Restaurant, the first full-service Tokyo-style sushi bar, opens
- 1974: Boldt Decision upholds the treaty rights of Native Americans to 50 percent of fish harvested
- 1976: Toshi's Teriyaki opens first location
- 1977: Seattle Mariners baseball team formed
- 1978: American Indian Religious Freedom Act passed
- 1979: Microsoft (established in 1975 in Albuquerque) moves to Seattle suburb of Redmond
- 1979: P-Patch Advisory Council forms

MODERN DINING GROWS

- 1980: Mirabeau opens as first view restaurant (forty-sixth floor of Seattle First National Bank)

- 1982: First pint of Redhook Ale sold in Seattle, kicking off microbrew craze
- 1982: Costco opens first warehouse store on Fourth Avenue in Seattle
- 1989: Chef Tom Douglas, with his wife Jackie Cross, opens his first restaurant, Dahlia Lounge
- 1989: Gwen Bassettil starts Grand Central Bakery, introduces Seattle to Como loaves and artisan bread (first sold homemade bread and jam in 1960s on Lopez island)
- 1991: James Beard Awards established; Capril Pence of Fullers named Best Chef Northwest category
- 1993: Amazon.com founded
- 1993: *Sleepless in Seattle* released
- 1993: Leslie Mackie opens Macrina Bakery to introduce artisan breads and pastries
- 1997: Allrecipes.com is founded as CookieRecipe.com
- 1999: Eric and Sophie Banh open Monsoon, Seattle's first upscale Vietnamese restaurant
- 1999: US Endangered Species Act lists nine Puget Sound salmon runs as endangered

TWENTY-FIRST-CENTURY MILESTONES

- 2000: Experience Music Project opens
- 2009: Link Light Rail service begins, making the circuit from SeaTac Airport to downtown
- 2010: City declares 2010 the "Year of Urban Agriculture," inspiring a fresh wave of locally grown cuisine
- 2012: Plastic shopping bags banned
- 2014: Fifteen-dollar minimum wage hike impacts restaurants
- 2016: Seattle Library Foundation panel of major chefs tries to define Seattle cuisine and "Pacific Northwest Cuisine" and has no definitive answer
- 2016–2017: MOHAI features "Edible City" exhibition, documenting high points of Seattle's food history

1

❖ ❖

The Material Resources

Mountain Ranges, Volcanoes, Glaciers, and the Sea

When the tide is out, the table is set.

—Coast Salish saying

Salmon swim, oysters and geoducks bubble, and whales and sea lions cavort in sparkling seas, while blackberries, acorns, fiddlehead ferns, and wood mushrooms add their succulence to the lush greenery and beautiful vistas of Pacific Northwest forests, mountain slopes, and meadows. The distinct geology and ecosystem surrounding greater Seattle gives it a food profile unlike any other city on the planet. The menu offered by this northern landscape reflects a rich biodiversity spawned by the region's enviable combination of fresh and saltwater, a location between two mountain ranges, and a mild climate.

Three forces influence the hospitable environment fostering the region's indigenous foods. First is the region's location along the eastern arc of the Pacific Ring of Fire and the surrounding mountain ranges, the Coast, Cascade, and Olympic Ranges, plus Vancouver Island's Insular Mountains. Created over thousands of years—along with several drowsing volcanoes, most notably ghostly Mt. Rainier anchoring the skyline only sixty miles south of Seattle—these jagged mountain ranges are still revealing themselves. Add in the rich biodiversity of the Salish Sea with its islands and estuaries, tides, and straits stretching between the United

States and Canada, and you discover a second influence. Both features reflect the Pacific Northwest's placement at a dynamic intersection of oceanic and continental tectonic plates, one of the youngest and most geologically active areas on earth. The push and pull, slipping, sliding, and colliding of these crustal plates below the ocean and the earth's surface over the past 220 million years of tectonic activity has spawned the mountain ridges, valleys, rivers, and fjords encircling Seattle. Islands rose, rocks were thrust upward into jutting peaks, and ancient seas became valleys. These earthly changes, movements, and eruptions are ongoing; indeed, seismic monitoring today testifies to the region's continued geological activity.

The third force creating Seattle's geography is hidden in plain sight. It involved extreme climate change and mammoth sheets of ice covering the Pacific Northwest during the last great Ice Age or Pleistocene period. During a glacial period about twenty thousand years ago, the Fraser Glaciation, which moved southward from Canada as part of the Cordilleran Ice Sheet, covered the Puget Sound region with a massive ice sheet more than three thousand feet (one kilometer) deep—"as high as six stacked Space Needles," estimates David B. Williams in *Too High & Too Steep: Reshaping Seattle's Topography*—and formed the significant vertical and

A ghostly view of Mt. Rainier looking across Lake Washington. *Courtesy of MOHAI, [Seattle Historical Society Collection], [7644].*

horizontal landscape seen around Seattle today. The huge plates of ice and frigid temperatures also created fierce weather and winds, determining which plants and animals survived on the land and in the sea. When the climate warmed around ten thousand years ago, the massive ice sheet retreated, allowing the Pacific Ocean to merge inland and connect three fjords: the Strait of Juan de Fuca, Puget Sound, and the Strait of Georgia. This created the Pacific Northwest's most significant inland waterway today, the Salish Sea.

THE SALISH SEA

Water. It may be the most important element in Seattle's dynamic landscape: water in the form of tides and waves, as erosion, as surface runoff, racing in rivers and streams, and cascading over waterfalls. The Pacific Northwest is all about water, and not just what falls from the skies; Seattle's average annual rainfall is thirty-eight inches, ranking forty-fourth among other US cities, although the Olympic Peninsula's rain forest records more than sixty inches annually, making it the wettest place in continental United States. Proximity to the Pacific Ocean, along with eons of uplifts and erosion, underlie modern precipitation patterns, river flows, and mountain glaciers. The region's mighty rivers, from the Fraser River winding through British Columbia, the Nisqually River south of Seattle, and the Skagit River to the north, all spill lavish amounts of freshwater into the Salish Sea, creating a verdant environment for wildlife and seafood. Which brings us to the most significant geological feature of Seattle's landscape: the Salish Sea.

Named in honor of the original people who inhabited the region, the term *Salish Sea* represents a new nomenclature for the waters surrounding the greater Seattle region. As Audrey DeLella Benedict and Joseph K. Gaydos note in *The Salish Sea: Jewel of the Pacific Northwest*, the designation and name for this multi-fingered body of water stretching west from Seattle into the Pacific Ocean was only officially approved and recognized in 2009 by American and Canadian government agencies. The waters of Puget Sound, the Strait of Juan de Fuca, and the Strait of Georgia, along with the ecosystem and coastline edging Washington State and British Columbia, with myriad anonymous islands, inlets, deltas, bays, beaches, tidal flats, and shoals, now make up the Salish Sea.

Puget Sound anchors Seattle's position along this vast inland sea. A southern waterway with a two-hundred-mile perimeter considered an extension of the Strait of Juan de Fuca, Puget Sound laps the front steps of the city and stretches northwest to encircle the San Juan archipelago. The English explorer Captain George Vancouver gave Puget Sound its name in 1792 when he sailed through the Strait of Juan de Fuca on his mission to chart coastal regions of the Pacific Northwest.

With its continuous tidal flow and blending of freshwater and the sea, the Puget Sound's system of estuaries is vital to creating and sustaining Seattle's marine ecosystem and indigenous foodways. As described by Arthur R. Kruckeberg in *The Natural History of Puget Sound Country*, "Some call Puget Sound a 'miniature ocean,' others portray it as one of the largest systems of estuaries in the world, and those with a biological basis describe it as 'one of the most productive bodies of water in the world.' Indeed, Puget Sound is the most distinctive feature of the landscape in Western Washington."

FLORA AND FAUNA

As a bountiful consequence of the Pacific Northwest's dramatic geological history and resulting temperate climate along with dependable fall and winter rainfall west of the Cascades, this region, particularly the Salish Sea, houses a mighty ecosystem. The diversity of salt and fresh waters combined with the topography of mighty maritime forests of giant red cedars and lush mountain meadows gave rise to a rich and diverse menu of indigenous foods. As a result, food resources of the Pacific Northwest have always been naturally abundant, sustaining generations of native people, along with the first settlers and immigrants. Abundant sea life such as whales, fish, and shellfish, along with seals, sea lions, and sea otters, provided resources for food and clothing. On shore, land-roaming mammals, from the woolly mammoths that wandered the region some fourteen million years ago (until the last ice age ended their migrations) to modern-age beavers and bears, deer, mountain goats, squirrels, rabbits, migrating birds, and more, provided sustenance along with materials for everyday living. Add native plants as another source of nourishment, and the area is indeed richly endowed with edible vegetation. The following section reviews indigenous food items of the Pacific Northwest still enjoyed today in Northwest cuisine, linking Seattle's modern residents to the region's earliest inhabitants and surrounding landscape.

FROM THE SEA

With the Salish Sea creating a dynamic ecosystem, fish, shellfish, and sea-going mammals were significant food sources for the first humans inhabiting the region surrounding present-day Seattle. Large mammals such as humpback whales were coveted, requiring both practiced skill and community commitment to capture and prepare for valuable protein. Smaller creatures roaming inlets, bays, and islands—sea lions, seals, and sea otters—were also pursued. While no longer found on modern menus, these animals were important in creating a sustainable diet for the region's first residents. In contrast, smaller, easier-to-harvest sea creatures found in habitats at the water's edge, along with many fish species, especially the magnificent wild salmon, continue to captivate our appetites and define Pacific Northwest cuisine.

Wild Salmon

Few fish have as mythic a legacy or are as linked to people and place as the Pacific salmon. In many ways, the story of salmon is the story of life in the Pacific Northwest. Salmon arrived first in this region and have been swimming in waters here for more than twelve thousand years. Adopted as a spiritual icon for the region's native tribes, who view wild salmon as a gift from the Creator as well as food, the salmon's annual spring-into-summer migration is celebrated as a time for both thanksgiving rituals and feasts. Careful to take only what they needed, these aboriginal tribes have always respected and fostered a relationship with the mighty fish. Certainly, wild salmon are the key reason native people stayed in place in this region instead of migrating to find food.

A *pelagic* fish, meaning a species inhabiting the middle, or pelagic, zone of the ocean and lakes, salmon are born in freshwater pools and streams far inland, and as juveniles, swim far downstream to enter the cold Pacific Ocean. Salmon are also classified as *anadromous*, a term derived from a Greek word meaning "running upward," a reference to their lifestyle of migrating back to their natal streams and lakes to spawn. At one time, wild Pacific salmon populations ranged from the Bering Strait off southern Alaska to the rivers of northern California.

During the annual salmon runs from April to August (timing overlaps for the various species, meaning runs have a peak, but not a definite end and beginning), along streams and rivers, at waterfalls and rock outcroppings, native fishermen danced on scaffolds built over the water, casting dip nets and aiming spears to snare migrating salmon. Nutritionally rich, salmon, whether eaten fresh, smoked, or dried, have been essential to human survival in the Northwest and feeding families throughout winter. Teachings, songs, and ceremonial feasts mark the salmon migration. As Elizabeth Woody, a Native American writer, outlines in her essay in *Salmon Nation: People and Fish at the Edge*, the Columbia River Inter-Tribal Fish Commission describes the salmon's revered place in native culture:

> [G]reat spiritual comfort is derived from the first salmon whose journey ends with a feast held in its honor. Together, tribal members and salmon weave a unique cultural fabric designed by the Divine Creator. What the mind cannot comprehend, the heart and spirit interpret. The result is a beautiful and dignified ceremonial response to the Creator in appreciation for the willingness of nature to serve humankind.

There are five species of wild Pacific salmon, all members of the trout family. Many Seattleites can name them all, as well as identify their favorite and tell you when the first fresh catch is available in local markets. Highlights from the North Pacific Anadromous Fish Commission's descriptions of these five salmon species follow.

1. Chinook (*Oncorhynchus tshawytscha*), also named King, Tyee, Tule, or Chin Blackmouth. The largest species in terms of size, growing up to three feet long and weighing thirty pounds; annual migration starts in spring and runs through fall.
2. Chum (*Oncorhynchus keta*), also named Dog, Calico, or Keta. Second largest Pacific salmon species; adults weigh eight to fifteen pounds; spawning grounds are typically at river mouths; annual migration takes place late summer through the winter to spring.
3. Coho (*Oncorhynchus kisutch*), also called Silver or White. Sleek and silver, adults typically weigh eight to twelve pounds; annual run takes place early summer through early fall.
4. Pink (*Oncorhynchus gorbuscha*), also named Humpback or Humpie, a reference to its humped back during spawning season. Originates in both Asia and North America, recognized as the most abundant Northwest salmon species (and is the primary species used for canning); small when compared with other salmon species, averaging two to four pounds; averages only eighteen months in the ocean; annual run takes place every two years.
5. Sockeye (*Oncorhynchus nerka*), also called Red (a reference to the species' intensely colored flesh and coloring during spawning season). The second most abundant species, with both ocean-going and river populations; smaller fish, growing from 1.5 to 2.5 feet and weighing four to fifteen pounds; annual run is summer through early fall.

On occasion, steelhead (*Oncorhynchus mykiss*), Washington's official state fish, a member of the trout family and a favorite Pacific Northwest fish, is listed as a Pacific salmon species, but it is not anadromous and lives only in freshwater lakes and streams.

Newcomers to the Northwest in the pioneer era once marveled at seeing migrating salmon clustered so densely one could "walk across a river over them." Commercial fishing for Pacific salmon began in the 1860s and has never stopped, although it now has limitations in modern times due to diminishing stocks. In his essay in *Salmon Nation: People and Fish at the Edge*, Seth Zuckerman reveals the downward trajectory of the Pacific Northwest's commercial salmon industry: "In 1970, commercial ocean salmon fishing in Washington, Oregon and California brought in annual average catch valued at $180 million, and was responsible for 7,200 jobs in fishing, fish processing, and supporting industries. By 1997 . . . that figure had dropped to $26 million."

Today, all five species are listed in some habitats as threatened or endangered under the 1999 Endangered Species Act. Threats to salmon in the Pacific Northwest are cumulative and include logging (which leads to forest runoff and erosion that then clogs streams), industrial pollution, farm field runoff, and various human factors such as overfishing, urban development, massive hydroelectric dams built along many significant migration watersheds in the 1930s that have blocked salmon runs, and significant climate change that has adversely affected ocean temperatures.

To combat these challenges, salmon runs today are aided by an extensive region-wide hatchery system that even goes so far as to transport juvenile fish in trucks around dams so they can have safe passage to the ocean. Heightened awareness of the interconnections between our shared habitats and salmon survival has also spurred broad-based community action at local, state, and federal government levels to restore habitats and protect the Pacific Northwest's watersheds for this cherished fish—with varying success. Neighborhood activist groups clean backyard streams and agitate for daylight, removing culverts blocking fish passageways, and drains along roadways are stenciled with alerts to remind everyone not to dump toxic liquids because these waterways connect to salmon habitats. As an indication of a changing mindset, after considerable public agitation for two decades and, finally, federal approval, beginning in 2011 and continuing to 2014, two dams crossing the Olympic Peninsula's forty-five-mile-long Elwha River, which spills into the Strait of Juan de Fuca, were removed—a huge step in salmon watershed restoration and a process outlined in detail by Michelle Nijhuis in her August 2014 *National Geographic* article. Now more than ever, wild Pacific salmon, a treasured symbol of culture and place, maintain their power to awe and enchant us.

Oysters, Mussels, Clams, and Geoducks—Oh, My!

Close to land and an accessible food source, the Salish Sea's tidal flats and estuaries have long proven a hospitable home for oysters, mussels, and clams, as well as a very odd creature, the geoduck. It was a truly inspired being who first discovered that these bivalves were edible, and then developed methods for farming them.

Oysters especially feast on the estuaries' algae, which in turn thrives on nutrients in the ebb and flow of rainwater filtering into the sea. A natural terroir based on a distinctive profile of salts, minerals, and algae species, twice-daily tidal movements, water depth, and water temperature, these elements all influence an oyster's flavor. (In fact, oysters are one of the only foods named—like wine appellations—for their region of origin.) Happily for seafood fans, the Pacific Northwest is home to a native species of oyster, the tiny (3.5-inch) Olympia oyster (*Ostrea conchaphila*), hailing most often from the tidal flats of Willapa Bay. Although almost lost in the 1930s and 1940s due to pulp mill pollution discharging into Puget Sound waters and over-harvesting, today, thanks to the perseverance of oyster farmers, the Olympia oyster is again thriving in South Puget Sound.

The Pacific Northwest's oyster roster has expanded in modern times to include two oyster species transplanted from Japan, probably originally on the bottoms of Japanese trade boats: the jumbo Pacific oyster (*Crassostrea gigas*), which can grow to twelve inches and is the key player in Washington State's modern commercial oyster industry, and the Kumamoto (*Crassostrea sikamea*), raised here since the 1900s. In recent years, the European Flat (*Ostrea edulis*), sometimes mistakenly called the Belon, and the Eastern oyster (*Crassostrea virginica*), a species transplanted from the Eastern seaboard, have begun being farmed in Puget Sound. Clustered in groups of irregular fluted ivory and black shells, with new shell growth showing an iridescent violet, oysters are farmed in cultivated beds throughout the inlets and estuaries around Puget Sound from Hood Canal to Tottingham Inlet. Many oyster farms are family run and go back five generations, yet another testament to the region's sustainable ecosystem. Bivalve fans will find more oyster information, along with tempting recipes, in Cynthia Nims's cookbook, *Oysters: Recipes That Bring Home a Taste of the Sea* (2016).

Clams and mussels are also on the roster of bivalve mollusks thriving in the Salish Sea's intertidal habitat of mixed sand, gravel, and mud beaches. The region's most common hardshell clams are the Pacific Razor clam (*Siliqua patula*), Manila (*Tapes philippinarum*), and Native Littlenecks (*Protothaca staminea*), with Butter clams, Cockles, and Macomas also on the Washington State Fishing & Shellfishing clam list. Next, add two primary species of mussels inhabiting coastal waters: Foolish (*Mytilus trossulus*) and California (*Mytilus californianus*). Identified by dark blue-black oblong shells, and at home in shallow coastal waters, these bivalves cluster in dense mats on rocks, pilings, floats, and pillars, or, in the case of the California mussel, on wave-washed rocks in the straits of the Salish Sea. Their humorously termed "independent living style" makes mussels especially attractive for commercial harvesting.

No catalog of the Pacific Northwest's seafood would be complete without describing the most unusual clam to inhabit Salish Sea waters: the geoduck (*Panopea generosa*). Pronounced "gooey-duck," the word is from the Lushootseed dialect of the Salish tribes and means "dig deep." The giant clam is native to coastal Pacific waters but found most abundantly in mudflats along the shores of Puget Sound and other Salish Sea waterways. The world's largest burrowing clam—it can weigh up to two-and-a-half pounds, including its shell, with a siphon up to two feet long—it digs its burrow in a bed of mud, sand, or gravel, two to four feet below ground level. A briny flavor and somewhat crunchy meat make it more appealing to taste than observe. Considered the grandfather of bivalves because many live to be fifteen years old or more—although most are harvested within three to five years—geoducks are as exotic now as they were when first discovered.

Dungeness Crab and Spot Shrimp

Although there are myriad species of crab scuttling along the seabed of the Salish Sea, the most cherished Pacific Northwest crustacean, the Dungeness crab (*Metacarcinus magister*), stands out as the rock star. A resident for eons among eelgrass beds and the sea floor throughout the region and along the West Coast, from Alaska south to Santa Barbara, California, these sweet, meaty crabs with distinct reddish-purple coloring move toward shore as the tide changes from low to high. Named after the Dungeness Spit, christened by Captain George Vancouver with this name because it resembled a similar point he knew on the English Channel, and adopted by settlers living in the town of Dungeness, Washington, the crabs are harvested using baited crab pots, the traditional native method. Since the mid-1800s, Dungeness crabs have been a significant economic resource for the region (and all along the West Coast), taking off in the 1920s with the inauguration of refrigeration.

The commercial crabbing season for Native Americans in the Northwest generally opens December 1 and slows by summer, while the summer crabbing season for recreational fishing opens July 1 (following the molting season) and again, early to late September, with the non-tribal commercial season starting October 1. Details are available online at the Washington Department of Fish & Wildlife, Fishing & Shellfishing website (http://wdfw.wa.gov). In line with a 1994 federal ruling, Dungeness crab harvests are also shared equally between Indian tribes and non-tribal fishermen in a commitment to sustainability. While once abundant, today both recreational and commercial crabbers must be licensed and record their catches; only five male crabs 6.25 inches or larger may be harvested daily to protect females and maintain the fishery.

The cold, deep waters of the Salish Sea also nourish several species of shrimp, including Spot shrimp, also known as Alaska Spot shrimp, Sitka Spot shrimp, and Puget Sound Spot shrimp. As the region's largest shrimp species—typically three to six inches long with pale orange shells—the sweet flavor of Spot shrimp makes them especially desirable. Like their crustacean crab cousins, shrimp are also caught using baited pots, with a season that runs from April to October.

Halibut

A denizen of the deep, the Pacific halibut (*Hippoglossus stenolepis*) is another revered resident of the Salish Sea and a significant food source from past to present. A mighty fish and a member of the flounder family, bottom-feeding halibut typically grow four to eight feet and can weigh from ten to five hundred pounds with dense, meaty white flesh. Also a managed fishery—since 1913 under the supervision of the International Pacific Halibut Commission—the commercial fishing season begins in early spring and lasts until late fall, covering the West Coast north into Alaskan waters. The recreational halibut fishing season in Puget Sound spans the month of May, with citizen fishermen, who primarily line fish, limited to one fish per day, but with no maximum size limit.

Pacific Herring

Tiny fish who flicker though the sea in huge silver schools, Pacific herring (*Clupea pallasi*) were once one of the most abundant fisheries in the Pacific Northwest. While these fish may swim in the open ocean, they move into shallower waters to spawn in "eelgrass beds, kelp and other seaweeds, as well as inshore rocks, pilings and any other fixed surface." The focus of a significant industry inspired by Scandinavian immigrants in the Pacific Northwest as well as along the northern California coast, the tiny fish were used for bait as well as processed for canned and pickled fish, oil, and meal. Alas, the herring fishery imploded in the mid-1960s due to overfishing and low reproduction rates, and to date has not recovered.

FROM THE LAND

As verdant with vegetation as the seas are packed with fins and shells, the terrain of the Pacific Northwest offers a lavish table of wild edible plants appealing to human palates. Mossy outcroppings, forest canyons, mountain meadows, and brambles in between provide an ideal habitat for berries, mushrooms, ferns, wild asparagus, chicory, clover, sorrel, dandelion, and more. At last count, according to foraging expert Tom Cervenka on his website NorthernBushcraft.com, the region is home to ninety-two wild edible plants. It's a list cultivated by twelve-hour days of summer sunlight that leave an orange glow behind mountain silhouettes late into the evening, and twelve-hour days of damp winter darkness encouraging green things to grow. Glacial soil, manageable rainfall, and temperate temperatures rarely falling below freezing around the Salish Sea create a hospitable environment for a veritable green feast. While the list of edibles is extensive, an overview follows describing some of the most popular categories of readily available wild foods.

Camas Bulbs

Called camas or Indian hyacinth (*Camassia*), the root bulbs of this perennial plant are its only edible part, but a part that sustained both native people and early settlers in the Pacific Northwest. A member of the asparagus family, recognized with six species (*Camassia leichtlinii* is identified as the primary species in Washington, Oregon, and British Columbia), its straight stalks appear each spring covering open fields and meadows, topped with lilac or dark purple flowers. The bulbs of the plant are harvested in the fall and then steamed twenty-four to forty-eight hours in an earth oven, or braised over a stone firepit to transform them into a nutritious jerky-like substance covered with a thin sugar-like film. Today, it is often used as an ornamental plant in gardens.

Salmonberries

The Pacific Northwest's volcanic origins, glacial transgressions, and deep forests with sunlit openings provide the perfect ecosystem for the salmonberry (*Rubus spectabilis*), an indigenous coastal shrub that reaches heights of six feet and stretches to a similar width. In early spring, the young plant shoots may be peeled and eaten raw. Succeeding the bloom of five-petaled, cupped magenta flowers, small orange-ish berries resembling raspberries appear by late summer.

Huckleberries

One of four species of perennial evergreens, the glossy green-leaved shrubs of Western huckleberry (*Vaccinium*) bushes thrive in both shade and sunlight. Around the Puget Sound lowlands, huckleberry brambles are covered first with pale pink blossoms in spring, and then single-stemmed dark red berries appear from midsummer until fall, while dark blue huckleberries are common in higher elevations. Wild huckleberries are another foraging staple for Native American tribes, who celebrate the huckleberry's seasonal harvest with First Berry thanksgiving rituals.

Blackberries

Wild blackberry vines are ubiquitous throughout the Puget Sound region, and the bane of many Northwest gardeners. But this rambunctious villain is the invasive blackberry, the exuberant Himalayan species (a cultivar developed by Luther Burbank) with plump seedy berries. The true native is the Coast Trailing blackberry (*Rubus ursinus*), a favorite with small, intensely flavored fruit that James Beard, according to Northwest Wildfoods (nwwildfoods.com), called "the uncrowned king of all wild berries," a designation repeated by Bethany Jean Clement, food writer for the *Seattle Times*, in her article "The Pacific Northwest's Better (and Native) Blackberry." For those on the lookout, the Coast Trailing blackberry grows particularly well in the warm San Juan Islands and in recently logged or burned areas, but it may also be found in Seattle environs.

Fiddleheads, Sorrel, and Other Edible Greens

The list of recognizable wild edible plants includes bitter cress and bitterroot, chicory, dandelion, false Solomon seal, goldenrod, mariposa lily, miner's lettuce, lamb's quarter, mustard, and more. Many were the foodstuffs of foraging native Pacific Northwest residents. In addition to these greens, modern foragers search for fiddleheads, the tender coiled shoots that ferns push out in early spring. With many varieties of ferns—the largest group of seedless vascular plants found on earth—careful identification is essential to make sure the edible greenery isn't mistaken for the shoots of poisonous plants such as hemlock. Other edible greens still popular today are found seasonally in farmers' markets and some local markets: Jerusalem artichoke (*Helianthus tuberosus*), mountain sorrel (*Oxyria digyna*), mustard (*Brassicaceae*), salsify (*Tragopogon* spp.), stinging nettle (*Urtica dioica*), watercress (*Rorippa nasturtium-aquaticum*), wild mint (*Mentha* spp.), and woodsorrel (*Oxalis* spp.).

Mushrooms

Not surprisingly, the Pacific Northwest's moist, wet climate is a nirvana for mushroom fans from summer through fall, providing an ideal nursery for hundreds of mushroom species. As a bonus, more than thirty edible "safe" fungi species grow in the region's mossy forests, on fallen logs, and beneath trees. Prized varieties include black morels and chanterelles, hedgehog mushrooms, and puffballs. Anyone foraging for mushrooms must follow careful identification checks since several species of Northwest mushrooms are deadly poisonous and should never be harvested or eaten without first verifying their classified name.

With this abundance of indigenous edibles from the very beginning of Seattle's food history, it is remarkable how many are still available in the twenty-first century and still celebrated for their Pacific Northwest origin.

2

❖ ❖

The Indigenous People
of the Pacific Northwest

Food is the essence of culture, from the collection, to the preparation, to the serving and then eating of food; it is what makes us who we are. It binds us to our families, our community, our history, our identity, and our home. The core cultural values around foods of Native Coast Salish peoples include: Food is the center of culture. Honor the food chain; Eat with the seasons; Eat a variety of foods.

—"Salish Bounty: Traditional Native Foods of Puget Sound," Burke Museum,
University of Washington (September 2013)

The actual arrival date of the first humans in the Pacific Northwest is uncertain, but both logic and archaeological evidence indicate it was after the last glacial period, or some thirteen million years ago, when the Cordilleran Ice Sheet and Fraser Glaciation melted. In the temperate climate that evolved, natural food resources became abundant and encouraged human migration, especially along inland waterways of the Salish Sea (an indigenous name meaning "salt water"). Some archaeological sites in the Puget Sound area date to ten thousand years ago and are found high in the Cascade Mountains, as well as along lowland rivers, bays, and beaches.

Along with its ancient human history, the city of Seattle is indelibly connected to its native heritage through its name, as well as by traditions, including food traditions. While Native Americans have a legacy in every region of the United States where words from their languages were adopted as place names for cities and geological features, in Seattle the connection is even more powerful because the city takes its name from Chief Seeathl (also known as Sealth and Seattle) of the Duwamish and Suquamish tribes, who played an important role in mingling indigenous people with the first white settlers developing a new village. Food was also often a link between the two cultures.

Native people living along the shores of the Salish Sea, and Puget Sound especially, had access to abundant food sources that defined their diet, determined their complex social, cultural, and political customs, and delineated their spiritual beliefs and values. Described by Native American author, theologian, and historian Vine Deloria Jr. in *Indians of the Pacific Northwest*, the region offered a natural cornucopia "where a great variety of salmon filled each and every river; where ducks and geese filled the evening sky; where berries literally dripped from the bushes at harvest time, and where crabs, clams, mussels, and oysters abounded."

Unlike nomadic tribes in other parts of North America, the abundance and accessibility of plants, animals, fish, and seafood available in the Puget Sound region and future site of Seattle made it possible for native inhabitants to develop a complex culture because they stayed in one place, only moving to "summer camps" during fishing and harvesting seasons. This arrangement allowed specific hunting and fishing techniques to develop, particularly for catching migrating salmon, along with methods to preserve food for cold weather sustenance. Substantial cedar longhouses and ceremonial structures in winter towns signified sophisticated communities where families shared resources, developed social connections, and observed seasonal religious ceremonies honoring the earth's natural bounty. As Coll Thrush notes in *Native Seattle: Histories from the Crossing-Over Place*,

> Natural resources, political power, and spiritual force circulated through these settlements in ways reminiscent of the networks enmeshing larger urban places in other parts of the world. . . . Each of these winter towns, along with nearby seasonal camps, resources sites, and sacred places was linked into a broader geographic community through webs of kinship, trade, and diplomacy.

Within this fertile setting of salmon and cedar, Seattle's Coast Salish tribes lived by the tens of thousands in numerous small, interrelated named towns and villages—Place of the Fish Spear and Little Canoe Channel are two examples—along a network of rivers and estuaries spilling into Puget Sound. Vine Deloria Jr. remarks that "the Puget Sound region was one of the most heavily populated areas north of Mexico City, before the coming of the white man."

Referred to as the *Lushootseed* (a word from the Seattle-area Salish dialect combining two indigenous words meaning "salt water" and "language") people because of their shared language, the Coast Salish and Puget Salish native inhabitants included (and still do) the Suquamish, Duwamish, Nisqually, Snoqualmie, and Muckleshoot (Ilalkoamiah, Stuckamish, and Skopamish) tribes. (Along the coast of Puget Sound, "Salish" is the name for a group of languages, not a specific tribe.) Other tribes calling the greater Seattle area home include the Tulalip and Puyallup nations, as well those from nearby coastal areas: the Chinook, Lummi, Quinault, Makah, and Quileute tribes.

The foodways of the Coast Salish native people deeply reflect the bounty of the surrounding landscape and the seasons of the Pacific Northwest. Overall, the traditional diet of Coast Salish natives was varied and highly nutritious. More than 280 species of plants, mammals, fish, shellfish, birds, reptiles, and marine life were identified by tribal elders and museum archaeologists as part of the Burke Museum's 2012 shared exhibition, "Salish Bounty: Traditional Native American Foods of Puget Sound." Says Elizabeth Swanaset, co-curator with Warren King George, of the Burke Museum's exhibition in partnership with the Tulalip tribe, "Coast Salish people followed the fish, the seasons, the tides—that was our calendar."

Although their river and coastal towns were stable year-round, summer was the season when native people moved to camps and shelters along waterways where they fished, foraged, and preserved food for sustenance during the dark, wet days of winter. Gathering and drying huckleberries, raspberries, and blackberries, along with mushrooms, acorns, and hazelnuts; collecting nettles, salmonberry shoots, tubers such as the wapato, and fiddlehead ferns; digging bracken and the potato-like camas roots to pound into cakes for drying; and harvesting honey, tree sap, and crab apples were summer and fall food activities, primarily undertaken by women and girls. (Some fall and winter hunting expeditions also took place, in which elk, deer, and bears living in the prairies and foothills of the Cascades were pursued. Mountain goat meat was considered a treat.)

Shellfish was also abundant for harvesting. Clams, geoducks, mussels, and oysters were harvested in shallow bays and on beaches by women and girls of the villages. Some were dried for winter, but generally most were prepared for a gigantic feast of fresh clams and oysters. Although crabs—concentrated along the northern end of the Olympic Peninsula—were plentiful in the spring, they were difficult to preserve and therefore typically provided a seasonal treat.

Another essential Salish food is the oil of the eulachon (*Thaleichthys pacificus*) or *oolichan*, its name in native dialects, a pelagic fish migrating once a year up coastal rivers to spawn. Along with salmon, seal, herring, eel, and whales, the oolichan (also commonly known as candlefish and smelt) is a source of a rich oil used to flavor bland vegetables or meats or enhance the flavor of fruits and berries, as well as to preserve them from spoilage. As the name candlefish suggests, and as J. B. MacKinnon describes in his post "The Salvation Fish" on Maptia.com, these small fish were so rich in oil, once dried, they could be lit and burned as candles.

The silvery-blue fish historically returned in such large numbers that they were easily captured by the thousands in large nets or in weirs.

Native people also netted migrating herring and sardines, fished for flounder (a bottom-feeding flat fish caught by spearing the fish on the bottom of mudflats), and, during winter months, caught steelhead trout, which also returns from the ocean to its spawning streams. Some Pacific Northwest tribes, especially the Makah, were deep-water ocean fishermen, both adept at and revered for their skills hunting whales, seals, and sea otters.

Foods were often steamed in fire pits, a method especially efficient for cooking larger amounts requiring immediate preparation. Food was also smoked on drying racks, roasted on vertical stakes placed around a fire pit, air-dried, and/or cooked in vessels that were tightly coiled baskets or watertight cedar boxes. To make the boxes, cedar stakes were split into an approximate shape, steamed until somewhat flexible, and then shaped, fastened with wooden pegs, and finally allowed to dry. The wooden panels would contract and pull together, making the pot entirely waterproof. Hot rocks might be added to cook liquids in the wooden pot, or it could be suspended above a low flame, cooking the contents slowly. This cooking method was used for soups and porridges prepared from various fresh and dried meats, fish, shellfish, and seafood.

Foods might also be suspended over fire pits for smoking on wooden racks or stakes over a low-heat fire. Smoking also was a preservation method for fish, meats, and shellfish, and some meats were wrapped in cedar bark or thick leaves to steam over hot rocks.

PEOPLE OF THE SALMON

But it was the sea and the mighty wild salmon that native people depended on most for food. With their homeward migrations every spring and summer after three or so years roaming the ocean, salmon are the iconic fish of the Pacific Northwest. For coastal tribes centuries ago, salmon made up 80–90 percent of their diet. This significant status as a food source and salmon's abundant runs in local waters gave the fish divine powers in native lore and stories, creating cultural links between the natural and spiritual worlds. The naturally fatty fish are also packed with flavor for their return runs home to their spawning streams, usually many miles and days long, during which they do not eat, which makes them even more appealing as food.

To honor the annual return of the five species of the pelagic fish (defined as fish living in the middle zone of ocean or lake waters, not on the surface, in reefs, or on the ocean floor) to their freshwater spawning grounds far upstream, native people held ritual celebrations to venerate what was perceived as a mystical passage. These rituals of respect held at gatherings along riverbanks were almost religious in nature, celebrating the first salmon caught in each river or inlet. This special salmon would be cooked over an open fire, barbecue-style, and then cut lengthwise, not crosswise, as Vine Deloria Jr. writes in *Indians of the Pacific Northwest*, "for fear that the salmon would get insulted and never return to the stream." (A useful belief because cutting a large salmon lengthwise is much cleaner and easier than crosswise.) In a special ceremony filled with singing and dancing, portions of the fish were shared among everyone, and the undamaged skeleton of the first fish was slipped back into the water, believing it would be reborn, to return again and provide continual sustenance.

To catch migrating salmon, Coast Salish people devised ingenious methods to accommodate the habits of each of the five Pacific salmon (*Oncorhynchus*) species—King (Chinook), Chum (dog), Coho (silver), Pink (humpback), Sockeye (red)—and their corresponding migratory calendar, paired with the features of various watersheds, which ranged from lakes, shallow estuaries, and rivers to freshwater lakes or tidal inlets. Fishing methods included weirs, dip-netting platforms with spears and gaffs, gill nets, reef netting, trolling, and set-netting techniques. Vine Deloria Jr. points out that the sophistication of these fishing techniques is rarely acknowledged, nor are the refined and long-standing property divisions denoting family fishing areas whose boundaries were important in determining ownership of the catch.

On freshwater lakes, catching the fish before they entered deep water was essential. Fishermen would station themselves at outlets of the lake where a river or stream exited and either spear or gaff the salmon (a gaff is a pole about six feet long with a hook at one end), and then haul it aboard a canoe in one swift motion.

For freshwater streams and creeks draining into saltwater inlets, large, ingeniously constructed weirs or twig fences were built across the Duwamish and other rivers—usually community property—to trap returning salmon. Fishermen then used nets to catch the fish. While weirs were community property, nets were privately owned by families and their use required asking permission of the owners. (This distinction between community ownership of catching fish and family ownership of preserving fish was totally misunderstood for decades by lawyers involved in fishing rights, who insisted that because native people shared the weirs, they had no concept of individual ownership property rights, which was used against them.)

Gill nets were also used on freshwater streams and creeks. Openings of the natural fiber mesh nets allowed small fish to easily pass through but snared the gills of larger fish. The Lummi tribe north of Seattle developed a skilled method of fishing known as reef netting, where a large net was extended between two canoes and then anchored to the floor of the bay or passage. As salmon swam into the camouflaged net, they could be easily caught. Split-second timing to make the catch was essential, requiring the head fisherman to have an almost mystical sense about the salmon. Other native fishermen developed trawling, long-lining, jigging, and set-lining techniques for fishing.

This photo taken in 1911 shows a traditional weir trap Native Americans built across waterways to catch migrating salmon. *Courtesy of MOHAI, [Museum of History & Industry Photograph Collection], [1983.10.PA11.79].*

Once caught, depending on the species and weather conditions, salmon would be prepared in any number of ways. Sometimes salmon was smoked, and other times, with a good dry wind, it could be cured by wind-drying. Sun-drying was risky because of high humidity. Salmon eggs, considered a great winter delicacy, were also dried and smoked.

Plank-roasting salmon as butterflied fillets (backbone and entrails removed) on Western Red Cedar or alder boards is a traditional Pacific Northwest native cooking method handed down and practiced today. The woodsy fragrance and natural oils of cedar and alder planks impart a distinct flavor to the salmon. Pinned onto planks standing vertically around a wood fire, the salmon cooks slowly, ensuring that the fish retains its natural moisture and fat.

FOOD AS A CURRENCY

With this abundance of food resources, it is not surprising Coast Salish tribes of the Puget Sound region developed an extensive and complicated trading system among themselves and neighboring tribes based on food. With the region's range of different plants and animals, the opportunities for trade were extensive between inland people and coastal tribes, even extending as far as present-day eastern Washington. The food trade was often based on exchanging dried and smoked salmon; oil from seals, whales, and dogfish; and a variety of other seafood and shellfish, in return for buffalo, antelope, and other meats. The Makah tribe traded whale meat and seal oil for salmon, and cedar planks for houses and canoes.

"The Puget Sound people, who had more salmon than they knew what to do with, often travelled across the snowy Cascades to trade for salmon that had come up the Columbia to the famous Celilo Falls," Vine Deloria Jr. comments in *Indians of the Pacific Northwest*. In addition, he writes:

> Because food and other trade items were so plentiful, people had to become specialists in order to produce unique commodities for trade. One could not simply smoke salmon because everyone did. Rather, the different villages had to develop specialty items that would be coveted by other tribes in order to participate in the trade. So no one grew very rich and no one was very poor. It was a system that worked out well for all.

For example, sockeye salmon was available on the western coast but did not run in any of the streams of the Strait of Juan de Fuca where the Makah and Clallam tribes lived. The Makahs did not have sufficient cedar logs for houses or canoes, so they traded whale and seal oil, along with dried herring roe, in exchange for salmon and cedar.

CULTURAL INTERSECTIONS, CHANGING DIETS

With the arrival of the first Europeans in the Pacific Northwest in the eighteenth and nineteenth centuries, native food resources became less about sustenance and more about trade. The Canadian/British-based Hudson's Bay Company and its spin-off, the Northwest Company, both promoted trade with Native Americans based on salted salmon and whale oil, plus sea otter and beaver pelts. The currency of exchange was often in guns, sugar, wheat, and whisky, which changed cultural interactions as well as native eating habits. Beef stew and corned beef hash frequently replaced roasted salmon and steamed clams. In 1855, the Point Elliott Treaty stipulated native people had to have access to their traditional hunting and gathering places, a step toward blending new and old food traditions. In 1866, the first salmon cannery opened on the Columbia River, producing cans of salted Chinook salmon. Within twenty years, more than fifty salmon canneries were operating along the Columbia River, many with Native Americans as employees. Food had become a commodity in the Pacific Northwest.

To support various trading posts, British traders also encouraged native people to raise vegetables for trade. Although technically not a vegetable, the potato, introduced first at Fort Langley on the Fraser River in British Columbia, became a hit. By 1838, the Hudson's Bay Company had formed the Puget Sound Agricultural Company to launch farming and ranching operations in the Puget Sound region, a measure of where things were headed.

From rich beginnings, Native Americans in the Pacific Northwest rapidly lost their homeland territory to white settlers, along with access to traditional foraging, hunting, and fishing grounds. Their populations were also decimated by smallpox and similar devastating sicknesses introduced by Europeans and Americans. Beginning in the 1850s, it became impossible to separate politics from the enormous social and cultural changes taking place and affecting the Coast Salish people's food choices, diets, and culture. The website for the Burke Museum of Natural History and Culture, burkemuseum.org, describes the effect of settlers on Native American food customs:

> Non-Indian settlers rapidly altered ecosystems and restricted access to lands and waters, making it increasingly hard for Coast Salish people to collect traditional foods. The reservation system was supposed to replace this loss, but instead it imposed new foods poorly suited to Native People's nutritional and cultural needs. Coast Salish people struggled to adapt and keep alive the cultural values that have always guided how and what is good to eat. That struggle continues to this day.

A Native American encampment north of downtown Seattle around 1885, most likely at the western end of Bell Street. After 1895, Native Americans were not allowed to live within city boundaries, and development would also have eliminated this site. *Courtesy of MOHAI, [Seattle Historical Society Collection], [2174].*

In another indication of this cultural clash, annual salmon runs—the sacred symbol of Pacific Northwest food resources—declined due to competition between native fishing, commercial fishing, and sport fishermen, along with habitat degradation. Although treaties signed in the 1850s ostensibly gave native people fishing rights in their traditional places, an influx of canneries increased commercial demand for salmon and promoted overfishing. As a result, efforts to maintain and manage native fishing rights in Western Washington unraveled and instigated decades of antagonism. Not until 1974 was managing and harvesting wild salmon again confirmed as a native right in a federal legal decision by Judge George Boldt. This federal ruling, known as the Boldt Decision, reaffirmed the right of nineteen Western Washington tribes recognized by federal treaties to 50 percent of the annual harvest (the remaining 50 percent was allotted to commercial and sport fishermen in Washington State) and again confirmed and elevated managing and harvesting wild salmon as a native right. As an outcome of this decision, the Northwest Indian Fisheries Commission was formed as a tribal governance body to co-manage, develop, and monitor sustainable fisheries in collaboration with state wildlife agencies.

Another treaty in 1994 supported tribal rights to harvest 50 percent of shellfish in treaty areas, also signifying how indigenous food resources and native people continued to play a significant role in managing the region's local food supply.

DISCOVERING TRADITIONAL NATIVE AMERICAN FOODS

Today, native people in the Pacific Northwest are again creating a living culture, overcoming barriers and revitalizing their relationship to traditional foods. The barriers are many—polluted shellfish beds, depleted or extinct fish runs, loss of access to land for hunting or gathering wild plant foods, forgotten recipes, the lure of fast food, and lifestyles leaving little time for food preparation and community feasts. Many Coast Salish tribes, schools, and community groups are now joining together to relearn the knowledge and values that have guided their people for generations. The appeal of these food traditions is their timelessness, outstanding nutrition, and both cultural and generational connections. The core values promoted through native foods include food as the center of culture, honoring the food chain, eating with the seasons, and eating a variety of foods. It is a rich legacy that deserves to flourish again.

While a new generation of Salish Coast people is discovering indigenous foods and cooking methods of their Pacific Northwest heritage, surprisingly few restaurants in the Seattle area offer authentic Native American dishes. One option: Catch the food truck named Off the Rez. Its menu of Indian tacos, burgers, chili, and fry bread was inspired by its owner Mark McConnell's appreciation for the Native American foods he grew up eating at family gatherings.

One of Seattle's legacy restaurants, Ivar's Salmon House on Lake Union, offers a more formal menu, but it also celebrates Pacific Northwest native food traditions. The scenic restaurant, a beautiful cedar replica of a Pacific Northwest Native American longhouse, brings alive the heritage of Pacific Northwest native people with its open-pit Native American–style barbecue, a source of alder-smoked dishes. The main dining room is filled with Native American artifacts and historical photographs of the Pacific Northwest, while spectacular views of Lake Union can inspire visions of native fishermen plying the waters in rugged cedar canoes. (On some days, there actually are practice canoes paddling past in preparation for one of the annual races.) Ivar's menu features Pacific Northwest seafood, including alder-smoked salmon, halibut, cod, clams, Dungeness crab, prawns, and many seasonal specials.

Two other restaurants, one west and one north of Seattle, also offer authentic tastes of Pacific Northwest native cuisine. Blackfish, a destination restaurant at the Tulalip Resort Casino on the Tulalip Reservation, is an hour's drive north of Seattle. Seafood is the star here too, and menu favorites include clam fritters and wild salmon cooked on ironwood spears over a charcoal and alder wood pit fire.

The second, Tillicum Village on Blake Island in Elliott Bay, offers an immersion into native culture. A half-hour ride from Seattle's waterfront aboard private boats operated by Argosy Cruises, the reconstructed native village is in a scenic natural setting with water vistas and a breathtaking straight-on view of Mt. Rainier (on clear days). It's an ideal opportunity for experiencing food, art, dance, and the history of the Coast Salish tribes. Guests to the island are served a veritable feast complete with salmon cooked on alder wood slabs using the traditional method; wild grain harvest rice; a Northwest stew featuring bison, beef, and venison; whole grain harvest rice; bread; salad; and more. The dessert, wild blackberry crisp, is the perfect ending to a Pacific Northwest feast.

3

❖ ❖

Early History

From Settlers to Loggers, Gold Diggers, and Celebrants at the Alaska-Yukon-Pacific Exposition

By all accounts, it was a drenchingly wet, stormy afternoon in November 1851 when twenty-two persons, five families of adults and children, disembarked from the two-masted schooner *Exact* and rowed ashore onto tidal flats of a low and sandy peninsula extending into Elliott Bay. The group (named the Denny Party after its twenty-nine-year-old leader, Arthur Denny) had traveled overland from Illinois to Oregon by covered wagon. Following a Portland stopover, the group headed north by ship to meet Denny's younger brother David, its advance scout, and two other friends, John Low and Lee Terry. The young men (David Denny was nineteen years old) had arrived together in September 1851 to stake a claim at *Smaquamox*, the Indian name of the place later renamed Alki Point by the white settlers.

Surrounded by the towering coastal forest of Douglas fir, Western hemlock, and red cedar trees, the group found a small, unfinished, and roofless log cabin constructed by the young men. Until other cabins were built, everyone packed into one room of the cabin. Nearby, a handful of newly arrived homesteaders—the Collins Party—was mapping out a pioneer farm alongside the Duwamish River estuary (the area became Georgetown in 1890), also the site of several tribal villages whose curious inhabitants visited the white settlers. The Denny Party's intent in journeying north was to establish a maritime commerce resource supplying San Francisco, which was booming following the 1849 gold rush in the Sierra foothills, with valuable Pacific Northwest commodities such as lumber and salmon.

From fur traders, trappers, and lumbermen, to miners, military personnel, missionaries, homesteaders, fortune seekers, and entrepreneurs like the Denny Party, Seattle's history intersects with the westward movement of Americans in the nineteenth century. An estimated sixty-five thousand travelers—both native-born Americans and European immigrants—journeyed to the Pacific Northwest between 1830 and 1860. For many overland pioneers, it was about following the Oregon Trail to Seattle by way of Portland and the Willamette Valley. This route followed in the footsteps of Meriwether Lewis and William Clark, who from 1804 to 1806 explored the Columbia River east of the Cascade Mountains, following the mighty river on its route to the Pacific Ocean. Other overland expeditions followed. In 1846, when the United States declared its sovereignty over the Oregon Country in a treaty establishing the boundary between American and British territories in North America—now the modern-day border between the United States and Canada—northward traffic increased significantly. The Oregon Donation Land Law passed by Congress in 1850 added more incentives for Americans to move westward to establish sanctioned claims on public lands. Disgruntled California gold prospectors also headed north in the late 1840s, seeking more reliable revenue sources.

After finding much of the Portland/Columbia River and Willamette Valley areas already claimed, pioneers moved north, settling first in the south Puget Sound region. In 1844, Michael T. Simmons and George W. Bush led an organized party to a site along the Deschutes River not far from the Hudson's Bay Company's outpost at Fort Nisqually. To endure their initial brutal winter, the group survived with help from nearby Native Americans who had introduced them to the area's natural food resources. In a short time, the outpost grew, expanding from a customs house to a general store, sawmill and gristmill (both constructed in 1847), and it eventually became Olympia, named the provisional capital of Washington Territory in 1853.

Farther north along the Puget Sound, in "New York Alki," the Denny Party's aspiring name for its new settlement—the last word was borrowed from the Chinook language and means "by-and-by"—the group celebrated its first Pacific Northwest Christmas in December 1851. The holiday meal included local foods such as wild goose, potatoes purchased from Native Americans, clam broth, and salmon.

Settler larders were also stocked with transported foods: barrels of flour, butter, and salted meat such as pork, plus sugar, syrup, tea, and coffee. As might be expected, these resourceful early settlers also tapped local edibles for daily meals. Gordon Newell, a dedicated chronicler of Seattle history, describes David Denny, in his lively history titled *Westward to Alki: The Story of David and Louisa Denny*, as "an ace hunter and fisherman" who supplied his extended family with food and acted as intermediary with Native Americans.

As the calendar turned over to 1852, winter weather intensified and supplies started running out. Arthur Denny, in his later memoir, *Pioneer Days on Puget*

Sound, recalled that "few vessels visited the Sound and it was a time of great scarcity and distress because barrels of pork, butter, and flour came around Cape Horn." Facing severe shortages, several in the Denny group paddled canoes to a nearby Duwamish tribal village on the Black River to trade for food. Denny also noted in this same memoir, "This was the hardest experience our people ever had, but it demonstrated the fact that some substantial life-supporting food can always be obtained on Puget Sound, though it is hard for a civilized man to live without bread."

In February 1852, recognizing that their New York Alki settlement didn't offer protection from storms or water deep enough for anticipated transport ships, Arthur Denny, Carson Boren, and William Bell explored and staked claims on the sheltered deep water on the east side of Elliott Bay (named in 1841 by Lieutenant Charles Wilkes, commander of the US Navy's oceanic exploring and surveying expedition, to honor his ship's chaplain, J. L. Elliott). Together, they moved their families to this new location with the intent of developing a small city. Today, this neighborhood is called Pioneer Square in honor of its heritage.

SEATTLE'S EARLIEST DAYS

As the early settlers arrived and set about constructing homes and business buildings in Seattle, the abundance of indigenous foods, as well as communities of Native Americans living close by to introduce harvesting and preparation methods, added a measure of security to their efforts. With a variety of edibles readily accessible around the Puget Sound, a basic requirement of survival was guaranteed, more so than in other areas such as dry and desolate eastern Washington. To illustrate the diversity of local foods discovered by settlers, historians Robert S. Fisher, in his essay "Mirror of Taste," and Clarence Bagley, in *History of King County, Washington*, both cite a letter by Rev. David Blaine, who arrived in November 1853 in Seattle with his wife, Catherine. In his first letter written in December of that year to family back East, Blaine describes in detail the native foods he found:

> As for fruit, we can very well live without it as the superabundance of berries here will serve as a substitute. These are all around during nine or ten months in the twelve. We have strawberries, raspberries, dewberries, salal berries, salmon berries, cranberries, whortleberries and wild grapes of a superior kind. These ripen successively and are picked by the Indians and brought in by the barrel. Cranberries and whortleberries are still hanging on the bushes in abundance. They are larger and more solid than our berries at home in the states.
>
> There is an abundance of game in the woods, consisting of deer, wild cattle (these belong to the Hudson's Bay Company but have run wild), bears, wolves, panthers, squirrels, skunks, and rats. Pheasants, grouse, gulls and ducks and crows are as tame as

hens at home. They are very numerous. There are also great many eagles, ravens, and cranes. Our Sound, or inland sea, besides its many other excellent qualities, abounds in fish of almost every variety. Salmon are very abundant, cod fish, herring, sardines, oysters, and clams. Whales come spouting along now and then. Halibut are caught at certain seasons of the year. The Indians do most of the fishing. The oysters here are of an inferior quality and small size.

With this cornucopia of seasonal edibles, pioneer women in the Pacific Northwest learned from Native Americans how to collect berries and green edibles, cook fish over open fires and in stewpots, dig for geoducks hiding in tide flats, and find clams and oysters in tidal inlets. Generally however, settlers craved familiar foods from their previous lives. Locally harvested foods such as venison and potatoes, traded or purchased from neighboring Native Americans, met the familiarity criteria, but others were commodities transported as household goods aboard ships. Seattle historian Clarence Bagley mentions Chile as the source of flour, and China for sugar, while ships sailing from East Coast cities around Cape Horn transported barrels of port and butter.

Adding to the culinary portrait of early settlers, in her book *The Way We Ate: Pacific Northwest Cooking, 1843–1900*, Jacqueline B. Williams presents a

In this sketch by Emily Inez Denny, Arthur Denny's oldest daughter, white settlers are shown bargaining in the 1850s with Native American traders at Alki Point. *Courtesy of MOHAI, [Seattle Historical Society Collection], [16468].*

fascinating and comprehensive investigation of the key elements of pioneer kitchens and cooking. Brought alive with first-person accounts from historical letters and diaries, Williams describes the three essentials cooks needed to feed their families in their new rustic surroundings: access to water, shelter, and channels for replenishing dwindling food supplies. She describes pioneer cooks as inventive and reliant on family recipes they brought with them to prepare meals with transported raw materials. (Cookbooks were still rare in this period; home cooks learned how to cook by watching relatives.) New foods were intriguing, but familiar "comfort food" dishes were preferred.

In this pioneer setting, cooking over an open fire in a cast-iron pot or Dutch oven was the standard method, and the same cooking technique relied on during settlers' overland journeys. Once a log cabin or log house was erected, with a fireplace if a family's menfolk or a neighbor was a skilled mason, cooking moved indoors. Otherwise, cooking could take place in a separate small cookhouse. As Williams outlines, floors in these log buildings and their kitchens were sometimes oilcloth but typically either dirt or split cedar log planks. Rarely were cook stoves present due to transport challenges related to their weight, but, surprisingly, Mary Denny (wife of Arthur Denny) arrived in 1851 with a small iron cook stove among the family's household goods, ready to set up in her pioneer household. Once homesteads were established, most early settlers also raised chickens, kept a cow or two, and planted kitchen gardens.

In the beginning, food items such as flour and pork were only available from commercial sources, which made Seattle's first residents dependent on maritime commerce and local retailers. Flour to bake bread, the familiar staff of life, was prized over almost every other ingredient. While the British at the Hudson's Bay Company outpost in Fort Vancouver planted wheat in 1828 and constructed a grist mill for grinding flour, it took several years before wheat fields were established near Seattle, and eventually most wheat came from eastern Washington farms. Food items arrived by ship at regular arrivals once word spread about the new settlement and its lumber resources. Ship captains would trade foodstuffs they'd brought as cargo to sell to settlers while loading lumber, thus establishing a mutually beneficial maritime commerce connection.

Charles Terry, a member of the Denny Party, was first to establish a retail store selling everything from hardware items to food. According to records, by late November 1851, Terry had opened a store on Alki Point with items he had shipped along with his family's household goods. Organized as a general store, his first sales were for axes, tobacco, tin ware, whiskey, and rye, all transported aboard the *Exact.* Later store orders included grocery staples such as barrels of pork, flour, molasses, sugar, mustard, lard, hams, and dried fruit such as raisins, all transported northward by merchant vessels from California. As competition,

Arthur Denny opened a retail store in the new Elliott Bay settlement, taking commercial goods off the hands of sea captains with no out-of-pocket costs and selling them on commission.

While timber shipments and wooden building materials were the primary source of cash income for early settlers, the abundance and proximity of seafood contributed to the town's developing economy. A key player in this diversification was David S. Maynard ("Doc" Maynard), who had made his way up the coast from Olympia in early spring 1852, arriving in the company of Chief Sealth. Aware of the commercial potential of salmon for the San Francisco market, Maynard staked his waterfront land claim among welcoming Denny Party members, establishing a hospital and starting a fish processing plant. His log cabin was constructed large enough to accommodate his living quarters along with a drugstore and a general store called the Seattle Exchange. In the first summer of operating his fish packing plant, his workers packed a thousand barrels of brined salmon. Unfortunately, historians note that the brine wasn't strong enough, probably because salt was an expensive and relatively scarce commodity then, and the fish arrived spoiled.

Most significantly, it was Maynard's personal friendship with Chief Sealth, leader of the surrounding Duwamish and Suquamish tribes, that inspired the new settlement's name. Sealth, who interacted and cooperated with white settlers, was a diplomat and visionary seeking a place for his people in a new cultural landscape. Although not consulted about using his name for the new town, which white settlers unanimously agreed was preferred over "Duwamps" (its original name), Chief Sealth acquiesced and is still honored today for his participation in helping to create the Pacific Northwest's most vibrant city.

In October 1852, another notable name in Seattle history arrived at the Denny Party's new Elliott Bay location. The person behind the name was Henry Yesler, an entrepreneur traveling from Ohio and seeking a waterfront location to build a steam-powered sawmill, the first on the Puget Sound. Finding a location in no time on land the others eagerly sold to him, Yesler built his lumber mill and soon employed most of the male settlers, along with many Native Americans. The lumber mill's forested and hilly setting gave rise to the term "Skid Road," a phrase originating from logs sliding down surrounding hills on greased runners to the mill, where they were processed and readied for shipping to California. (Today the road is named Yesler Way.)

Yesler also built a single-story log cookhouse that earned status as the town's first restaurant. With the lumber mill the primary source of employment for the town's men, Yesler insisted that his employees eat there: "All must be prompt at the mill, and this is why all were required to eat at the cookhouse," as John

Calibrick notes in his *HistoryLink* essay "Yesler, Henry L." As a center for meals and conviviality, the cookhouse also served as a site for community social and civic activities ranging from sermons by visiting ministers to Seattle's first court case and election. Although there are no existing records about what was served, Chuck Flood, in his book *Lost Restaurants of Seattle*, relays a mock obituary published in the *Puget Sound Weekly* in 1866 when the building was torn down. The mock obituary noted that the cookhouse was

> simply a dingy-looking hewed-log building about 25 feet square, a little more than one story high with a shed addition in the rear, and to strangers and new-comers was something of an eyesore. . . . No man ever found the latch string of the cook house drawn in or went away hungry from the little cabin door; and many an old Puget-Sounder remembers the happy hours, jolly nights, strange encounters, and wild scenes he has enjoyed around the broad fireplace and hospitable board of Yesler's cook-house.

However, historian William Speidel suspects that businessman Yesler was not without his compensation, noting that "naturally, Henry [Yesler] made a tidy profit on each meal sold" in his 1967 book, *Sons of the Profits*.

With the demise of the Yesler cookhouse (replaced by Yesler's Pavillion as the town meeting place), other eating places were constructed in the fledgling water-front town, notably the Seattle Restaurant and Coffee Saloon, an establishment opened by one of Seattle's early black settlers, Matthias Monet, which he converted two years later into an oyster house called Connoisseur's Retreat. Interestingly, Seattle's first African American settler, Manuel Lopes, is credited with opening the first official restaurant in 1852, on Commercial Street (now First Avenue) as both a restaurant and a barbershop. Although no records exist to say what was served (only that the restaurant was sold in 1859), Lopes was known for providing meals whether or not his customers had the money to pay. He is also described as one of Seattle's most colorful early settlers, who not only announced mealtimes—especially lunch—to the village by beating his snare drum but also led the annual Fourth of July procession, described as circling through the muddy township's maze of shanties punctuated by tree stumps.

By the mid-1850s, Seattle was a frontier town of wooden clapboard buildings constructed on a muddy flat and inhabited by loggers, millworkers, sailors, and miners. As word spread about its prosperity, the city grew as a trading and commercial center, and boarding houses and hotels such as Felker House—the city's earliest, opening in 1853—sprang up to provide inexpensive housing for hardworking, hard-living single men. Most ate their meals in the boarding houses and cheap bare-bones hotels that proliferated in the main commercial district.

This view of early Seattle (1878) looks south from Pine Street across Elliott Bay to Henry Yesler's lumber mill, with a faint glimpse of Mt. Rainier in the background. *Courtesy of MOHAI, [Lantern Slide Collection], [2002.3.496].*

In 1884, Seattle's first upscale hotel, the Occidental, was constructed in what is now Pioneer Square, with a separate dining room with entrances from both the street or within the hotel. An 1888 menu from the hotel (included in the University of Washington's special collection) lists sophisticated dishes such as baked striped bass à la Bordelaise, boiled sugar-cured ham with Champagne sauce, roast stuffed young turkey with cranberry sauce, duck with orange marmalade sauce, and dessert options including Charlotte Russe, Indian Pudding with hard sauce, pumpkin or apple pie, and cream puffs.

Clarence Bagley, in documenting Seattle's early history in *History of King County, Washington* (1916), reported that by 1876, the fledgling city's first annual business directory listed 12 restaurants among Seattle's 272 business establishments. Bagley also notes that during this era, "cattle still ran at large in the streets . . ." and in early morning "cows gathered in front of vegetable shops and 'mooed' for breakfast." Humans were still well looked after. The dining room of the Brunswick Hotel near the waterfront docks served soup, salads, and

Opened just off Pioneer Square, where James and Mills Streets (now Yesler Way) intersect, the Occidental Hotel with its separate dining room was considered the grandest hotel in Washington Territory. *Courtesy of MOHAI, [Seattle Historical Society Collection], [1581].*

fish, with a bakery known for wedding cakes, while two restaurants in the area boasted all-night lunch counters, one advertising it served "everything the market affords in eating and drinking," while also noting it "employed no Chinese," which reflected racial tensions of the time. Street corner vendors also sold hot dogs, eggs, candy, and popcorn at popular intersections until a city ordinance in 1892 stopped their sales.

Overall, the city's economy expanded between 1870 and 1880, to include a small gold-mining segment, plus coal mining, farming, wheat, and fruit shipments from eastern Washington, along with small manufacturing, dairy production, and a northern fishing industry including halibut and salmon fisheries in Alaska. Leaving its frontier persona behind, Seattle looked west with the 1882 launch of a trans-Pacific steamship route. By the 1890 census, Seattle's population totaled slightly less than forty-three thousand, a number achieved despite the Great Fire of 1889 that devastated the city's downtown business district.

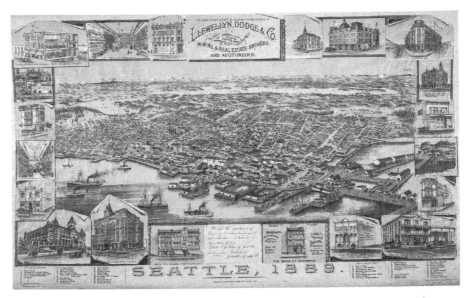

An aerial view of Seattle looking northeast toward the Cascade Mountains before the huge fire in 1889, with advertisements for various city businesses around the edge of the map. *Courtesy of MOHAI, [Seattle Historical Society Collection], [483B].*

THE GREAT SEATTLE FIRE

A city milestone and a catastrophe, the Great Fire of Seattle on June 6, 1889, roared through twenty-five blocks including four wharves of the developing business district, almost all wood-framed houses and buildings, turning everything, including all the area's restaurants and cafés, to ashes. Caused by a glue pot in a downtown woodworking shop catching fire, the inferno wasn't helped by limited water access from a private water company, low water pressure, and a low tide too far out for fire hoses to reach seawater. Business owners regrouped quickly, however, housing businesses and restaurants in tents, and the city immediately launched a massive building campaign, with new building codes requiring brick, stone, and iron construction instead of wood. Laborers and transient workers flooded into Seattle to rebuild the area, creating a need for more saloons, taverns, boarding houses, and cheap hotels. Unlike Seattle's early days, this time there was a need for higher-end accommodations and restaurants.

One of the only downtown restaurants rebuilt after the fire was the Merchant's Cafe, which reopened in 1890 in today's Pioneer Square. This historic bar, according to Clint Lanier and Derek Hembree in their book *Bucket List Bars: Historic Saloons, Pubs and Dives of America*, offers a snapshot of Seattle's early history.

The original wooden two-story building was replaced by a brick building with a liquor store/café on the bottom floor and a hotel on the upper two floors. Almost 130 years later, the doors to Merchant's Cafe are still open, making it the oldest standing restaurant in Seattle. Today, diners can order food named for Seattle's early history, including Klondike Mozzarella Nuggets, Yesler Sliders, and Doc Maynard's Prawn Skewers, or order a beer at the intricately carved bar shipped around Chile's Cape Horn in the late 1800s.

Several other saloons that opened in Pioneer Square after the fire are still operating, particularly the J & M Café and the Central Café. Each has been bought and sold numerous times and had colorful histories as speakeasies and brothels. The Central Café, dating to 1892, was originally called Watson Brothers Famous Restaurant. Never known for its food, in the 1970s—after being purchased by two young Boeing engineers, Bob Foster and Jamie Anderson—it hosted legendary Seattle musicians such as Jimi Hendrix, Alice In Chains, Nirvana, and Soundgarden and earned a footnote in Seattle's musical history book.

In another change following the Great Seattle Fire and reflecting Seattle's positive economic status, boarding houses turned upscale. Now called "residential hotels," they catered to business travelers and offered meals in on-the-premises dining rooms. While not restaurants in the traditional sense—there were no menus and guests weren't given food choices—available food usually served buffet-style was an incentive to book a room. One of the first residential hotels was the Otis, which opened in 1902 on Summit Avenue in Pioneer Square.

As Hattie Horrocks mentions in her history of Seattle's restaurants, the city's hotels also added dining rooms in the late 1890s to cater to well-off clientele and business travelers. The Grill Room at the Butler Hotel built in 1893 at Second and James Streets featured cold storage and an open refrigerator permitting patrons to select their steaks and other meats that were then cooked to order. Other downtown hotels serving meals in this era included the Snoqualmie, the Arlington, the Diller, and the Rainier Grand. The Waldorf Hotel on Pike Street is recognized for having the first twenty-four-hour coffee shop.

Hotels outside the downtown area also served meals. The Alki, which opened in 1895 near the site of the Denny Party's landing, was famous for its chicken dinners and touted as "well worth the ferry ride" to West Seattle, as observed by Hattie Horrocks in her manuscript, *Restaurants of Seattle*. High on a hill above the downtown business area, the spectacular Denny Hotel (also known as the New Washington Hotel) provided guests with views of Mt. Rainier, Mt. Baker, and the Olympic Range from the dining room and bar. According to Horrocks, the menu from August 19, 1904, listed an elaborate range of choices including clam chowder and several varieties of fish. Unfortunately, the imposing hotel was torn down in 1906 as part of the Denny Regrade project. In its place, a new version of the New

Washington Hotel was built in 1908 at Second and Stewart Streets (today called the Josephinum and used for low-income housing and a Catholic church). As Horrocks also mentions, the May 1913 menu from this hotel's dining room offered Olympia oyster stew, fried Olympia oysters, loin of lamb, beef tenderloin, and veal chops with vegetables ranging from stuffed eggplant and carrots and peas in cream to cauliflower and asparagus.

THE ALASKA-YUKON GOLD RUSH, 1896–1899

The Great Seattle Fire proved to be a catalyst for the city's next growth period, which expanded its range and access to food commodities, and was also spurred by a rivalry with Tacoma at the southern end of Puget Sound. The Northern Pacific Railroad line ending in Tacoma in 1883 had launched the fierce competition. As University of Washington professor Linda Nash pointed out in a 2016 lecture, in its early years, Seattle was all about being a non-stop source of supplies to San Francisco, from wood to salmon, from coal to whale oil—at least until the severe national economic depression from 1893 to 1897. Tacoma also pursued this path, but with the 1893 arrival of the Great Northern Railroad into Seattle, with its route from St. Paul, Minnesota, Seattle surged ahead. More settlers arrived directly to the growing city, while the drastic grading of hills above the central district prompted more business development. The railroad's arrival also inspired small food-processing businesses to develop and produce bread, beer, and cheese, while local farms exchanged produce, meat, potatoes, and some grains, adding to the city's solid commercial base.

One bright spot during this economic recession were gold searches in the Yukon Territory and interior Alaska. In July 1897, as anticipated, the SS *Portland* arrived with a cargo of solid gold from the Klondike River area in Canada's Yukon Territory. Word about the fortunate strike rocketed like wildfire from Seattle to other West Coast cities. The news described Seattle as a gateway to the north, prompting expeditions to form with would-be gold miners who could easily travel to Seattle by train. Almost overnight, the city's businesses became staging grounds for Alaska-bound expeditions. Fortune seekers arriving for their journey north not only needed to purchase food, tents, clothing, and supplies for their journeys to the faraway gold fields but also had to be housed and fed before their departure. Local merchants, the Seattle Chamber of Commerce, and city officials seized on this opportunity, developing a successful publicity campaign to convince the world Seattle was the only place to be outfitted for the journey as "The Gateway to the Gold Fields." Grocers, general stores selling hardware and expedition equipment, and clothing suppliers all rose to the occasion. A special edition of the *Seattle*

Post-Intelligencer published on October 13, 1897, promoted Seattle to prospective Klondike miners with this information: "There are numerous good restaurants of all grades in the city and any number of good boarding houses."

Restaurateurs weren't the only ones benefiting from the gold rush. Seattle's hoteliers and boarding house owners booked sold-out properties, while merchants had a monopoly in providing miners with the supplies and food they would need to last a year. The *Seattle Post-Intelligencer*, on October 21, 1897, also emphasized that Seattle's Klondike goods were manufactured specifically for the Arctic, with "her meats being especially cured and her butter packed." The region's food industries received a major boost from the demand for dried fruit, flour, and potatoes. A boat ride away from downtown Seattle, farmers and processors on Whidbey Island began producing tons of dried potatoes as an innovative way to earn income from a traditional crop. As described in the Klondike Gold Rush, Seattle Division, History & Culture section of the website for the Seattle Unit of National Park Service records (www.nps.gov), "some 30,000 to 40,000 of the estimated 70,000 'stampeders' (prospectors) who arrived to be outfitted for their Klondike expeditions bought their 'ton of provisions' in Seattle."

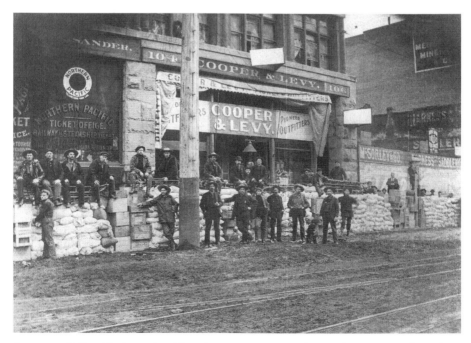

A group of Klondike-bound gold seekers in 1897, standing with provisions from the Cooper & Levy grocery store (on First Avenue South), one of many outfitters in the city. *Courtesy of MOHAI, [Seattle Historical Society Collection], [401].*

While rowdy miners were eating and drinking at taverns and saloons, an alternative to Seattle's rough-and-tumble gold rush establishments also flourished in 1888. That year, a trio of business pioneers and entrepreneurs—Thomas Burke, William Peters, and John Leary—decided to distinguish themselves from city riffraff and open a private club for entertaining, socializing, and conducting business. The result of their efforts: the swanky, members-only Rainier Club. Given that egalitarian territorial law in this era did not allow private clubs to be established, the Rainier Club was first listed as an exclusively male boarding house and restaurant. Ten years later it reincorporated as a private club, which it remains today. As for dishes served in its elegant dining room, when Honorable George Meyer, secretary of the navy, attended a private dinner at the club in 1910, he was served an upscale meal of Drayton Harbor Oysters, Dungeness crab flakes, fricassee of capon, and filet of Eastern beef. This sophisticated dining tradition, with its focus on seasonal Pacific Northwest ingredients by the club's exclusive chef, continues today.

Seattle's Klondike-infused gold rush officially ended in 1899, but the boom had lasting effects. The surge in commerce persuaded the Northern Pacific and the Great Northern railroads to upgrade their Elliott Bay dock facilities to streamline moving goods and raw materials between ships and trains, and vice versa. Imports and exports expanded, with British Columbia, Vancouver, Alaska, Hawaii, the newly acquired US territory of the Philippines, and the Far East now accessible in a thriving new trade network.

THE 1909 ALASKA-YUKON-PACIFIC EXPOSITION

Having established Seattle as a gateway to Alaska, Canada's Yukon Territory, and Asia with the Yukon Gold Rush, the city and state's leaders (Washington had become a state in 1889) were determined to continue promoting the region and supporting its economic development. The outcome of their efforts: the city's first world's fair, the Alaska-Yukon-Pacific Exposition, held between June 1 and October 16, 1909, attracted more than three million visitors. Constructed on the forested campus of the young University of Washington, which had moved to the site in 1895 from its downtown campus, A-Y-P (the fair's shortened name) was designed by the Olmsted Brothers with its primary sightline focused on Mt. Rainier. This view inspired the line "the World's Most Beautiful Fair" in an advertisement for the Great Northern Railway promoting a scenic railroad journey over the Rocky Mountains to Seattle in the *Washington* (DC) *Evening Star*, March 14, 1909. While Japan and Canada were the only foreign governments to erect pavilions, the presence of exhibits and displays from the US territory of Hawaii and the Philippines (turned over to the United States at the end of the Spanish-American War) added

international flavor. Closer to home, many communities in Washington State produced displays to showcase their history and key products, from historical artifacts
to prized agricultural items.

New and familiar foods to taste were part of the Alaska-Yukon-Pacific fair's experiences. "The Pay Streak" arcade, the fair's entertainment and refreshment area
with souvenirs and carnival rides, also featured booths themed around the Yukon
gold rush with costumed miners and Native Americans, while thirsty fair-goers
could buy glasses of lemonade at a Japanese-style kiosk or "pea nuts" from a grab-
and-go stand. Adding to the fair's international atmosphere, the Chinese Village
was constructed by Ah King, a successful businessman in Seattle's Chinatown. The
display's three buildings included a stage with a theater troupe from Shanghai, as
well as a teahouse and a restaurant serving authentic chop suey.

In its intent and premonition, the 1909 Alaska-Yukon-Pacific Exposition established Seattle as a city with international connections, both in business and in
food fascinations. The next chapter of the city's culinary history promised to be
delicious on many levels.

4

Immigrant and Migration Patterns

Seattle's Melting Pot of Global Culinary Traditions

Like most others who have done the impossible, they were dreamers.

—Peter Ebbesen, Danish immigrant, 1868

Swedish and Norwegian pancake breakfasts, dim sum, and steaming bowls of *pho* are three culinary hints of Seattle's diverse ethnic population. While some immigrants arrived in the city more than 150 years ago and others are newly settled, for all, food is a significant link to homeland cultural traditions and identity. Whether seeking jobs, asylum, or adventure, the culinary traditions and vibrant flavors immigrants brought to their new home influenced what Seattleites eat today.

Seattle's immigrant history with its multiple culinary traditions mirrors immigrant patterns in other parts of the United States. Driven by economic crisis, as well as social, political, and religious discontent, two waves of European immigrants arrived in the Pacific Northwest between 1840 and 1914. In this period, nearly fifty-two million Europeans left for overseas destinations, with thirty-five million coming to the United States. The first wave arriving in Washington Territory from 1840 to 1880 was primarily from Great Britain, Ireland, Germany, the Netherlands, and the Nordic countries, plus transplanted Canadians. The second wave of immigrants arrived between the 1880s and the outbreak of the First World War, with the majority coming from Southern and Eastern Europe.

In the 1850s, Washington Territory remained one of the last frontiers in the United States, with a non-Indian population estimated at one thousand. Attracted by America's reputation for welcoming immigrants, jobs in burgeoning industries—including farming, fishing, maritime, forestry, coal mining, shipbuilding, and railroad construction—and a landscape familiar to many, particularly those from Nordic countries, immigrants headed to Seattle in record numbers. Disenchantment following the 1849 Gold Rush in Northern California and the liberal 1862 Homestead Act were contributing factors. The significant impact of expanded railway lines was also critical: in 1883, a connection between Seattle and Tacoma with the Northern Pacific Railway Company was completed, and another in 1893 with the Great Northern Railroad. Both lines made transport from East and West Coast cities more direct. Add the 1897 Yukon Gold Rush, and Seattle became a boomtown. According to the 1910 US Census, the number of non-native inhabitants had exploded to 250,000, with 23 percent of the population consisting of foreign-born immigrants. The 1910 census also indicated that 26 percent of the state's population were first- or second-generation residents from Nordic countries, followed by 31 percent from Canada, Great Britain, or Ireland.

Although immigrants arrived in a region blessed with an abundance of natural resources, for most (Scandinavians excepted) these resources were unfamiliar ingredients, and people preferred to cook comfort food recipes from their home countries. Family recipes had to be tweaked to substitute what was locally available; yet, over time, these so-called foreign ingredients, flavors, cooking techniques, and ethnic dishes brought by immigrants became woven into Seattle's culinary tapestry.

As regional and international transportation and commerce expanded, ingredients could be imported across long distances, making it easier to re-create authentic dishes at home and in restaurants. Local food resources also expanded, as Italian and Japanese immigrants established truck farms in outlying areas and provided fresh produce to city residents. Neighborhood cafés operated by immigrants were primarily about economic opportunity for the owners, who could sell inexpensive food to customers craving flavors from home, like "Mother used to make," and offer community with others from their homeland.

Although immigrants from every corner of the globe have settled in Seattle, the following overviews focus on culinary contributions and traditions of immigrant groups having the most impact on the city's food culture.

NORDIC IMMIGRANTS

A tour of greater Seattle in the early 1900s would have offered plenty of places to stop in for a two-cent cup of coffee and *wienerbrød*, a flaky buttery almond-paste pastry beloved by Scandinavians. In that era, there were eleven Scandinavian bakery/ cafés in the area—full-service bakeries with adjoining coffee shops (called a *kaffé stuga* in Norwegian or Swedish)—evidence of the city's many Danish and Swedish immigrants who were skilled bakers. These coffee shops, notably Scandia Bakery & Café, founded by Swedish immigrants Gast and Anna Backman and located at 902 Howell Street, were gathering places for Nordic immigrants craving the company of their countrymen and -women in a foreign land, along with favorite foods of their homelands.

In Seattle, settlers from the countries of Sweden, Norway, Denmark, Finland, and Iceland had many fellow immigrants to join them in coffee conversations. Economic distress, population growth, social inequities, agricultural crises, famines, plus political, personal, and religious factors all motivated Nordic emigrants to embark for America. They were also lured by glowing "America letters" from relatives who had already immigrated, extensive in-home country advertising by American steamship and railroad companies, along with newspaper reports about business opportunities. The Homestead Act of 1862 allowing anyone over the age of twenty-one to apply for a 160-acre parcel of federal land was also motivating, a huge opportunity compared with Nordic cultures in which only the eldest son inherited the family farm.

Nordic immigrants arrived in the Pacific Northwest in two waves. First came rural farmers with families who could afford to immigrate. The first European to settle in King County was a Dane, Matts Pedersen, who claimed 160 acres in 1865 in what is now the town of North Bend. Many of the men had seafaring and lumbering experience, allowing them to quickly acclimatize to the Seattle region. Many of these new settlers had first immigrated to Midwestern farms and cities, and they brought to the Northwest not only foodways from their homeland but also dishes already adapted to local ingredients. By the beginning of the twentieth century, the second immigration wave arrived: single women joining relatives, along with laborers and craftsmen from Scandinavian coastal towns and cities.

The city of Ballard (a separate city until annexation by Seattle in 1907), with its first land claim dating to 1852, was the residential hub for Nordic immigrants. In 1890, it was a thriving independent city, one of the largest in the new state of Washington, with 1,636 residents. Immigrants flocked here to work in lumber mills, shipyards, and cedar shingle mill factories (at one time, more cedar shingles were produced in Ballard than any other place in the world) along Salmon Bay. By 1905, Ballard's population had reached ten thousand due to maritime and shipping industries; since 1914, the Alaska Fishing Fleet's homeport has been Fishermen's Terminal, just south of Ballard. Even more significantly, the area resembled home for many Nordic immigrants, from the surrounding Olympic and Cascade mountain ranges to the many neighborhood social clubs, community centers, Lutheran churches, coffee shops, and bakeries.

Given the modest backgrounds of most Nordic immigrants, whether living in town or on a dairy farm outside Seattle, eating and entertaining occasions occurred almost exclusively at home or at family gatherings. Family meals were a lot like home-country meals because of the similarity of Pacific Northwest ingredients: simple, seasonal, and often seafood-based, with salmon, herring, and halibut being the fish of choice. Scandinavian immigrant families also foraged in Northwest forests for berries and mushrooms, continuing a tradition based on the harsh northern climate of their homelands, where food was about survival as much as sustenance.

Special occasion entertaining for Pacific Northwest Nordics also brought out traditional foods adapted and prepared using local ingredients. Steaming pots of strong coffee were a must, to go with home-baked treats such as Swedish pancakes served with local strawberries and wild blackberries. On extra special occasions such as birthdays, weddings, Midsummer, *Syttende Mai* (May 17, Norway's Constitution Day anniversary), and Christmas, cardamom bread, fancy marzipan-filled cookies, butter cakes, *kransekakes* (pyramid-type cakes constructed from almond rings), and imported lingonberries would be served.

Ritual foods of the Christmas holidays were also important to Nordics living in the Pacific Northwest. Abundant local ingredients similar to ingredients of the home country made it possible to closely duplicate original Scandinavian recipes. Local farmers would prepare *pinnekøtt*, a main course dish of dried lamb or mutton, while herring was abundant and available for pickling. Some ingredients, such as Norwegian *lutefisk* (salted and dried cod fillets), were imported. Prepared for community dinners at area Sons of Norway Lodges, the reconstituted codfish served with butter, bacon, and potatoes was—and still is—an edible connection to homeland holiday traditions.

Scandinavian restaurateurs were also part of Seattle's vibrant mid-century food scene. In 1941, Swedish immigrants Siri and Matts Djos opened the Chalet Restaurant across from the University of Washington campus and served a daily *smörgåsbord*. The enterprising couple also opened Dalom, a "Cultural Center and Swedish Dining Room" on the corner of Boren Avenue and Spring Street, which also featured a traditional *smörgåsbord*. Downtown shoppers could have also eaten at A Little Bit of Sweden, a *smörgåsbord* restaurant on Sixth Avenue.

Although all are now gone, in the middle of the last century, Scandinavians also opened restaurants serving traditional foods. The Selandia Restaurant, which opened in 1948 on Elliott Avenue, was run by Danes and was a favorite for its scenic views and authentic *smörgåsbord*. The Norseman's Cafeteria on Market Street in Ballard was opened in 1960 by Einar Johnsen to serve meals with familiar ingredients to both first- and second-generation immigrants. The last of the traditional restaurants, Scandia Café, owned and operated by its Finnish owner, Tom Miller, served pickled herring and meatballs on Friday nights and featured a Sunday brunch complete with Swedish pancakes and lingonberries.

Any overview of Seattle's restaurant history—Scandinavian or otherwise—must mention Ivar Haglund. A restaurateur, Seattle port commissioner, and musician, Haglund is the wit behind the phrase "Keep clam," along with a multitude of other clever sayings. Born to immigrant parents from Sweden and Norway, in 1938 he opened Seattle's first aquarium and then added a fish-and-chips shop on what is to-day Pier 54. His first full-service restaurant, Ivar's Acres of Clams, opened in 1946 next door to the original fish-and-chips shop, and it is still bustling there today. The restaurant chain, boasting both fine-dining locations and fast-casual fish-and-chips shops, has grown to twenty-four locations.

Seattle's Scandinavian culinary heritage is also still thriving today in several retail shops and bakeries, although on a smaller scale. While the venerable Olsen's Scandinavian Foods on Market Street originally opened in 1960 as Johnsen's Scandinavian Foods, with name changes by subsequent owners, it closed in 2009. Engstrom's Home Bakery (1940s–1960s) in Ballard has also closed, but other Nordic emporiums are going strong. Both Larsson's Bakery on Twenty-Fourth Avenue Northwest in Ballard, which has featured traditional Danish pastries since 1974, and Nielsen's Danish Pastries, founded in 1962 by Danish immigrant and classically trained pastry chef John Nielsen, are nirvana for anyone seeking Scandinavian sweets. Nielsen's is renowned for its flaky, buttery *kringle* rings, authentic Danish pastries, cardamom bread, and traditional marzipan cookies that can be taken home in signature pink boxes or served with steaming cups of coffee or espresso in the cozy café. A newcomer to Seattle's Scandinavian bakery/café scene, Byen Bakeri opened in 2013 on the north side of Queen Anne, specializing in mostly Norwegian artisan breads, cakes, and pastries, including the "almighty kringle," as anointed by Meredith Barrett in a *Seattle Met* article (October 2013).

Anyone craving *smørrebrød, lefse,* or *kvaefjordkake*—a meringue and cream layered indulgence also known as "The World's Best Cake"—knows to head for Scandinavian Specialties in Ballard. From fish cakes to liver paté, this family-owned emporium prepares traditional Nordic foods according to its own recipes, "imports" homemade *lefse* (Norwegian potato flatbread) from the town of La Con-ner just north of Seattle, and stocks a wide range of Scandinavian-made cheeses and cold-water shrimp, along with ingredients and kitchen tools and myriad Scan-dinavian gift items and books, also sold online and by mail order. When December arrives, orders for traditional *pinnekjøtt* (authentic salted and smoked lamb ribs served at Norwegian Christmas dinners) always sell out.

Seattle's Swedish Cultural Center, Sons of Norway Lodge, Northwest Danish Association, and Nordic Museum, the only museum in the world celebrating all five Nordic countries, carry on Scandinavian culinary traditions at various seasonal and monthly events and cooking classes. The Nordic Museum also hosts an insight-ful permanent exhibition about the Scandinavian immigration experience.

While Seattle's Scandinavian heritage is not as robust as it once was, the 2018 opening of the new, modern Nordic Museum on Market Street gave it a shining new community center. The surge of interest in New Nordic cuisine has also revived appreciation for Scandinavia's culinary legacy in the Pacific Northwest, even more relevant today with its seasonal seafood and locally sourced focus.

ASIAN IMMIGRANTS

> Given our perch on the Pacific Rim . . . the culinary traditions of Japan and China, Korea and South Asia are fused into Seattle's very existence. By some measures, Thai food is more popular than pizza. But lately, something is different. Gone are the days when Japanese food meant simply sushi and going for Chinese meant plates you'd never actually see in China. Some of these newcomers faithfully recreate traditions of their native countries, while others take gleeful liberties.
>
> —Allecia Vermillion, "The Best New Asian Restaurants in Seattle,"
> *Seattle Met*, February 2016

If there is one element distinguishing Seattle's food history and cuisine from other areas of the Pacific Northwest, it is the Asian-Pacific influence. Immigrants from China, Japan, Korea, the Philippines, and Vietnam, as well as the Pacific Islands, all brought authentic flavors, cooking techniques, and culinary traditions to the Puget Sound region. Each Asian immigrant group has a different story, but, together, the food they farmed, processed, and cooked has made an indelible contribution to Seattle's food biography. A special exhibition in 2011–2012, "From Fields to Family: Asian-Pacific Americans and Food," at Seattle's Wing Luke Museum of the Asian Pacific American Experience, an affiliate of the Smithsonian Institution located in Seattle's historic Chinatown district, described it this way:

> The foods a modern Northwest diner chooses to eat, what they consider different, new and even comforting are often imported tastes and aromas, textures and techniques from Asian Pacific American communities. A steaming bowl of phở is as easy to get as a cup of coffee. Noodles made from wheat, rice or even rarer grains are now commonplace, whether udon, soba, glass or egg.

The impact of Asian cuisines on Seattle's restaurant culture is undeniable. In 2015, the *Huffington Post* and Yelp combined their user data to identify which five cuisines were most disproportionately popular in each US state. In Washington, four of five Asian cuisines ranked higher than the national average: Vietnamese ranked 181 percent higher, Thai was 125 percent higher, Korean was 103 percent higher, and Japanese was 88 percent higher. ("Fish and Chips" ranked second in the state, coming in at 175 percent above the national average, a position most likely related to the abundance of fresh fish in the Puget Sound.)

Chinese Immigrants

Chinese were the first Asians to migrate in large numbers to Washington State, arriving in the 1860s and 1870s when China suffered from war and civil unrest along with periodic flooding and famine, especially in South China around Guangzhou (Canton). The vast majority of Chinese immigrants from this area ended up in Seattle, which explains why Chinese food in Puget Sound initially was Cantonese.

Heavy recruitment abroad by railroad, mining, and logging firms inspired most Chinese immigrants to come to Seattle. In the 1860s, the first Chinese workers settled along the eastern edge of what is now Pioneer Square. Mostly single men, they came by steamship and rail, crowding into cheap boarding houses while looking for employment. Maxine "Max" Chan, a food historian who focuses on the evolution of Chinese cuisine from the 1850s, explained in a personal interview how Chinese immigrants brought a variety of dried foods with them—fish, mushrooms, preserved eggs, spices, herbs—on their long voyage to the United States. These foods not only provided sustenance aboard ship but also were a connection to comfort foods from home.

Many Chinese immigrants also toiled in canneries along the Columbia River and in Alaska from April to October during salmon fishing season. Thousands of Chinese men, and later Filipinos, would gut, slime, clean, and prepare the salmon for canning. The workers hammered the cans into shape over iron cinders, filled, soldered closed, and then cooked the contents. This all changed in 1909, when a machine with the racist name "the iron chink" made its debut at the Alaska-Yukon-Pacific Exposition; shortly afterward, machines replaced Chinese railroad workers on the fish processing lines.

Seattle's first official Chinese resident, Chin Chun Hock, arrived in Seattle in 1860 as a domestic worker less than ten years after the first white settlers landed at Alki Beach. According to Doug Chin in *Seattle's International District: The Making of a Pan-Asian American Community*, Hock worked for eight years and saved enough money to open his own general merchandise store, the Wa Chong Company. The first Asian-owned retail business in the United States, the store sold sugar, tea, Chinese goods, and—a few years later—opium. After Chinatown burned in the Great Seattle Fire of 1889, Chin Chun Hock—by then a wealthy Chinese merchant and labor contractor—rebuilt a "new" Chinatown just east of today's International District. Soon other businessmen began building cheap restaurants and boarding houses for the transient laborers who were flooding into the small, densely populated area built on stilts over tidal flats.

In a photo taken around 1900, this man standing in a flood of fresh salmon illustrates how Chinese immigrants were crucial at canneries to sort, clean, and then can the fish. *Courtesy of MOHAI, [George and Louisa Frye Collection], [1990.45.20].*

Chinese vendors sold ice cream from wheelbarrows and peddled vegetables grown nearby on family farms to restaurants and households around town. Most vegetables were grown in two large garden areas: one on the site of today's Seattle Center, and the second along the Duwamish River south of the city's commercial area.

In 1896, the arrival of the Nippon Yusen Kaisha steamship marked a significant milestone in Seattle's culinary history because it allowed local Chinese merchants to receive direct shipments of foodstuffs from China. Dried ducks, sweet-smelling roots, bamboo bales, herbs, smoked meats, tea, and assorted packaged goods were now available directly, and Seattle's Chinese merchants quickly became wholesale suppliers to restaurants, general stores, and work camps.

Once the railroad extensions were completed and mining diminished, hundreds of Chinese laborers were out of work. This prompted many to open restaurants offering inexpensive food to their own community. Most small Chinese restaurants were run as husband-and-wife businesses; the husband served as cook and

A street scene in the International District in 1934, a neighborhood settled in the 1920s by Seattle's Chinese immigrants, who were soon followed by other immigrants from Japan and the Philippines, attracted by the area's Asian businesses, restaurants, and affordable boarding houses. *Courtesy of MOHAI, [Museum of History & Industry Photograph Collection], [1986.5.7828.4].*

dishwasher in the kitchen, while the wife worked the front of the house as waitress, barmaid, and cashier. Eventually, these eateries attracted patrons outside their native ethnic group and became more profitable business enterprises.

Early restaurateur and successful businessman Ah King (born in 1863) also played an important role in bringing Chinese food to Seattle. After working in logging camps to earn money, Ah King opened a restaurant in 1897, and then, in 1908, founded the Ah King Company (also known as the King Chong Lung Company), which sold Chinese groceries. Known as the "mayor" or "king" of Chinatown, he traveled to China in 1908 at his own expense to select Chinese curios and goods for the "Chinese Village" at the 1909 Alaska-Yukon-Pacific Exposition, where he also opened a restaurant and a hot corn stand.

Between 1920 and 1940, many Chinese-owned restaurants had an "American" food section on their menus, which included items such as steaks, chops, potatoes, salads, and sandwiches, along with chop suey. According to Seattle food historian

The Tanagi grocery store, located at 653 King Street next to Russell Meat Market, with its front showing vegetables, fruit displays, and scales of the 1930s. After World War II, the Tai Tung restaurant took over the space. *Courtesy of Wing Luke Museum, [2000.015.029]*.

Max Chan, Chinese restaurant cooks began incorporating economical and available local ingredients into traditional dishes. Chan is quick to emphasize that this does not imply the dishes lacked authenticity, only that they were nontraditional. Clams, salmon, Dungeness crab, and geoduck (popular in stir-fry dishes) soon began appearing in home kitchens and on Chinese restaurant menus.

Seattle's oldest surviving Chinese restaurant, Tai Tung, established in 1935, still serves traditional fare today at 655 South King Street in the International District. It originally catered to single men from China and the Philippines who worked on railroads and in canneries. Lonely without their families, these hardworking men would sit day after day on swiveling stools at long counters in restaurants where they could socialize and eat. As described by author Rachel Belle in a 2015 KIRO (710 AM) radio interview, Harry Chan, the current owner of Tai Tung and grandson of the founder, recalled the men sipping cups of coffee and savoring almond cookies while waiting for shuttles to the canneries. "The transport would come and take them off to work. Then, in the evening, they would come back here and that's when they would have their dinner combination plates: one, two, three." Diners enjoying today's menu at Tai Tung can order the same three combination plates served in 1935. The only thing changed is the price. Combination plates started with soup of the day and included pork chow mein, sweet and sour sparerib, or pork egg foo young, always served with plain white rice.

Although it does not have the historic legacy of Tai Tung or other local restaurants, Fortuna Café today preserves an important culinary tradition: glutinous Chinese rice dumplings used for Seattle's annual Dragon Boat Festival. Considered a lost craft, few millennials, or even their mothers and grandmothers, make these dumplings at home any longer. Once upon a time previous generations of grandmothers would labor to make dumplings next to their daughters-in-law and grandchildren in an assembly line, but today the dedicated staff at Fortuna Café is the only active source.

Ruby Chow: Roast Duck Diplomacy

Seattle's most prominent Asian American politician may be Gary Locke, who served as the governor of Washington from 1997 to 2011, as well as US ambassador to China and secretary of commerce during the Obama administration. But one of the city's earliest Asian American politicians was a female restaurateur, Ruby Chow. She and her husband Ping (a Chinese opera star) opened the first high-end Chinese restaurant outside the International District in 1948 in an old mansion on Broadway and Jefferson Streets, a predominantly black neighborhood. Friends in Chinatown warned her that she would be bankrupt in sixty days. The restaurant flourished for thirty-one years.

Ruby Chow's was a popular hangout at a time when segregation ruled. Celebrities including Sammy Davis Jr. and Sidney Poitier were guests. Politicians were regulars and her swanky, exotic restaurant became a place to schmooze, cut deals, and raise money. She became a community leader—a bridge between Chinatown and the rest of Seattle. In 1973, Chow was the first person of color elected to serve on the King County Council.

While in office, Chow combined food and politics by hosting dinners for Washington State's active governors, including Dixie Lee Ray and Dan Evans. Her most controversial move was leveraging a roast duck to prevent locating a prison work release program in a federal building in Chinatown. Chow got on a plane and flew to Washington, DC, to meet with Senator Warren Magnuson, according to a former aide interviewed on a KUOW-FM (NPR) radio program. As recounted by Ruby de Luna in her radio program describing the state's history through the prism of food, "The colorful thing . . . is that [Chow's husband] Ping roasted a duck and she took it with her to give to Senator Magnuson. Her staffers called it 'roast duck diplomacy.'" While it's uncertain whether the duck swayed the senator, plans for

Ruby Chow at home in her kitchen around 1960 with a bundle of fresh Asian long beans. *Courtesy of MOHAI, [Museum of History & Industry Photograph Collection], [1986.5.21497].*

the work release program didn't get far. Ruby Chow served three terms on the King County Council, and her legacy lives on through her son, Mark, who was a former King County District Court judge, and her daughter, Cheryl, who served eight years on the Seattle City Council.

Tsue Chong Noodle Company: Four Generations Bringing Noodles and Good Fortune to Seattle

When he arrived in Seattle in 1917 from a small village in the Guangdong province of South China, Gar Hip Louie had the good fortune to recognize a business opportunity. He started out with a hand-cranked noodle machine, similar to a home pasta machine. Working from a small storefront on Jackson Street in Seattle's original Chinatown, he wrapped the fresh noodles in newspapers and then delivered them to local customers, as Leora Bloom described in a 2016 article in the *Seattle Times*.

Four generations and a century later, the Tsue Chong Company still prepares Rose Brand Chinese noodles in the International District, but now in a thirty-eight-thousand-square-foot building. Louie's great-grandson Timothy Louie is president of the company, which produces about ten thousand noodles every day. The company produces seventeen different lines of noodles, including dumpling wrappers for wonton, gyoza, and egg rolls, as well as fresh, steamed, and dried varieties of noodles. All noodles are prepared from four basic ingredients: flour, salt, water, and eggs. Grossing four million dollars per year, Rose Brand noodles are shipped throughout the Pacific Northwest. The top seller, according to Louie, is still the freshly made rice noodles. Like his great-grandfather one hundred years earlier, Timothy Louie emphasizes the importance of delivering the noodles immediately to local stores.

The Tsue Chong Company can also claim a second source of food fame. In the 1950s, when fortune cookies gained popularity in the United States, Timothy Louie's grandmother, Eng Shee, decided to try her hand at making the American-invented product. The fortune cookies became a huge success, prepared by hand until the 1980s, when the family figured out how to automate the process. Today, as the company's website describes, machines wrap and fold thirteen cookies per minute, each with a fortune paper wrapped inside (five hundred different messages are available), yielding six finished cookies every three seconds, or almost eighty thousand fortune cookies per day.

In 2010, as Lornet Turnbull described in the *Seattle Times* on February 17 of that year, the US Census Bureau contracted with the Tsue Chong Company to produce a fortune cookie with a special message: one side of the fortune read, "You will find fame and fortune"; the reverse side read, "Put down your chopsticks and get involved in Census 2010!" As part of a creative outreach strategy employed by the Census Bureau to encourage participation from historically undercounted populations, the Tsue Chong Company distributed more than two million fortune cookies to restaurants and grocery stores. (Not always evident, ethnic census participation determined congressional representation and funding, as well as locations for community facilities such as schools, hospitals, and new housing developments.)

Mon Hei Chinese Bakery: Baking Happiness

Authenticity and pleasure was what the Mon Hei Bakery was all about. Its name, "Mon Hei," means "a thousand years of happiness." The first Chinese bakery in Seattle, it opened its doors in 1978 in the International District and was run by the Chan family. Seattle residents who adored baked goods discovered it and were quick to rave. Favorites from the daily selection were the traditional *Gai Mai Baos*, cocktail buns, moon cakes, rice cakes, chicken hand pies, silky egg tarts, and, above all, heavenly soft Chinese-style sugared doughnuts. A bonus was the café area of the bakery, a welcome spot that attracted both locals and tourists visiting the International District. Stacks of pink bakery boxes waited along inside walls to be filled with bakery treats. Although it has been closed since December 2013, when the historic century-old Louisa Hotel that housed the bakery caught fire, hopes remain fervent that it will reopen soon.

Japanese Immigrants

> What really defines a city's food scene is not its four-star restaurants but its most plebeian cuisine—the glorified street fare that no one thinks about but everyone eats. San Francisco has its super burrito, Philadelphia its cheesesteak. . . . Someday Seattle's hallowed salmon, voluptuous berries, and cloud-kissed mushrooms may be eclipsed in the national imagination by another local specialty: teriyaki.
>
> —Jonathan Kauffman, "How Teriyaki Became Seattle's Own Fast-Food Phenomenon," *Seattle Weekly*, August 14, 2007

There is a reason teriyaki is often called "Seattle's own fast food." It has everything to do with the many Japanese immigrants who brought their energy, resources, and cooking skills to the Pacific Northwest. The culinary legacy of this ethnic group is evident in the city's affection for Asian restaurants. An integral ethnic group in many facets of Seattle's history, Japanese immigrants first arrived in the 1890s, after Japan lifted its ban on emigration in 1885. Even then, vital links between Seattle and Asia were forming. In 1896, the first regular commercial steamship line was established between Seattle and Japan, opening a major gateway for transporting lumber, coal, wheat, and metals to the East, and returning with Asian products such as soybean oil, silks, tea, ginger, and straw matting. Despite the breakdown during World War II, the link has thrived and maintained its importance.

The first Japanese immigrants arrived in the Pacific Northwest for jobs in railroad construction, logging, mining, fish processing canneries, and agriculture. This wave in the 1890s primarily came from the rural prefectures of Hiroshima, Yamaguchi, and Okayama, and included fortune seekers, students, young men avoiding the military draft, unemployed veterans of the Russo-Japanese War, and younger sons unable to inherit family land and farms. The 1908 Gentlemen's Agreement between the United States and Japan restricted the immigration of laborers but allowed wives. Called "picture brides" in arranged marriages, these women were often from the men's home villages. The majority of immigrant men, however, expected to work in the Northwest and then return to Japan, where many had left wives and families.

At the end of the nineteenth century and into the early twentieth century, a vibrant Japanese district emerged in Seattle. Initially centered around Pioneer

Square, but eventually moving eastward along Yesler and Jackson Streets to form *Nihonmachi*, or Japantown, this vibrant community hub both served and insulated newly arrived immigrants and their families. A landmark from this early era was the Star Restaurant, which was opened in 1888 by Kyuhachi Nishi and Azuma Nisho. The Panama Hotel, constructed in 1910 by the first Japanese American architect in Seattle, served as a starting point for many immigrants. By the beginning of the 1910 decade, even more Japanese arrived to run farms, shops, restaurants, inns, and boarding houses and to work in Alaskan canning factories.

As historian Doug Chin notes in his insightful book *Seattle's International District: The Making of a Pan-Asian American Community* (2001), Japanese immigrants did more than help build Seattle; they also played significant roles in developing local farming, regularly bringing their goods into Seattle, supplying produce stands and restaurants in the International District. Many also had stands at Pike Place Market when it opened in 1907, although their presence later instigated discrimination efforts by white vendors. As a constraint, Japanese farmers could only sell goods they grew themselves, a regulation not required of other vendors. Japanese immigrants were also essential in running, and eventually owning, several area dairies, learning skills on farms where they were employed.

The Pacific Northwest and Seattle were especially hard hit when the United States declared war on Japan, and when on February 19, 1942, President Franklin Roosevelt signed Executive Order 9066. This directive forced 110,000 Japanese Americans living on the West Coast to leave their homes, farms, and businesses for forcible internment in ten inland prison camps. In Seattle, Japanese Americans were estimated to operate 140 retail grocery stores, including the iconic Uwajimaya grocery store, 67 market stands, and 57 wholesale houses, according to a survey by the Japanese American Citizens League, which was submitted to the Tolan Congressional Committee on National Defense Migration. Many were born in the United States or had been in the United States for more than three decades. Internment meant almost complete destruction of their communities and livelihoods.

After Japanese Americans returned to Seattle in 1945, only a few Japanese restaurants, tea houses, and grocery stores reopened, and *Nihonmachi* was gone. Even more heartbreaking, few families regained their land and farms.

Later, Nishi leased the Virginia Café. Bush Gardens (now closed), a Japanese restaurant hot spot in the International District after World War II, had its heyday with both returned Japanese Americans and adventuresome Caucasian residents.

With the popularity of Asian—and Asian fusion—cuisine rising since the 1980s, particularly sushi, Japanese restaurants have flourished in Seattle. But before these modern Asian food trends arrived, savory-sticky teriyaki reigned as the city's most popular Asian fast-food dish, complete with a few local twists.

Teriyaki—Seattle's Favorite Fast Food

Newcomers to Seattle soon notice the ubiquitous white boxes carried around by downtown and South Lake Union workers at lunchtime—and dinnertime, too. The contents of the box are usually teriyaki, the fast-food-type dish featuring a heap of sticky, salty sweet, soy sauce–seasoned grilled chicken atop a giant mound of steamed rice. Some call it Seattle's favorite fast food. In her 2008 *Seattle Met* magazine article, "The Restaurants That Changed the Way We Eat," Kathryn Robinson noted that within Seattle proper there were "more than three times as many teriyaki joints as there are McDonald's, Burger Kings, and Jack in the Boxes put together."

The culinary love affair started in 1976 when Toshihiro "Toshi" Kasahara arrived in Seattle from Ashikaga, Japan, and opened a Toshi's on Lower Queen Anne. The teriyaki chicken plate with rice and a cabbage salad was a dinnertime steal at $1.85. From this first location, in 1990, Kasakara expanded his concept by opening franchises around the city, to street malls and street corner storefronts. He would start a shop, bring it to a level of profitability, sell the shop, and open a new location, rarely owning more than two at any given time. By the time he retired in 2003, there were more than thirty Toshi's Teriyaki spots around Seattle.

One of Kasahara's first employees, Yasuko Conner, followed her employer's business model and recipe concept to open her own chain of nine restaurants. Other entrepreneurs followed suit. As Joseph Warren reveals in his article "Seattle-Style Teriyaki," there were 107 places in King County in 1992 with "teriyaki" in their name, and by 1996, there were 196. In 2007, the number rose to 519 teriyaki restaurants in Washington State. New shop owners represented many nationalities, from Chinese to Vietnamese, Mexican, and Indian, but Korean Americans really gave the dish its Seattle style by seasoning it with ginger, garlic, and sesame oil.

Teriyaki easily and deliciously adapts to many ethnic flavors in Seattle. Thai is usual, but even Hawaiian has appeared. It's also not surprising to find many Vietnamese *phở* shops with a teriyaki dish now on their menu. The dish is even versatile enough to accommodate the corn dog teriyaki version served at Tokyo Gardens in the University District (a restaurant owned by a Nepali immigrant with a chef originally from Puebla, Mexico). As a measure of culinary mingling, Tokyo Gardens also offers Nepalese dumplings, Japanese dumplings, and sushi. South of Seattle in the Tukwila suburb, a Somali restaurant serves a halal chicken teriyaki.

Korean Immigrants

Kimchi has been universally considered one of the hottest food trends in the United States since 2015, and happily for Seattleites, the authentic spicy pickles—prepared from cabbage, cucumbers, radishes, and turnips—are easy to find in local

Korean markets and small family-owned restaurants, as well as in many of the city's major grocery stores. Along with standard Asian ingredients such as rice, tofu, soy sauce, and plenty of vegetables, Korean food leans toward spicy, seasoned with red peppers and ginger, sesame seeds, and oil, plus green onions. It's all available here, especially for food explorers heading toward the city of Shoreline just north of Seattle. While Korean Americans "may be [Seattle's] least visible ethnic community," according to Carey Giudici in her 2001 *HistoryLink* essay, with a little searching, Korean culinary icons ranging from *bibimbap* (Korean barbecue) and *bulgogi* (Korean-style marinated grilled meat) to *mandu* (Korean dumplings) and *chap ch'ae* (Korean noodles) are served in many places.

Like many immigrants, Koreans arrived in the Pacific Northwest in search of employment and cultural freedom. Japanese colonization of the Korean peninsula after defeating China in the Sino-Japanese War (1894–1895) and subsequent oppression of Korean culture compelled many discontented Koreans to leave their homeland. Korean men and women came to the Pacific Northwest in waves starting in the early 1900s through World War II and the Korean War.

Almost all Koreans who came to the United States in the first immigration wave took up residence in Hawaii. To escape the harsh working conditions on the sugar plantations, Koreans who could manage the financing left Hawaii, moving to the West Coast in the early 1900s. Those moving to urban areas found work by starting restaurants, vegetable stands, and small shops, or by working as tailors and carpenters, while others toiled in the West's coal and copper mines. More recently, since the 1970s Korean immigrants have been a significant group in the Pacific Northwest, owning one-third of the state's convenience stores.

In Seattle, Korean immigrants settled in the University and Central Districts, as well as to the north, in the cities of Shoreline and Edmonds, and to the south, in Federal Way and Tacoma. Korean Americans today are more than sixty thousand strong in the greater Seattle region, owning more than three thousand businesses. Between 1970 and 1980, King County's Korean population increased by 566 percent, compared with the rest of the United States.

Among this population, contemporary Korean Americans operate casual family-owned restaurants and ethnic eateries such as Korean Tofu House in the University District, Kimchi House in Ballard, Kimchi Bistro on Capitol Hill, and Old Village Korean Restaurant in Shoreline, noted on its website as the "only Korean restaurant in Washington State that has charcoal BBQ burners built into the [dining] tables." Korean Americans also spurred Seattle's surge of teriyaki shops in the 1970s, including Yak's Deli in the Fremont neighborhood, creating a "Seattle-style" version of the Japanese dish by enhancing its flavor with more seasonings.

As Korean food becomes mainstream and trendy, places like Chan, on an alley in Pike Place Market, are destinations for modern takes on ethnic dishes.

Korean-Asian fusion restaurants have also earned a place among Seattle's hot ethnic restaurants, particularly Trove, Revel, and Joule from Chefs Rachel Yang and Seif Chirchi, which regularly earn applause for their interpretation of Korean street food prepared with French techniques. Marination Station on Capitol Hill and its sibling, Marination Ma Kai in West Seattle, successfully blend Korean with Hawaiian flavors. A newbie in the International District, Tofully, has also recently earned acclaim for its spicy pork bulgogi with "just the right amount of heat," according to Julia Wayne's September 2014 *Seattle Magazine* article, "The Best Korean Restaurants in Seattle."

Filipino Immigrants

Sinigang, pancit, lumpia, kare kare, adobo, and *dinuguan.* Few Seattleites recognize these traditional Filipino dishes, even though Washington State is home to the third-largest Filipino population in the United States, with nearly one million Filipinos living in King, Pierce, and Snohomish Counties. Equally baffling: with so many Filipinos living in Puget Sound, why are there only a handful of Filipino restaurants? Influenced by Spanish, Chinese, and Malaysian cooking, the ingredients and flavors from the Philippines are similar to other Asian cuisines embraced by Seattle diners. Why, then, does Filipino food have such a low profile among local diners, both Filipino and non-Filipino?

One reason may be that Filipino families have a home-cooking culture and prefer to eat traditional food at home: Why dine out when what Mother prepares is always better than anything ordered in a restaurant? Irbille Donia, cofounder of two Filipino pop-up restaurants, has another theory. In a 2014 *Seattle Weekly* interview with writer Nicole Sprinkle, he attributed the scarcity of Filipino food in Seattle to some element of shame related to the country's complicated history of being colonized for centuries. Donia said that people "take a lot of the colonialism to heart and stay away from bridging those cultures. But that's what makes food really beautiful, the infiltration of cultures." He also added that non-Filipino diners are put off because the traditional one-pot stews aren't "pretty" and the food is messy because it's traditionally eaten with fingers.

Colonized by the Spanish in 1542, the Philippines—an archipelago of more than 7,641 islands between the South China Sea and the Pacific Ocean—was sold to the United States in 1898 for $20,000,000 after the Spanish-American War. The islands became a US territory in 1898; shortly afterward, the first immigration wave occurred. Living in an American territory gave Filipinos the unusual legal status of "nationals" rather than "aliens"; they were not required to carry a passport and could enter Seattle without restrictions. Quickly, Filipinos became a more attractive labor force than the Japanese and Chinese. With the passage of the

Pensionado Act in 1903, Filipinos also had an opportunity to study in America; the University of Washington enrolled the highest number of Filipinos of any institution in the United States, which in turn brought more people who ultimately settled in Seattle.

The first large migration of Filipinos to Seattle began in the 1910s, with people arriving primarily as uneducated laborers to find seasonal employment in lumber mills, coal mines, and canneries along the Columbia River and in Alaska. Since many workers were single men, they stopped in Seattle on their way to agricultural fields and fruit orchards in eastern Washington. Some stayed on in Puget Sound, working on berry and hop farms in South Park, Renton, Kent, Woodinville, Auburn, and Bellevue. With one Filipina woman for every thirty men, most of the first Filipino families in the Puget Sound were interracial, with marriages between Native Americans, African Americans, and other Asians.

The Asian Exclusion Act of 1924, which severely curtailed Chinese and Japanese immigration to the United States, was a boon for Filipino laborers. In 1928, there were nearly 4,000 Filipinos working in Alaska's canneries. During the summer, they worked twelve-hour shifts cleaning, processing, and canning salmon. Most were housed in run-down barracks, eating poor food in different mess halls with different menus from white workers. On their way to and from Alaska, many Filipino laborers stayed in single-unit apartment hotels, often at the Eastern Hotel on Maynard. It was in these hotels that men gathered to discuss the harsh conditions of canning salmon, and in 1933 workers were inspired to form the Cannery Workers' and Farm Laborers' Union Local 18257, considered one of the most militant unions on the West Coast.

Considering that home cooking is a standard of Filipino culture, it is surprising that in the 1920s and 1930s only one dedicated Filipino grocery store was recorded: the V. M. Laigo Company, which was owned by a labor contractor. Over the years, a sprinkling of small mom-and-pop markets served local communities, but it wasn't until 2010 that a major Filipino-focused supermarket—Seafood City—opened in Tukwila just south of Seattle. It was followed in 2016 by another California-based chain that opened in Rainier Valley—Island Pacific Market, which boasts large cafeteria-style restaurants selling prepared food to eat in or take out.

Filipino-owned restaurants, shops, and clubs in the 1920s clustered around Maynard Avenue and King Street, a neighborhood nicknamed "Manilatown." The neighborhood overlapped with Chinatown and catered to single, male migrant workers. Popular restaurants included the Manila Corporation Restaurant (Sixth Avenue and King Street), which served Filipino and Spanish dishes and operated a pool hall next door; the Philippine Cafe; and the New Manila Cafe, now the site of Hing Hay Park in the International District. As Filipino immigrants moved into other neighborhoods around the city, Manilatown faded, as did its small restaurants. Although limited in number because most Filipino families ate at home, a few Filipino restaurants appeared in mainstream parts of the city and were frequented by everyone.

Oriental Mart in Pike Place Market, which Mila Apostol opened in 1972, is the oldest and one of the only Filipino restaurants in the city. (Kusina Filipino on Beacon Hill, which opened in 2002, is the only other well-known traditional Filipino restaurant in Seattle.) Originally a grocery store, Oriental Mart was described by Charles Mudede in an article in the alt-weekly *The Stranger* "as a family kitchen in a public space." The family-owned restaurant is famous for *sinigang*, a soup composed of salmon tips and invented by Filipino laborers at the canneries in Alaska who were allowed to take the leftover fish tips home. Rich in fat, the discarded salmon tips transformed into a flavorful dish.

Inay's, a legendary Filipino restaurant opened by Ernie Rios in 1991, served comfort food cafeteria-style and quickly became a popular gathering place for Seattle's Filipino community for the next twenty-five years. In 2012, Inay's (which means "mom's" in Tagalog) began hosting innovative Monday night pop-ups called "Food & Sh*t." The dinners were the vision of Chera Amlag, an educator and baker, and her husband George "Geo" Quibuyen, an emcee for the local hip-hop act Blue Scholars. Once the restaurant closed, the couple continued Food & Sh*t as an online resource "to explore historical and current threads in Filipino cuisine," as noted on their website (foodandsh-t.com), and they also curate popular pop-ups presenting traditional Filipino dishes with a Northwest twist; a recent pop-up featured *lumpia* egg rolls prepared with salmon instead of the usual beef or pork. The couple also opened Hood Famous Bakeshop in 2014 in Ballard to showcase Amlag's desserts, such as an *ube* (purple yam) cheesecake that weaves Filipino flavors into a familiar American classic.

Other pop-ups and food trucks have also introduced Seattle diners to Filipino food. One of the first pop-ups was Kraken Congee, which was started in 2013 by three friends from culinary school: Irbille Donia, Garrett Doherty, and Shane Robinson. Much to their surprise, three hundred people showed up at the first event. The trio used congee, a simple rice porridge found in many cuisines throughout Asia. For Filipino cooks, congee is a base for various key ingredients. These may be duck confit accented with Chinese five-spice, or pork-stuffed squid enhanced with salty black squid ink. Some Filipino cooks have even braised a salty-tangy version of pork-belly adobo in soy sauce and vinegar. In 2015, Kraken Congee opened as a brick-and-mortar restaurant in Pioneer Square.

Seattle's burgeoning food truck culture claims a half-dozen or so Filipino food trucks and food carts roaming around the city. These serve up traditional dishes but also offer contemporary interpretations of favorites recipes, often integrating Vietnamese or Hawaiian influences.

While few Filipino chefs own their own restaurants in Seattle, as the rise of Filipino food trucks and grocery stores indicates, the scene may be changing. In 2015, Allison Austin Scheff predicted in *Seattle Magazine* that a Filipino food movement was about to break out in Seattle due to a "spirited, proud group of young Filipino chefs" who were launching pop-up restaurants.

Vietnamese Immigrants

Phở, a steaming bowl of aromatic noodle soup, may be the national dish of Vietnam, but it is also often considered a culinary staple in Seattle. In 2016, a Yelp search returned more than 260 restaurants in greater Seattle with the words "*phở*" or "Vietnamese" in their names.

With the fall of Saigon in 1975, thousands of Vietnamese refugees found asylum in Washington, ultimately shaping Seattle's culinary landscape with vibrant flavors and textures from Southeast Asia. One man bears much of the responsibility for this phenomenon and the strong presence of Vietnamese food in Seattle: former governor Dan Evans. In 1975, Evans was so disturbed by California governor Jerry Brown's opposition to welcoming Vietnamese refugees that he invited them to Washington State. Governor Evans established a resettlement camp at Camp Murray, a National Guard camp in Tacoma, encouraged local families to accept refugees into their homes, and urged employers to hire these refugees. Two years later, there were six thousand Vietnamese living in Washington with 2,500 residing in King County.

Rochelle Nguyen, who fled from Vietnam in 1975 when she was nine years old, was among the first families to arrive at Seattle's Camp Murray. Speaking in an interview about local Vietnamese refugees on PBS station KCTS-9 in a special program on April 23, 2015, Nguyen remembered, "They helped us adapt to American customs and the culture: macaroni and cheese, peanut butter sandwiches, you know—cereal. And I didn't know why we had pancakes with very sweet syrup, and then there's bacon that is salty. So it just tasted really strange."

By 1980, Washington State had the fifth-highest population of Vietnamese in the United States. The arrival of "boat people" created the second wave in the 1980s as more refugees escaped from the Communist regime and fled to the United States. A third wave arrived as part of the US Humanitarian Operation Program, which connected Vietnamese American family members, former prisoners from "re-education" camps, and Amerasian children of American servicemen. As reported in the 2010 US Census, Washington State had the third-largest population of Vietnamese, with almost seventy-six thousand people; Seattle ranked as the eleventh-largest city with the most residents from Vietnam, a population reaching more than thirteen thousand immigrants.

Vietnamese refugees arriving in Seattle were unlike those settling in other parts of the country. Their transition was easier because King County was already home to two generations of Asian immigrants. "Markets serving the Asian community, such as Uwajimaya and other small grocery stores in Seattle's Chinatown/International District helped Vietnamese retain their culinary culture," wrote Nhien T. Nguyen, editor of Seattle's *International Examiner*, in an essay titled "Building a Vietnamese Community from Scratch: The First Fifteen Years in King County."

Small grocery stores selling authentic Vietnamese food also opened in homes, basements, and garages, along with tailor shops that made *ao dai*, traditional Vietnamese dresses. Lani and Tommy Wong, ethnic Chinese from Vietnam who arrived in Seattle in 1977, opened one of the first Vietnamese shops, the Mekong, on Rainier Avenue South. The shop sold everything from fresh fish to spices and woks, to rice and candy, as recounted in *The Rainier Valley Food Stories Cookbook*. Forty years later, the shop is still going strong with second-generation clientele.

Other Vietnamese businesses opened in the late 1970s on Jackson Street from Fifth to Twelfth Avenues, creating a four-block area called "Little Saigon." Seattle residents from other neighborhoods began venturing into Little Saigon to try "exotic" Vietnamese food, such as French-influenced Vietnamese sandwiches made with fresh baguettes and topped with special ham, peppers, pickles, carrots, paté, and soy sauce.

Seattle's first *phở* restaurant, Phở Bach, started out as Cat's Submarine in 1982, serving American-style cold-cut sandwiches. But within a few months, Vietnamese customers frequenting the International District markets on weekend shopping trips began requesting comfort foods from home. Within a year, all the American-style sandwiches disappeared, and the fragrance of *phở* wafted from the kitchen when Phở Bach opened its doors as the city's first *phở* restaurant.

SOUTHERN AND EASTERN EUROPEAN IMMIGRANTS

Jewish Immigrants

With such an abundance of salmon here in Seattle, why is it so difficult to find salmon's favorite partner: a terrific bagel? The first Jewish immigrants arrived in Seattle in the mid-1800s, and Washington State today has the fifth-largest Jewish population in the United States, but only one Jewish delicatessen exists in all of Puget Sound (and it isn't even kosher). Tracing the history of Jewish immigration in the Pacific Northwest sheds light on these culinary conundrums.

Seattle's early Jewish immigrants were not affected by the New York influences defining most American Judaism and its culinary traditions. Partly this is because Seattle's Jewish community was founded by two very different Jewish cultures: the

Ashkenazi from Central and Eastern Europe and the Sephardic Jews from Spain, Turkey, Morocco, and Greece, descendants of Jews expelled in 1492 at the beginning of the Spanish Inquisition. Although both groups celebrated the same holidays and were connected by common beliefs, they didn't speak the same language and brought with them very different cultural and culinary traditions. Sephardic Jews from Spain had never tasted matzo ball soup, while Jews arriving from Germany did not use fragrant Moroccan spices.

The story of Seattle's first Jewish resident begins in 1845 when Adolph Friedman, a twenty-four-year-old Latvian adventurer, arrived in Washington Territory. He was soon followed by waves of ambitious, entrepreneurial German and Eastern European Jewish immigrants, all ready to gamble on starting businesses in what was still considered the Wild West. By 1870, Washington Territory had a Jewish governor, Edward S. Salomon, and five years later, Seattle had its first (and only) Jewish mayor, Bailey Gatzert.

Seattle's Jewish community changed dramatically at the turn of the century with the arrival of the first Sephardic Jews: Solomon Calvo and Joseph Policar from Marmara in northwest Turkey (present-day Armenia), and Nessim Alhadeff from the Greek island of Rhodes. Calvo and Alhadeff started peddling fish and eventually founded retail/wholesale fish companies: Calvo's Waterfront Fish and Alhadeff Palace Fish Company, whose motto was "If it swims, we have it." They, along with other Sephardic Jews, also opened produce and flower stalls in what became, in 1907, Pike Place Market. The market, in turn, became a de facto community center for what was the nation's third-largest population of Sephardic Jews.

In the early 1900s, Jewish restaurants and bakeries dotted what was known as "Kosher Canyon," an area in the Yesler Way corridor of Seattle's Central District. A hub for Jewish families, the area provided immigrants with synagogues (three synagogues present in 1933 reflected the three Jewish cultures coexisting in Seattle) for religious, social, and educational functions, plus small kosher butcher shops, bakeries, and groceries such as the Twenty-Eighth Avenue Market at 2401 Yesler Way, all run by Jewish shopkeepers and their families.

By 1917, there were approximately 1,700 Sephardim living in one Seattle neighborhood and close to 8,500 Ashkenazi Jews in other neighborhoods, each with separate synagogues. The large number of Ashkenazim can be attributed to the pogroms mounted against Jews in Eastern Europe in the nineteenth and twentieth centuries. Because they were not as likely to observe Jewish dietary laws, their neighborhoods had fewer kosher markets, butcher shops, and restaurants. Differences existed between these two sects; Ashkenazi kids called Sephardic kids "Mazola," while Sephardic kids called Ashkenazi kids "Schmaltz," both names referring to kinds of fats.

Seattle's Pike Place Market was founded in 1907 with many vendors from the Sephardic community. According to Megan Hill in an article in the April/May 2016 issue of *Jewish in Seattle* magazine, the Market became a new home for many Sephardic immigrants. A Sephardic immigrant central to developing Seattle's Jewish community was Morris Tacher, owner of The Turkish Restaurant and The Cozy Corner in Pike Place Market. Both served as social hubs for the Sephardic community, places described by Naomi Tomkey in her article for *The Forward* (May 31, 2015), where "immigrants and their families from Turkey, Syria, and the Greek island of Rhodes could *come can gana*," a Ladino (the Judeo-Spanish language that most of the Sephardic immigrants spoke) phrase meaning "eat with a good appetite." Tomkey also notes how the Market bustled with "Sephardic shop owners, their (also Sephardic) employees, and Sephardim who worked downtown and came to the restaurant[s] to hang out."

The documentary film *The Sephardic Jews and the Pike Place Market*, produced in 2001 by Stephen Sadis also illustrates the intersection of Sephardic Jews with Pike Place Market. Lucille Spring, whose father, "Pinky" Almeleh, was a produce stand vendor, called it a "secular synagogue" given daily involvement there for many Sephardic immigrants. Sol Tacher, the son of Morris Tacher and also interviewed in Sadis's film, notes how essential the Market was to the Sephardic community contributing to the community's growth plus its role building Seattle.

Today, three vendors with ties to Seattle's Sephardic legacy remain at the Market: Pure Food Fish Market, Three Girls Bakery, and Sweeties Candy. Their ties to Sephardic immigrant history are family-related and active. Pure Food Fish Market, founded in 1957 by father and son Jack and Sol Amon, showcases seafood from wild salmon and halibut to Dungeness crab and sea scallops, and also ships fish cross-country to fulfill orders from Jewish families and stores. As Naomi Tomkey notes in her article in the *The Forward* (May 31, 2015), "The slight disconnect of a Jewish vendor selling shellfish harkens back to a century earlier, when Sephardic vendors . . . struggled with the challenges of running a business that had to stay open on Saturday, the Market's busiest day. Still, no matter what, they always shut down for the High Holidays." Both Three Girls Bakery, opened in 1912, and Sweeties Candy, opened two decades ago, are also owned and operated by Sephardic families with long-established Market ties.

Jewish Restaurants and Bakeries

Contemporary Seattle does not have a Jewish bakery culture. It is not uncommon for Jews in Seattle to come back from a visit to New York City with bagels, rye bread, and rugelach stuffed into their suitcases. Yet this was not always the case. One of Seattle's earliest bakeries, the New York Bakery, was opened in 1899 on

Jackson Street by Sam Mosler. Brenner Brothers, another of Seattle's earliest bakery-deli shops, opened in 1900 and started with door-to-door deliveries from a horse-drawn wagon by its owner, Abe Brenner, an immigrant from Austria. Eventually, he and other family members set up shop in the Central District with its ready-made customer base for bagels, challah, pastries, and famous loaves of light and dark Russian rye bread. Alas, the final loaf was baked in 1997.

Schwartz Brothers Bakeries, a commercial wholesale bakery that opened in 1973, sells private label baked goods for major grocery stores, as well as products under its own name to major supermarket chains. It was established when brothers John and Bill Schwartz could not source any cheesecake or pies to sell to customers at their newly opened spot, the Sandwich Shop and Pie Place. The bakery is certified kosher, although Schwartz Brothers–owned restaurants, such as Chandler's Crab House, are not. Several other Seattle bakers also have kosher certifications, including Krispy Kreme Doughnuts (the SoDo neighborhood store only), Einstein Bagels, and Tsue Chong Noodle Company (its fortune cookies are also kosher).

Surprisingly, Goldberg Deli in Factoria is the only legitimate Jewish-style delicatessen in greater Seattle, but it is not kosher. Although welcomed with great fanfare in 2011, Stopsky's on Mercer Island closed three years later, despite being named one of America's best delis by *Food & Wine* in an article by Elizabeth Sherman, and despite being described as one of the "new artisanal Jewish delis" by the *New York Times* in an article by Julia Moskin. As of 2017, only four restaurants (all vegetarian)—Pabla Indian Cuisine, Bamboo Gardens, Teapot Vegetarian House Restaurant, and Island Crust Café—were certified kosher by Va'ad Ha Rabanim, an independent, nonprofit regional kosher certification agency.

Greek Immigrants

Given their cultural passion for good food served to family and friends, it's no surprise to learn that, at one time, Greek immigrants in Seattle "owned and operated more than 75 percent of Seattle's downtown restaurants and candy stores," according to Robert Fisher in "Mirror of Taste: The Restaurant as a Reflection of the Changing Appetites of Seattle." Most of these restaurants, however, featured "American food." This offering consisted of oysters, steaks and chops, eggs and omelets, salads, and potatoes, plus pie for dessert, or basically an Americanized menu reflecting this immigrant group's keen desire to fit in alongside their Pacific Northwest neighbors.

Reflecting immigration patterns in the rest of the United States, a second influx of immigrants from Eastern and Southern Europe arrived between the 1880s and 1916. By the 1910 census, Washington State was home to 4,177 residents with Greek heritage, with the majority living in Seattle and Tacoma.

Like the majority of Seattle's immigrants arriving at the turn of the twentieth century, Greek immigrants came to the Pacific Northwest via the railroad. At first, most were unmarried laborers who either worked on regional railroads as train staff and maintenance workers or managed fruit and tobacco stands, neighborhood markets, candy stores, shoe-shine parlors, and numerous restaurants in downtown Seattle.

Seattle's hub of Greek immigrants was centered around St. Demetrios Greek Orthodox Church, originally founded in 1894 as the Greek-Russian Church, and renamed in 1915. To this day, St. Demetrios, in the Montlake neighborhood, is a center for Greek American cultural events, hosting a hugely popular annual festival showcasing authentic Greek dishes such as baklava, spanakopita, gyros, and more to sellout crowds.

As Greek immigrants assimilated, they moved into restaurant management and operated cafés throughout the city. Some reflected their owners' heritage with names such as the Apollo and the Acropolis, but others were all-American: Busy Bee, Boston Café, Sapho, and Golden Gate, for example. Few survived into the 1960s, a casualty of a maturing population and lack of interest from the younger Greek American generation. The few remaining original Greek eateries include the Athenian Seafood Restaurant and Bar in Pike Place Market, opened in 1909 by three brothers of the Pappadakis family. The spot was first a bakery, then a luncheonette, and finally a full-service restaurant that's still a favorite today. In contemporary times, Greek restaurateurs include Thomas Soukakos (the mover and shaker behind Capitol Hill's favorite brunch spot, Vios) and Peter Canlis (the visionary behind Canlis Restaurant).

Italian Immigrants

Seattle doesn't have a "Little Italy," but it does have a "Garlic Gulch" where most Italian immigrants settled, in the area around Rainier Avenue and Atlantic Street. Less than 1 percent of the four million who emigrated from Italy to the United States between 1880 and 1920 to escape severe poverty came to Washington State. In 1910, there were only 3,454 Italian immigrants living in Seattle. Most were men who had arrived on the East Coast and then worked their way westward working on railroads, changing to coal mining or farming work once they arrived. A small number of families also came to Seattle; in 1915, the number of Italian immigrant households clustered in the "Garlic Gulch" of Rainier Valley was estimated to be 215, with smaller Italian immigrant communities clustered in Georgetown, South Park, First Hill, South Lake Union, and West Seattle. This total may be compared with the total city population in the 1910 census: 51,042 families.

Although the total number remained small, Italian immigrants played a significant role in developing Seattle and its culinary landscape. Many became truck farmers in the fertile Rainier Valley, growing produce to supply city markets, especially Pike Place Market. Others worked in construction and flour mills. By 1915, Frank Marino, the leading truck farmer in Seattle, estimated that most Italian households engaged in farming. With Seattle surrounded by some of the best gardening land in the West, and only seventy-five dollars required to farm on leased land (anyone with several hundred dollars might buy land outright), deciding to pursue farming for a livelihood was an easy choice.

Italian truck farmers were key to establishing Pike Place Market in 1907. Among them, Giuseppe "Joe" Desimone was both an Italian immigrant farmer and a major player in establishing Pike Place Market to give the area's truck farmers a place to sell directly to customers and skip the middleman. With his direction for keeping maintenance costs to a minimum, Pike Place Market stalls were rented at reasonable rates, allowing farmers to afford them year-round.

Another legacy from the city's Italian immigrants appears every May, when many Seattle backyards are fragrant with white clouds of blooming Italian prune plum trees, a prelude to the sweet purple-black oval fruit falling off trees and being cooked into compotes and jam later in the summer. Anyone with an Italian plum tree in their yard knows the legacy of their good fortune and happily shares the bounty.

As expected and outlined in *The Rainier Valley Food Stories Cookbook*, edited by Mikala Woodward, Italian immigrants brought "rich cultural traditions with them, and at their heart was food." This passion for food propelled some into new careers. Giglio Gai, an immigrant from Roccella, Italy, established a successful wholesale and retail bakery operation—Gai's Seattle French Bakery—into the city's largest baking company and the top specialty bread baker in Washington State. Family owned and operated, the bakery was one of the first to sell presliced bread, and in the 1970s and 1980s expanded its business by supplying fast-food restaurants. In 1992, the company merged with San Francisco French Bread.

Looking for a bakery where cannoli and wedding cakes reign? Head south on Rainier Avenue South to find Borracchini's Bakery. Founded in 1923 by Italian immigrants Mario and Maria Borracchini, who came to Seattle from Florence, the bakery still thrives today as a family business. As specialists in traditional Italian baked goods, the store also offers a full-service deli with an in-store eating area and sells a wide variety of Italian grocery items.

Food, particularly sausages, inspired another innovative Italian entrepreneur. Hugo Kugiya of the *Seattle Times* offers a brief history of the company founded by Constantino Oberto. According to Kugiya, Oberto founded Oberto Sausage Company in 1918 as a specialty meat producer with a repertoire of salami, capocollo, pastrami, linguica, and other cured meats. After his father's death in 1943, sixteen-year-old Art Oberto took over the business while finishing high school and soon built it into a significant family-owned corporation selling its specialty meats to area delis and grocery stores. With the tag line "Oh boy! Oberto!" the company is now a $100-million-a-year business and acclaimed as the largest producer of beef jerky in the United States, a product expansion that the company pursued in the late 1950s.

Cheese lured Angelo Merlino away from a dangerous coal mining job to start a business in 1900 importing various Italian cheeses, pasta, bulk olive oil, and other foodstuffs. The store he opened became hugely successful, an impetus for him to start importing Italian food by the container load. Although Merlino's is now owned by the Biesold family, Angelo Merlino's grandson, Armandino Batali, carried on the family tradition by opening Salumi Meat Company in the Pioneer Square neighborhood. (And yes, Armandino is the father of the famous chef Mario Batali.)

Italian immigrants and their restaurants are reviewed in chapter 7, but for immediate gratification, many Seattleites head for DeLaurenti Specialty Food & Wine shop at Pike Place Market, where it has been a cornerstone ever since the post–World War II era. Founded by Pete DeLaurenti, and then run by his son Louis DeLaurenti, the shop was purchased in 2001 by Pat McCarthy and a partner to ensure its continuation as a community resource. Almost like a general store of edibles, it's the top place in town to taste and buy cheeses from every part of the globe, along with cured meats, crackers, olive oil, breads, wine and bubbles, dips, dolmades, paté, and more.

MEXICAN AND LATINO IMMIGRANTS

Immigrants from Mexico and Latin America first arrived in the Pacific Northwest in the 1790s as crewmembers on early sailing expeditions exploring the Olympic Peninsula. Others arrived following the turbulence of the Mexican-American War (1846–1848) and found work as fur trappers, miners, mule-train wranglers, cattle ranchers, and farm laborers, with the majority settling in Eastern Washington. Rosario Romero from Sonora, Mexico, is credited with starting the region's sheep herding industry in this part of the state. One of the state's first Mexican restaurants has a historic tie to this area, but only because the first business endeavor of Carmelita Colon and her husband didn't work out. In the 1860s, the enterprising couple settled in Walla Walla to run mule-pack supply trains to Idaho. When this business failed, they opened their Mexican restaurant.

During the Mexican Revolution (1910–1920) many Latino families permanently immigrated to Eastern Washington for agricultural jobs such as harvesting sugar beets, potatoes, and other labor-intensive crops. In 1941, things changed drastically for Latinos in this area because of the internment of thousands of Japanese Americans. Large-scale farms were desperate for workers to harvest produce. As a result, a government-approved program called the Bracero Program gave growers a green light to employ "guest workers" directly from Mexico. Joining immigrants already in the state, the two groups worked together and prevented farms from losing their produce.

In the 1950s, Latino families in rural Eastern Washington began moving to Seattle seeking employment in the area's booming postwar economy. Others moved for agricultural jobs in the fertile Skagit Valley, just north of Seattle. Like other immigrants before them, they did not settle in one Seattle neighborhood, but moved into multicultural areas such as the Central District and Rainier Valley. Here, the new arrivals introduced the flavors of their homeland by opening bakeries, grocery stores, and taquerias selling Mexican foods.

Until the 1960s, there was little evidence of traditional Mexican cooking in Seattle, except in private homes. This all changed because of one woman: Lucy Lara de Lopez. Known as the "godmother of Seattle's Mexican restaurants," she was originally a schoolteacher from the small village of Cuautla—three hours by car from Puerto Vallarta and two thousand miles south of Seattle. Lopez not only brought Mexican food to Seattle but also forever changed the destiny of residents of her small hometown.

When Lopez arrived in 1957 there were only three Mexican restaurants in Seattle, and two of them were owned by gringos, according to a 1994 article in the *Seattle Times* by Ignacio Lobos, who interviewed Lopez. After working as a babysitter, and then in a clothing factory, Lopez became a dishwasher at Los Amigos Mexican, a restaurant owned by Ernesto Gonzales across from the Paramount Theatre. Gonzales taught her to cook Mexican food with a Southwestern twist (Tex-Mex). A few years later, she became a cook at Bob's Chile in downtown Seattle, owned by Henry Naon, a Jewish American restaurateur who, in 1967, helped Lopez to open her own restaurant on Seventh Avenue and Pike Street.

Hiring relatives and friends from her hometown of Cuautla to staff her restaurant, Lopez effectively launched many of Seattle's Mexican restaurants. Many employees who came north from the tiny town eventually opened their own restaurants, including Azteca, Mazatlán, Las Margaritas, Torero's, Jalisco, El Tapatio, Tacos Guaymas, Maya's, and Acapulco. In fact, in 2005, the *Puget Sound Business Journal* estimated that three hundred Mexican restaurants in Washington were started by entrepreneurs from this small town. The success of these restaurant owners in Seattle enabled them to pay for municipal improvements in their hometown, from constructing a town plaza and a health clinic, to building roads and a $1 million bullfighting ring.

Although most of the Cuautlan-owned restaurants feature "family-style dining" with combination plates and lots of melted cheese, Lopez's legacy remains active. Several Seattle food trucks sell traditional Mexican fare, while a few trendy nontraditional Mexican restaurants are clustered on Capitol Hill. Perhaps the Mexican restaurant with the most "Seattle soul" is the festive and funky Aqua Verde Cafe and Paddle Club on the shore of South Lake Union. Opened in 2002, the water-front venue offers views of downtown skyscrapers and kayaking before margaritas, including a paddling tour through Portage Bay's houseboat district made famous in *Sleepless in Seattle* (the hugely popular romance film released in 1993, and directed and co-written by Nora Ephron), with a menu of freshly prepared traditional Mexican dishes.

The 1970s and 1980s brought Spanish-speaking immigrants from Central and South America, as well as refugees fleeing political turbulence in Guatemala, El Salvador, Chile, and Nicaragua. This new wave has introduced fresh flavors and culinary traditions to Seattle's evolving culinary landscape.

Today, more than fifteen Mexican and Latin American grocery stores are listed in the Yellow Pages for greater Seattle. El Mercado Latino in Pike Place Market, established in 1988, is one of Seattle's oldest Mexican grocery stores and is a favorite of hot sauce fans with its large wall of 100+ varieties. White Center's Castillos Supermarket, established in 2005, also reflects Seattle's ethnic diversity. The store offers a wide range of Asian products, but primarily stocks goods from Mexico, El Salvador, Honduras, Peru, Colombia, Brazil, Venezuela, and other Latino countries—foods that, according to an in-store slogan, "will remind you a bit of your beloved country."

AFRICAN AMERICAN MIGRATION

African Americans arrived in the Pacific Northwest in three waves. In the beginning, they came in small numbers not sizable enough to qualify as a migration. The Oregon Territory in the 1800s had no laws prohibiting African Americans from owning property, unlike much of the rest of the United States. For adventurous African Americans looking for opportunity, Seattle and the West provided new homes and employment opportunities. In Seattle's frontier days, blacks were more likely to own restaurants over any other form of business—except barbershops. Matthias Monet, an early black settler, opened the Seattle Restaurant and Coffee Saloon, which he later converted into an oyster saloon and chop house. Manuel Lopes, also African American, earned a name for himself with his barbershop and restaurant, both opened in 1852.

Completion of the railroads to Seattle was another factor bringing black residents to the city, since railroads had mostly black staff. Along with the Yukon Gold Rush, these events spurred an economic boom with work opportunities attracting new residents. A bonus: In the 1880s there was no official segregation policy—discrimination was more subtle—and many African Americans were eager to leave the post–Civil War South to find employment in a peaceful environment.

Black entrepreneur William Gross (sometimes spelled "Grose") was also notable during this era. He owned Our House restaurant in the Pioneer Square business district and made no differentiation between guests. While there are few records of food served at boarding houses, it is certain that bread, coffee, and hot porridge were staples. After his establishment was destroyed in the 1889 fire, ever the entrepreneur, Gross started over by building other successful businesses in the East Madison area.

Social changes started in the early decades of the twentieth century when racial divides intensified due to conflicts involving unionized workers. Seattle was then a highly unionized town susceptible to strikes. As a result, black workers found jobs in Seattle in 1917 during the butchers' strike, and again in 1919 during a dockworkers strike. Several groups of black miners were recruited in 1919 from the South to replace striking miners in the Newcastle and Franklin coal mines south of Seattle, but overall when compared with other U.S. cities during this period the number of African Americans arriving here was small. For work, most remained in domestic service occupations. As reported by University of Washington professor Quintard Taylor in his detailed chronicle about Seattle's black residents, *The Foraging of a Black Community*, "the vast majority of black Seattleites between 1900 and 1940 were working class people, but a small middle class of professional and business owners (about 15 percent of the 1940 population) emerged to provide a variety of services to the community." Among these were restaurant and boarding house owners, plus grocery store owners, including the North American Produce Company. As the city grew, customers for black businesses changed. No longer primarily white, they were more often black, but black-owned stores also had to compete with Asian- and white-owned businesses for the same black customers. For the most part, blacks shared the Central District neighborhood with Jewish residents. They also managed Chinese-owned jazz clubs in Chinatown in the 1940s and 1950s.

World War II was a major catalyst for black migration to the Northwest. Defense jobs in shipyards and airplane factories urgently needed to be filled, and color barriers disappeared; by 1945, 80 percent of Boeing's production workers were black women. Boeing was the largest area employer at this time, but there were also twenty-nine shipyards operating (plus navy facilities in Bremerton, and Pacific Care and Foundry Company in Renton building tanks), and Professor Taylor estimates that Seattle's black population grew by 300 percent starting in 1942.

On the food scene, many African Americans arriving in this era were from the South. They brought with them traditional dishes such as fried chicken, collard greens, grits, cracklings, cornbread, and peach cobbler. Showcasing these soul food classics, family restaurants such as Kingfish Café on Capitol Hill and Ms. Helen's Diner in the Central District were always packed, but, alas, both are now closed.

Seattle's black superstar restaurateurs are still small in number, but their restaurants have big appeal and creativity. Chef Edourado Jordan's Salare is a standout, making deep dives into his African American culinary heritage. Donna Moodie, owner of Marjorie, and Tarik Abdullah, chef at Morning Star Brunch and Midnight Mecca pop-ups, as well as a culinary educator at Hillman City Collaboratory, are acclaimed for presenting classic dishes from their culture. New places such as Jackson's Catfish Corner in Rainier Valley, Ms. Helen's Soul Food Bistro on Capitol Hill, and Simply Soulful in Madison Valley are all recent hits expanding the tradition of African American food in Seattle.

MODERN MELTING POT: FROM REFUGEES TO TECH GEEKS

In such a diverse city, with an embarrassment of riches in food choices such as ramen, xiao longs bao, pho, pizza, gnocci, burgers and French fries, to name a few, are we still pigeonholing non traditional European fare as "ethnic"? Our city is a passport to the food world—maybe it's time to tear down the verbal borders.

—Seattle chef Lisa Nakamura, owner of Gnocchi Bar, as quoted by
Bethany Jean Clement, *Seattle Times*, July 13, 2016

Consider the diversity of restaurants within a few blocks on Rainier Boulevard in Columbia City that diners can choose from: Senegalese specialties at La Teranga; upscale Vietnamese seafood at the Salted Sea Seafood and Raw Bar; Japanese cuisine at Wabi-Sabi Sushi Bar; dishes inspired by Jamaica, Barbados, and Puerto Rico at Island Soul Caribbean Cuisine; Thai at Spice Room; Sicilian cuisine at La Medusa; and classic American diner food at Geraldine's Counter. These small independently owned restaurants reflect the culinary traditions of Seattle's earliest as well as most recent immigrants.

Since 2010, more than 16,500 refugees from forty-six countries have come to Washington State, with two-thirds settling in King County. Whether they are refugees fleeing civil wars in East Africa or highly educated software engineers from India lured by high-tech opportunities, immigrants who come to Seattle in the twenty-first century continue to bring their rich culinary traditions and new flavors to the Pacific Northwest.

Historically, Seattle has welcomed immigrants for many years as a sanctuary city, dating at least to 2003. Its political leaders continued this tradition in 2017 with a renewed commitment in the wake of the Trump administration's ban on immigrants. While this is a political statement, the city also puts its money where its mouth is by supporting programs that focus on food as a way to help immigrants successfully integrate into a new culture. Established in 2014, the Restaurant Success program supports immigrants and minority groups who want to open restaurants by helping them navigate unfamiliar health department regulations as well as complicated legal and permit processes. A partnership between the Washington Restaurant Association, the state of Washington, and the city of Seattle, the program provides translation services plus resources and information in multiple languages. Anthony Anton, president and CEO of the Washington Restaurant Association, as quoted in an article by Erika Sommer in the *Seattle Globalist*, said, "This isn't going to solve all their problems but hopefully it makes it just a little bit easier. For a lot of people that come to this country, restaurants are their way to kind of own their piece of the American pie and the American dream."

Project Feast, a not-for-profit organization established in 2013, offers hands-on culinary-focused vocational training programs to refugees and talented immigrant home cooks as a way to gain their footing in Seattle's food industry in Seattle. As described on its website, projectfeast.org, Project Feast connects immigrants "to opportunities to make a living and share their wealth of food knowledge with our greater Seattle community, a place with hunger and passion for excellent food. In the process, our participants become deeply integrated into local communities and economies. We enrich all of our lives, one cook at a time."

Although immigrants from around the globe are settling in Seattle in the early twenty-first century, those with the largest numbers or most impact on the region's culinary profile are as follows.

African Immigrants

Ethiopian Immigrants

The first Ethiopians in Seattle were college students who arrived in the late 1960s and early 1970s to study at the University of Washington. Most of them intended to return home, but their plans changed in 1974 when Emperor Haile Selassie was ousted, bringing unrest and instability that soon escalated into war and famine. Thousands of Ethiopian refugees began arriving in Seattle in the 1980s, which created a demand for Ethiopian foods, spices, coffees, and teas. According to Joseph W. Scott and Solomon A. Getahun, authors of *Little Ethiopia of the Pacific Northwest*, the first Ethiopian immigrants were males who did not know how to cook and were unfamiliar with Western food. This created entrepreneurial opportunities for the few Ethiopian women in Seattle. Several started informal food services in their homes or opened licensed mom-and-pop eateries that served home-cooked meals Ethiopian-style, including thick, flavorful stews (*wat*); berbere, a complex blend of chile peppers and spices; and injera, a sour, spongy flatbread made with teff, an ancient grain. Seattle's first Ethiopian restaurant, Kokeb, opened in 1982 in the University District. Owned by four Ethiopian and American families, it introduced a new cuisine to the city and operated for thirty years.

Although Ethiopia is a small country, it has more than eighty different ethnic groups, multiple indigenous languages, and two dominant religions—the Ethiopian Orthodox Church and Islam. Most people, however, share a common food culture, which involves eating with one's fingers by using pieces of spongy pancake-like injera bread to scoop up meat and vegetables. In *The Rainier Valley Food Stories Cookbook*, Alysan Croydon, an ESL teacher at the Refugee Women's Alliance, describes how her students couldn't get teff to make injera and had to substitute wheat to make something they called "911" or "emergency injera." As more East African immigrants arrived in Seattle, including those from Somalia and Eritrea, teff, the primary ingredient for breads in all three cuisines, became available in the ethnic grocery stores that began opening in the Rainier Valley.

Ethiopian food and ingredients also offered challenges and new opportunities for local food producers. Butcher Bob Ackley, the owner of Bob's Quality Meats, relates in *The Rainier Valley Food Stories Cookbook* how his Ethiopian customers kept requesting "red meat, no fat." After finally figuring out that his customers wanted tiny chunks of red meat with no fat, a characteristic of their culture's traditional lean meat style used in rich, spicy stews, Ackley found a supplier in Ferndale who began raising low-fat beef cows, a result of the type of feed they're given, to meet this requirement. Blends of hot spices such as *mitmita* and the classic berbere—a mix of ground chili peppers, ginger, garlic, cumin, dried basil, fenugreek, and coriander, along with several other dry spices—are signature Ethiopian ingredients. Small local companies managed by immigrants started producing these spices for their fellow Ethiopians. This also prompted a demand for specific curries and sauces, plus teff and chickpea flour, to name a few key ingredients in Ethiopian cooking.

By 2010, more than twenty-five thousand Ethiopians lived in the Seattle area, according to the US Census, making it one of the largest communities of Ethiopians in the United States. The scores of Ethiopian restaurants and small grocery stores in Ethiopian communities in the Central District, Rainier Valley, and Pinehurst neighborhood reflect this immigration pattern. The names of Seattle's Ethiopian restaurants often signal what area of Ethiopia or which ethnic group the owners hailed from and often have political undertones, according to Scott and Getahun in *Little Ethiopia of the Pacific Northwest*. For instance, the original owners of Seattle restaurants Addis Ababa, Mercato, and Arada came from the Shoa province, while a restaurant named Assimba signifies an impregnable mountain hideout in northern Ethiopia that served as a military base for one of the anti-government armies. Scott and Getahun note that through the restaurant names, "Ethiopians can safely feel that certain restaurants where they dine will provide both psychological comfort and the sustenance they desire."

In 2017, Yelp listed more than thirty Ethiopian restaurants, which were not only patronized by immigrants but also gaining popularity with Seattleites eager for new culinary experiences. Restaurants ranged from Cafe Selam ("Cafe Peace" in Amharic), which opened in 2003, to Wonder Coffee and Sports Bar, a combination Ethiopian restaurant, burger joint, and sports bar that opened in 2013 in the Central District.

Somali Immigrants

King County's Somali community started with a small group of college students and engineers in the 1970s and 1980s but has grown exponentially as thousands of refugees fled violence and famine following Somalia's 1991 civil war. Although several sources say Somalis are the largest refugee group in King County, their cuisine is relatively invisible outside of their neighborhoods in Kent, Auburn, Tukwila, and Rainier Valley, with only a handful of Somali restaurants. Several reasons are a factor in this: traditionally, Somalis eat at home, and most Somalis in Seattle are Sunni Muslims who adhere to strict dietary laws and, therefore, find it easier to eat at home. Also, because close to 60 percent of Somali immigrants arriving between 2002 and 2013 came from camps, as reported by the Migration Policy Institute (MPI), it's logical that restaurants are economically and culturally not a focus for this community. Like many countries with Muslim cultures, it is mainly men who frequent restaurants. The traditional separate dining areas for men and women also make Somali restaurants less appealing to a broader population.

Juba Restaurant and Cafe, which opened in 2011 next to a mosque in Tukwila near SeaTac airport, is a popular meeting place for Muslim men to gather for lunch after prayers, as well as a convenient stop for Somali cab drivers and airport workers. Juba also welcomes women and families, who eat in separate dining rooms, as well as the occasional non-Somali diner. Nicole Sprinkle in the *Seattle Weekly* (January 26, 2016) makes Juba's cuisine sound like a foodie paradise. Her overview of the menu describes traditional dishes, including chunks of spiced goat meat, a large flavorful salmon fillet, and half a roasted chicken ringed by fluffy piles of rice thick with flavors of butter and cardamom. She also notes that the menu includes several preparations of salmon, which is not a traditional ingredient in Somali cooking, and quotes a Somali friend who said, "Living here, we have become addicted to salmon. . . . I love that; it's the story of food everywhere, the assimilation of regional influences creating an entirely unique riff on the original."

South Asian Immigrants

Basmati rice, according to Amy Bhatt and Nalini Iyer, the authors of *Roots & Reflections: South Asians in the Pacific Northwest*, is now "as much a part of the cultural landscape of the Pacific Northwest as fresh-caught salmon." This is primarily due to the thousands of highly educated professionals from South Asia who have flocked to Seattle, lured by opportunities at technology giants Microsoft and Amazon as well as jobs in the aerospace and biomedical industries. These, however, are not the first immigrants from India to arrive in Seattle. A small number of early settlers from South Asia first arrived in the early 1900s to work on the railroads, in lumber mills, and as farmers and fishermen. There is little evidence of these early Indian settlers or their culinary history because many were driven out by discrimination such as the "anti-Hindu" Bellingham Riots in 1907.

The next group of South Asian immigrants didn't arrive until the 1940s when students came to study at the University of Washington. Since then, Seattle's South Asian population has grown slowly but steadily. When the technology boom hit in 1990, it increased from four thousand to more than sixty thousand in 2010, with the largest percentage living in Redmond (Microsoft's headquarters), Kirkland, and other cities on the East Side.

As Bhatt and Iyer describe in to *Roots & Reflections*, immigrants who migrated after World War II "did not find staple ingredients such as long grain rice, yogurt, or spices easily available," and relied on people traveling from or to South Asia or those visiting larger American cities to bring back ingredients they needed. Like immigrants before them, the new arrivals learned to substitute ingredients and pooled resources in order to cook traditional dishes. Some even drove to Vancouver to stock up on supplies from the Punjabi markets there or found similar ingredients at Uwajimaya, the Asian grocery store in the International District focused on East Asian cuisine. Aware of the potential sales, in 2017 Uwajimaya opened a second location in Bellevue near the Microsoft campus that stocks okra, dal, and various pickles used in South Indian dishes.

Beginning in the late 1980s, strip malls known as "Little Indias" began sprouting in suburban neighborhoods near Microsoft, such as Redmond and Bellevue, to serve South Asian families. There might be a restaurant, bakery, a small grocery store with a halal meat counter, and a video store. In many families, both husbands and wives are software engineers, which makes having neighborhood food sources welcome. To accommodate home cooks, major grocery chains on the Eastside began offering a wide selection of Indian spices, vegetables, and prepared food. The retail warehouse chain Costco—headquartered in Issaquah—also stocks a selection of Indian ingredients along with South Asian curries, breads, sweets, and frozen dishes. Although affluent high-tech professionals are not averse to eating at restaurants, they are more likely to choose Western or other ethnic restaurants. Why go to a restaurant for home-style Indian food if it's better at home? This may also explain why there are not a significant number of Indian restaurants in Seattle despite the large immigrant population. Most Indian restaurants in Seattle are small neighborhood cafés, and a few are strictly vegetarian, appealing to Hindu and Jain diners. When Pabla, a modest pure-vegetarian (no dairy or eggs) restaurant and grocery, opened in 1998 near the Boeing factory in suburban Renton, it was an instant success with South Asian Boeing engineers. It also quickly began attracting non-Indian vegans and vegetarians, as well as African immigrant Muslims and Orthodox Jews, since it is one of very few kosher restaurants certified by the Va'ad HaRabanim of Seattle.

The number of South Asians working at tech companies has also been a major factor in Seattle's food truck culture, which generally serves traditional street food and first began rolling up to park near Microsoft and Amazon campuses. Sometimes technology and food overlap. In 2014, software engineer Kathi Josho, who grew up in the Mumbai-Pune region of Western India, left her job at Microsoft to open a food truck—Roll OK Please—serving grilled flatbread wraps filled with either marinated meat or grilled paneer, mint chutney, and pickled onions. Her food truck not only travels onto the Microsoft campus but also roams Seattle and throughout the Eastside.

Seattle's food scene is decidedly richer on multiple levels because of the many immigrant groups, both past and present, who moved to the Northwest to make the city their home. From soup pots to sauté pans, noodles to fish steaks, crab cakes to cheesecakes, *kringle* to doughnuts, teriyaki, pad Thai, and numerous other tasty examples, Seattle's culinary heritage with its many ethnic resources is a delectable bonus to residing here. Adventurous eaters are guaranteed to always find something new to twirl on their forks and taste.

5

Growing and Sharing the Bounty
From Field to Fork

This market is yours. I dedicate it to you, and may it prove a benefit to you and your children. It is for you to defend, to protect and uphold, and it is for you to see that those who occupy it treat you fairly. . . . This is one of the greatest days in the history of Seattle, but it is only the beginning, for soon this city will have one of the greatest markets in the world.

—Thomas P. Revelle, member of the City of Seattle Council, 1907, quoted in Alice Shorett and Murray Morgan, *Soul of the City* (2007)

Fish fly, oysters are weighed, sample apple and peach slices find fingers (and then mouths), flats of blueberries are carried off, and tourists stroll amid Hmong flower ladies, potters and painters, street buskers, and aromas of coffee and croissants. Vendors talk with customers and visitors may discover new edibles such as fiddlehead ferns and Alaskan King crab. That's a very short list, but it's another typical day at Pike Place Market. Described as the "Soul of the City" by historian and author Alice Shorett in the title of her 2007 book outlining the Market's colorful and tumultuous history, Pike Place Market is a living witness to Seattle's food history. A historical look at the city's markets and purveyors bringing food to kitchens and dinner tables must start with Pike Place Market. As the oldest continuously operating public food market in the country for more than a century, it is both landmark and legacy, as well as a several-times survivor of urban environmental politics.

Consider onions the instigator. Since the price of onions had soared tenfold between 1906 and 1907, an increase blamed on middlemen and price fixing, who wouldn't want an alternative for buying onions, a cooking staple? An option was organized through progressive civic efforts. On a gray, soggy Saturday—August 17, 1907, to be exact—a dozen or so farmers parked their horse-drawn wagons on a street between First Avenue and Pike Street above Western Avenue, which ran from the top of the bluff down to the waterfront. With vegetables and fruits grown on an estimated three thousand small farms in the highly fertile Duwamish, White, Cedar, and Kent valleys, and Puget Sound islands surrounding Seattle, these farmers could sell directly to customers, eliminating the middleman. Alice Shorett estimates in *Soul of the City: The Pike Place Public Market* that "half [of the farmers] were native-born Americans; the rest were new arrivals, mostly from Europe, though there were some Chinese and a growing number of Japanese and Filipinos." As records document, on that first Saturday, shoppers turned out in droves, creating havoc in their stampede to buy fresh produce at prices lower than usual rates. Despite the first-day frenzy, the market was a sellout and a huge success. On the following Saturday, more than seventy farmers turned out, again selling every apple, onion, egg, chicken, and potato on their wagons. Pike Place Market was open for business.

The backstory of Pike Place Market's beginning and its farmers is linked to the city's system of middlemen, price gouging, a community-focused city councilman, and a newspaperman. To give the story context in numbers, Seattle's surging population between 1890 and 1910 impacted many city activities. It was a place where people could find employment in a variety of jobs related to the Yukon Gold Rush, rebuilding San Francisco after its 1906 earthquake and fire, available land, and railroad routes. Charles P. LeWarne outlines the region's population numbers in his introduction to Mary Wright's *More Voices, New Stories*, with details taken from Calvin F. Schmid and Stanton E. Schmid's book, *Growth of Cities and Towns, State of Washington*:

> Seattle's population more than doubled during the first decade of the 20th century. In 1890, 42,837 people lived in the city. By 1900, there were 80,671 and a decade later an astounding 237,194. In the statehood year of 1889, King County was the state's largest county, with 63,989 residents tallied in the following year's census. The number climbed to 110,053 over the next ten years and doubled to 284,638 by 1910. Four of every ten county residents live in its largest city.

To this picture, add changes happening while Seattle grew in the first part of the twentieth century, and the location of Pike Place Market makes sense. From the original core settlement around Yesler's Wharf and between First and Third Avenues, downtown expansion activity moved north and west toward Denny Avenue and First Hill, reflecting the city's challenging hilly geography and the slow process of filling the southern tide flats. As Roger Sale explained in *Seattle, Past to Present*, many downtown buildings accommodated offices and residences, hotels and boarding houses, with rich and poor living side-by-side, employed and job seekers, with minimal distinctions between groups. He describes this early downtown Seattle as having no heavy industry but says:

> It did have furniture and cabinet makers, machine shops, groceries, laundries, dress-makers, meat and fish merchants, and in a great many instances the owners and employees of these businesses lived there or nearby. The boarding houses accommodated not only transients like salesmen and sailors, but also jewelers, engineers, teachers of anything from the violin to penmanship, clairvoyants, midwives, retired couples. There were rooms not just for the single and the childless but also for families and groups of families.

And everyone had to eat. In an era with limited refrigeration, seeking out and acquiring food was a daily necessity.

So how was grocery shopping accomplished in early Seattle? Small, independent grocery stores existed in some neighborhoods for purchasing staples. A directory from 1885 to 1886 listed just twenty-two grocers in the entire city. But with farms nearby, in the early twentieth century, distribution methods for locally grown fresh foods included door-to-door sales, with some farmers driving horse-drawn carts and eventually trucks through residential neighborhoods or to hotels and restaurants. However, due to time constraints for most farmers, the main sales method involved farmers selling to wholesalers on lower Western Avenue, then known as Produce Row. By all accounts, the inequitable system was rife with fraud, controversy, and high prices for local shoppers and grocery stores. Many times farmers were not paid, or they were paid far below the retail price for their produce. Choice foodstuffs would frequently be shipped to large-scale exporters. Enter Tomas P. Revelle.

Revelle had moved from Maryland to Seattle in 1898 to serve as a Methodist minister. He attended the University of Washington and received a law degree. In June 1906, he was elected to the Seattle City Council. Aware of the middleman controversy for produce sales, he took up the farmers' cause and determined the best solution would be establishing a public market for direct sales. As it happened, Seattle's city council had passed a resolution in 1896 authorizing a public market in response to the severe depression from 1893 to 1897, but that decision was tabled during Seattle's Yukon Gold Rush boom. In June 1907, Revelle pitched an ordinance to the city council designating Pike Place as Seattle's new public market area following the terms of the 1896 resolution. While the city council considered Revelle's ordinance, Colonel Alden J. Blethen, publisher of the *Seattle Times*, issued a series of news stories aimed at exposing the fraudulent tactics of the wholesale commission houses. On August 5, 1907, the city council

90   *Chapter 5*

passed Revelle's ordinance establishing Pike Place as the site for an ongoing public farmers' market and setting up the Pike Place Market Preservation and Development Authority as landlord.

To create the actual physical market, Frank Goodwin, one of Seattle's early real-estate developers and a self-taught architect, saw an opportunity. He already owned the Leland Hotel at the western end of Pike Street, as well as undeveloped land north and west of Pike Place. While five buildings in the Pike Place complex already existed—the Economy Market, LaSalle, Livingston-Baker, and the Leland and Stewart buildings—there was no money to build others. Knowing an arcade was needed to protect vendors from inclement weather, in 1908, Goodwin built the Market's first arcade with seventy-six stalls for produce vendors. In 1910, the city extended the arcade, but Goodwin, with his realtor brothers and eventually his nephew, Arthur, owned most of the additional buildings constructed over the years. In 1914, Frank Goodwin built additions to the original market buildings by going downward and westward. In 1916, he took over the lease on the building on the corner of Pike and First Avenue and renamed it the Economy Market, with additional vendor stalls. With city support between 1910 and 1920, awnings and stalls were added to the original structures. Automobiles also had to be accommodated.

Shoppers at Pike Place Market around 1911 choosing produce from local farmers in stalls both outside and beneath the new covered arcade area. *Courtesy of MOHAI, [Museum of History & Industry Photograph Collection], [1983.10.6868.2].*

Overcrowding was one issue that Pike Place Market needed to deal with. Alice Shorett reports in *Soul of the City* that, in 1917, 5,217 farmers rented stalls, although most were short term, for one or two days. She also notes that a 1917 proposal for a $600,000 Market expansion prompted a study by the Seattle Municipal League. This report said that "the city with a population of 340,000 was served by 550 grocery stores, 160 butcher shops, 35 delicatessens, and 12 market buildings includ[ing] the Corner Market, Sanitary Market, Pike Place, and Economy Market" and did not support the expansion proposal.

All things considered, Pike Place Market was hugely popular in the 1920s and promoted itself with the slogan "Everything for the Table under One Roof." From fish to fruit, eggs, meat, and lettuces, Seattle's shoppers were assured of fresh, affordable food, seasonal availability, and building relationships as they got to know their vendors and farmer suppliers. The decade saw a post office and library added to Market services, along with the first coffee shop and a space for selling doughnuts.

Looking into Pike Place Public Market around 1915 following the construction of the Corner Market on First Avenue and Pike Place. Trolley cars, horse delivery vans, cars, and bustling shoppers all testify to the Market's place at the center of a growing city. *Courtesy of MOHAI, [PEMCO Webster & Stevens Collection], [1983.10.140.5].*

In 1922, when the Goodwin brothers proposed renting the most visible market stalls to wholesalers to ensure year-round produce availability, protests erupted from farmers. However, these "high stalls" have had permanent vendors since that date. As shared by Alice Shorett in *Soul of the City*, Mark Tobey, who would later become important in saving the Market, used his artist's instincts to describe Pike Place Market on his first visit in 1922:

> I walked down this fabulous array of colors and forms. So many things are offered for sale—plants to be replanted; ropes of all kinds; antiques; Norwegian pancakes made by an old sea captain, to be eaten on one of four stools on the sidewalk looking in. I hear the calls to buy—"Hey, you, come over here for the best tomatoes in the Market." Across the street are open shops under long burnt-orange-colored awnings.

THE IMMIGRANT EFFECT AT PIKE PLACE MARKET

Pike Place Market was a point of entry for many immigrants arriving in Seattle. The list is long and includes immigrants from Japan, the Philippines, Italy, Greece, and Sephardic Jews who brought with them a work ethic and strong sense of community. Jeffrey Craig Sanders notes in *Seattle & the Roots of Urban Sustainability*, "By 1940, sixty to eighty percent of 'wet-stall,' or lower stall, vendors were Japanese Americans." Many immigrants involved in the Market are described in an earlier chapter, but the list is long of vendors who stand out for their role in establishing the variety of foods available at the Market, and several more are worth mentioning here.

Examples in this group include Pasqualina Verdi, who moved to Seattle in 1949, an Italian truck farmer who sold home-grown produce ranging from arugula to dandelion greens for thirty-six years at a metal table stand; Dan Zido, who, after arriving from Poland and working at a Seattle sausage factory, started Dan's Meats in 1916 with a partner and became full owner in 1924; and Italian immigrants David Mossafer and his brother-in-law who opened the Quality Fruit Shop in 1912 on the corner of Pike Street and Pike Place. In 1928, Mossafer with Ness Peha started United Fruit Company, Seattle's first locally owned chain of supermarkets, but lost this business during the Depression years. Numerous Sephardic Jews, most immigrants from the island of Rhodes, also found their way to Seattle and to Pike Place Market. David Levy bought the City Fish Market, while others—Selemo Calvo, Jacob Pelicar, Jacob Feinberg—established their own fruit stands. Angelina Mustelo arrived from Italy and opened a small grocery store in 1928 staffed by her daughter, Mamie-Marie, who married Peter Ramond DeLaurenti. The couple eventually bought out Mustelo and renamed their store DeLaurenti's, which was—and

Showing off her bounty of strawberries around 1919, this Asian American woman was one of many local farmers selling fresh vegetables, berries, apples, and dairy products at Pike Place Market. *Courtesy of MOHAI, [Museum of History & Industry Photograph Collection], [1983.10.1593.1].*

still is today—celebrated for its wealth of premium Italian food products and treasure chest of cheeses from around the world. For example, there's not just one Brie cheese but at least a dozen choices, ranging from buttery soft with a full fat content to more pungent versions. Knowledgeable cheesemongers will recommend cheeses, offer tasting samples, and carefully slice every individual order—another example of Market traditions remaining vibrant for today's food fans.

Among recent immigrant stories, in 1982, Pike Place Market joined the Indochinese Farm Project, a program organized to help Hmong and Mien immigrants from Vietnam and Laos become self-sufficient through farming. Over the years, more than thirty Hmong and Mien families have come to the Market to sell gorgeous flower bouquets and fresh vegetables from farms in the surrounding area. Their participation again proves the importance of Pike Place Market in welcoming newcomers to the Pacific Northwest and renewing the connection between local farms and food.

THE BENEVOLENT GODFATHER OF PIKE PLACE MARKET

Looking back in time again to the Market's roster of immigrants, Giuseppe "Joe" Desimone is a star. Born in 1880 to an Italian tenant-farming family, he arrived in America in 1897 at age seventeen eager for success. Making his way to Seattle's Rainier Valley where an uncle lived, he worked for hire until he had saved enough money to lease a truck farm in Georgetown, and then a second truck farm in South Park. He and his young wife Assunta, also an immigrant from Italy, grew every vegetable possible in those days: potatoes, lettuces, celery, carrots, beets, turnips, yellow and green onions, cauliflower, corn, beans, and peas. Eventually, by 1928, their South Park farm covered seventy acres. Tall and distinguished with a handlebar mustache, Giuseppe delivered his produce in a Model T Ford truck to Seattle's many neighborhood grocery stores, hotels, and restaurants. He was the only farmer in 1922 to pay the seventy-five-dollar monthly fee for a permanent market stall.

In 1925, when Arthur Goodwin took over the Market Company from his uncles, Joe Desimone bought stock in the company, buying more in 1927 when another shareholder sold his interests. The latter purchase made him the second-largest shareholder and vice president of Pike Place Public Market Company. Following a series of ups and downs during the Depression, the Goodwins' involvement in Pike Place Public Market Company diminished, and in the 1940s Joe Desimone was left in the key role as company president. (By then, his son Richard was also involved in running the company.) His loyalty to the community of tenant farmers and producers at Pike Place Market enabled many to keep their stalls even during the height of bad times, something for which he is still gratefully remembered.

Richard Desimone, shown around 1946 in the delivery truck of the produce business established by his father, Giuseppe "Joe" Desimone, who emigrated from Italy to Seattle in 1897 and eventually became a majority owner of Pike Place Market. *Courtesy of MOHAI, [Seattle Historical Society Collection], [10720].*

With the start of World War II, Pike Place Market slipped into decline. One major building in the Market was demolished by fire in December 1941. Almost all Japanese American truck farmers in the area were sent to internment camps in May 1942, leaving numerous empty market stalls. Records show that in 1939 permits were sold to 515 sellers; in 1943, the number had dropped to 196. After the war, few Japanese American farmers were able to return to their land, and small farms selling directly to the public found it difficult to compete with the new trend of large farming conglomerates that shipped produce long distances by truck. Post–World War II also marked the beginning of car culture, which spawned suburbs and supermarkets. Fewer people lived in downtown Seattle, and most still there were poor. The Market took on a scroungy appearance with decaying structures and few customers.

In 1957, Seattle's city council reinstated the Market's ten-year lease on arcade space, but many questions arose about the Market's viability and longevity. The

1962 World's Fair positioned Seattle as a forward-oriented city. Was the Market part of this vision? For many the answer was "no." Eager planners presented an urban revitalization concept that would raze every building on the Market's twelve-acre site, replacing them with a huge parking garage for four thousand cars, a hotel, and a park. Another plan proposed a hockey arena, an office park, and a highway exit. In progressive Seattle, where discussion is valued, conversation over the future of Pike Place Market rapidly turned into a fierce debate.

URBAN RENEWAL VERSUS URBAN POPULISM

In 1968, the fate of Pike Place Market reached a boiling point and civic war ensued. The pro-Market side lined up behind the Friends of the Market coalition organized by city councilman Wing Luke. This group petitioned the Seattle city council to approve the Market's historic value in 1969 by gathering fifty-three thousand signatures on a petition. The council rejected the petition, instead voting for the urban renewal plan. University of Washington architecture professor Victor Steinbrueck (credited with designing the iconic Space Needle while working on assignment at John Graham Jr.'s architectural firm) countered this move by getting the council to approve the Pike Place Market area as a historic district according to the terms of the National Historic Preservation Act. Launching a grassroots fight as actions intensified, Steinbrueck proved to be a forceful and visible voice supporting the Market's survival.

Downtown businessmen counterattacked by attempting to reduce the designated historic area from 17 acres to 1.7 acres. At this move, the Friends of the Market coalition sued, saying the chairman of the State Advisory Council, Charles Odegaard, had exceeded his authority by reopening the question of the historic area's size, and asked in their court brief to restore the designated seventeen-acre site to the National Historic Register. The city filed to dismiss the case and was denied, but the case never came to trial.

In the meantime, the situation intensified when the federal government approved a $10.6 million Pike Plaza project that would completely destroy the Market. With the gauntlet thrown down, Friends of the Market launched an initiative campaign to gather signatures for a 1971 ballot measure. Their proposal was to establish a seven-acre historic district and maintain the Market as a public resource. Initiatives required 15,560 approved signatures to be listed on the ballot; the Friends gathered 25,478 signatures in less than three weeks. In November 1971, after intense debates across the city, the initiative passed, with 76,369 approving signatures and 53,264 disapprovals. To manage the new historic district, the city established the Pike Place Market Preservation and Development Authority.

Renovation for the Market's downtrodden buildings happened next. US senator Warren Magnuson engineered $60 million in federal funds to refurbish the Market's buildings and infrastructure. While these steps seemed to ensure smooth Market functioning, the pressures of high-maintenance expenses and demand to keep tenants' rents low prompted Market administrators between 1980 and 1983 to enter into "tax sale" contracts with various syndicates. These turned out to all be under the Urban Group, a New York–based financial group that now had a 90 percent controlling interest in Pike Place Market in exchange for a cash infusion of $2.93 million. The motivation: The Urban Group could use the Market as a tax write-off and a source of tax savings. But tax laws changed in 1986, eliminating the original tax write-off.

In 1988, the Urban Group threatened to take over the Market and redevelop the area in order to recoup its investment. A new fight to save the Market opened. The challenge was finding money to pay off the Urban Group and extricate the Market from its financial obligations while creating a cash flow. In the end, Washington's legislature kicked in money, as did many local investors. For the first time, the Market also launched its own public fundraising campaign with huge success as patrons purchased stylized pig hoofprints reflecting Rachel, the life-size bronze piggy bank celebrated as the Market's mascot. The brass hoofprints are embedded in sidewalks throughout the Market, and families often visit looking for their names.

Since the last uprising in the 1980s, Pike Place Market has thrived and prospered as both a retail outlet and a source of social service agencies and low-income housing for four hundred persons; operations include the Pike Market Senior Center and a Food Bank as well as the Pike Market Childcare and Preschool, and the Pike Market Health Clinic. The nine-acre historic site is one of the most visited destinations anywhere in the United States, a Seattle centerpiece, and a living testament to the city's sense of community and commitment.

TODAY'S BOUNTIFUL PIKE PLACE MARKET

The Market has long been about affordable and abundant food, but it's also about community and connections with its "Meet the Producer" up-front-and-personal focus. Today, more than eighty local farmers and fishermen sell their products at Market farm stalls seven days a week, 363 days each year. Honoring its historic mission, the focus is on fresh and high-quality foodstuffs. An equal number of craftspeople rent open tables to sell their wares, and street musicians draw tickets determining where and when they'll play each day. In 2015, the Market launched a Wednesday evening summertime market, along with downtown pop-up farmers' markets one day each week from June to October in four locations: City Hall,

Denny Regrade, First Hill, and South Lake Union. All markets are members of the Washington State Farmers Market Association.

In an affirmation of its future and significance as a vital part of Seattle's character, in June 2017, Pike Place Market expanded westward into a new MarketFront building overlooking Elliott Bay. Along with a pavilion with space for forty-seven farm and craft retail vendors, the building includes the Old Stove Brewing Company, Little Fish, Honest Biscuits, and Indi Chocolate. There is also a new neighborhood center and forty low-income studio apartments for seniors.

Add all these food and community riches together, stir with a good measure of endurance, and in mere seconds one can understand why Pike Place Market still represents the heart and soul of Seattle. Diverse, energetic, and a hub for exchange on multiple levels, the Market exists as an exciting resource of inspiration and validation.

DISCOVERING PIKE PLACE MARKET'S
FOOD AND COOKWARE SHOPS

While the Market's day vendors operate according to an established check-in system to claim their spaces, today's permanent retailers in surrounding buildings echo the vibrant community spirit and commitment to quality of their ancestors. From fish and meat shops to cheese purveyors and a fully functioning cheese producer, along with the original store of a national cookware chain, the variety of independent businesses heightens the Market's appeal. For example, Three Girls Bakery opened in 1912 and featured an upstairs ice cream parlor and coffee shop as well as a full-service bakery on the ground flour. Founded and managed by three women, the bakery earned attention as Seattle's first female-owned business. By 1919, the trio had opened eight more bakeries, plus a wholesale bakery. However, by 1925, only one location remained, and the women had stopped baking, instead selling baked goods from Brenner Brothers Bakery. Jack Levy, who bought the bakery in 1979 with his sister, brought baking activities back in-house. From shortbread to sandwiches, Three Girls Bakery is a Market institution that continues to satisfy and treat its customers.

Also a Market institution, Frank's Quality Produce was established in 1928 by the Genzale family. Still operated four generations later by Frank Genzale Sr. and Frank Genzale Jr., the stand is renowned for its bountiful and beautiful seasonal fruit and vegetable displays arranged daily by its engaging, helpful owners. Whether looking for ripe mangos, dragon fruit, or dill weed for brining pickles, in every way, Frank's personifies the best of the Market with top-quality seasonal produce and welcoming customer service.

Quality Cheese Inc. is another steadfast retailer, a fixture in the Market on Post Alley for more than twenty-five years. Known for its extensive selection of imported and domestic artisanal cheeses, along with accompaniments such as olives, cornichons, patés, and multitudes of crackers, the shop is an established food lovers' paradise.

Beecher's Handmade Cheese, an operation founded by entrepreneurial visionary Kurt Beecher Dammeier in 2003, is a Pike Place Market original. (A Seattle food original, Dammeier also owns the Pasta & Company chain of delis with a changing menu of seasonal take-home deliciousness.) With its storefront cheese-making operation, Beecher's sets Seattle apart as one of two metropolitan cities in the universe where commercial cheese-making takes place seven days a week in full public view. (The other city is New York, where Beecher's also operates a creamery and restaurant.) A look through the big windows at the corner of Pine and Pike Place Market shows milk from a local dairy being processed in huge stainless steel vats. Large paddles slowly churn the heated milk, activating the age-old chemistry that turns curds and whey into Beecher's handcrafted smooth, creamy, or hard cheeses. Walk inside for a closer look and grab a sandwich to go, choose a container of squeaky cheese curds, have cheese sliced, or enjoy a bowl of soup or Beecher's prize-winning mac 'n' cheese (it's also sold frozen to take home and cook). The usual line here of happily munching customers underscores Beecher's special Market status.

Cheese is the rock star in this grilled cheese sandwich that's a sophisticated version of the American classic. Made with Beecher's Flagship or Just Jack cheese, it's a winner, and shared here with permission from Kurt Dammeier's first cookbook, *Pure Flavor: 125 Fresh All-American Recipes from the Pacific Northwest*. A cooking tip: Any type of semi-hard cheese—for example, Cheddar or Gruyère—will produce a flavorful sandwich. Add slices of roasted turkey to create a heartier version. Either option is excellent with homemade tomato soup.

Toasted Tomato-Basil Sandwich

(Makes 4 sandwiches)

INGREDIENTS

¼ cup mayonnaise
1½ tablespoons whole grain mustard
2 dashes Tabasco® or other hot sauce
8 slices hearty artisanal white bread

4 ounces Beecher's Flagship cheese, or a semi-hard cheese, cut into 8 thin slices
2 tomatoes, sliced ½ inch thick
12 fresh basil leaves
2 ounces Beecher's Just Jack cheese, or a semi-soft cheese, cut into 8 thin slices

Toasted Tomato-Basil Sandwich (*continued*)

DIRECTIONS
In a small bowl, whisk together the mayonnaise, mustard, and Tabasco sauce to make a smooth sauce.

To assemble the sandwiches, spread half of the mayonnaise mixture on four slices of bread. Layer two slices of Flagship cheese, two tomato slices, three fresh basil leaves, and two slices of Just Jack cheese on top of each slice of bread. Spread the remaining four slices of bread with the mayonnaise mixture and place them, mayonnaise side down, on top of the cheese slices.

Heat a large skillet over medium heat and place the sandwiches into the pan. Cook until the cheese has melted and the bread is golden brown, about three minutes on each side. (Use a spatula to turn each sandwich so both sides cook.) Serve warm.

Every visit to Pike Place Market must include stopping and shopping at Pike Place Fish Market—where your selection is guaranteed to fly. No, fish don't have wings, but the teamwork between the fishmongers at this open-air shop as they toss a fresh, frozen-from-the-sea wild Alaskan salmon or a hefty halibut over the counter could make you think otherwise. The teamwork on display making fish fly is so tight, it's also proven the inspiration for employee training workshops. A key Pike Place merchant since 1930, the fish selection is seasonal and may include flash-frozen whole wild Coho salmon and whole wild King salmon from Alaska or off the Washington coast, along with whole Alaskan halibut, true cod fillets, and rockfish fillets. Shellfish options typically include Dungeness crab, Alaskan King crab, wild shrimp, and prawns. Specialty fish can range from yellow fin tuna fish and squid tubes to whole mackerel. A short walk into the main building leads to Pure Food Fish, another outstanding purveyor with a market legacy and a full selection of seafood in cases and spread over ice on multiple tables.

Nearby, on the corner of Stewart Street and Pike Place, baking fragrances drift from the doors of Le Panier Bakery. Founded in 1983 by co-owners Kristi Drake and Thierry Mougin, the bakery is a cornerstone of the Market's revival. It's also evidence that Julia Child's TV introduction of French cuisine went a long way to create an audience for authentic baked goods. Inside, display cases feature traditional French pastries, many adapted with seasonal flavors and ingredients. From croissants to individual brioche and elegant French baguettes, everything is prepared in the on-site bakery. For anyone craving authentic French *macarons*, this is an ideal destination. Colorful choices of the almond paste cookies span more than a dozen flavors ranging from lemon to lavender or pistachio. Welcoming tables and chairs invite staying a while to sip a coffee beverage and savor a pastry.

On the other side of the stove, the correct skillet can make the difference in recipe success. Sharing this knowledge and selling the "right" pan to home cooks was the mission of Shirley Collins when she founded Sur La Table in 1972 as a resource where serious cooks could find cooking equipment ranging from knives to bakeware, tabletop items, pottery, and cast-iron Dutch ovens. The first store was on Stewart Street in Pike Place Market in a refurbished secondhand store building. In 1995, Collins sold the company. Now a national chain with more than one hundred stores, the company is owned by Bahrain-based Investcorp. Even with its "big company" ownership, Sur La Table remains a Seattle original.

While this is a limited recap of favorite shops at Pike Place Market, the panoply of colors, sights, and sounds throughout the Market will enchant a first- or fiftieth-time explorer no matter which direction is explored. The connections between farmer, food, and customer are undeniable and alive everywhere.

SEATTLE'S EARLY GROCERS AND GROCERY CHAINS

While Pike Place Market was experiencing its roller coaster ride between success and distress, Seattle was growing slowly. In 1920, the city's population hovered around 316,000, according to census figures. Hit hard by the 1930s Depression (Seattle had its own Hooverville of mostly indigent men camping out in the tidal flats around Pioneer Square), and then a stagnant economy, growth was minimal before the outbreak of World War II. Until that point, neighborhood grocery stores were the norm, and the city had an abundance of independent chains and stand-alone retail stores. People had to eat, and entrepreneurs knew grocery stores could be a steady income source if scaled rationally. Most of these early groceries were strictly food stores, while others were expansions of stores that served as outfitters for Klondike Gold Rush explorers. Offering a spectrum of goods, they provided necessary edibles for home cooks of this era who typically shopped every day or every other day. The style of grocery shopping also changed in the decades between the world wars, from handing a list to a stockist or grocer (or phoning in an order) for fulfillment and home delivery to self-service shopping from stocked shelves and putting items into a basket for checkout and payment. Food prices also rose in this period, which made self-service a way for grocers to discount prices.

Examples from this lively era of grocery entrepreneurship in Seattle are numerous, with multiple mergers and consolidations. Top names and chains include Augustine & Kyer, which operated a large emporium from 1908 to 1938 downtown in the Coleman Building, complete with operators available to take phone orders and its own fleet of delivery wagons. The company also operated its own candy factory and bakery behind its flagship store and promoted a name-brand coffee. As a side business, the chain's president ran a large poultry farm in Kent, Washington, to provide eggs and chicken for grocery customers and the store's bakery. Augustine & Kyer expanded to five branch stores but, unfortunately, did not survive the Great Depression.

An early grocery chain that did survive Depression years was Eba Mutual Groceries, started in 1908 by Herman Eba, a transplant from Ohio who ran the first store with his son Earl in one of the Market's permanent Main Arcade stalls. The store was sold twice with name changes. In 1922, it was bought back by Earl Eba (his father was now deceased) and named Eba's Cut Rate Grocery. Between 1926 and 1929, Eba expanded his chain by purchasing four independent grocery stores in West Seattle, Capitol Hill, and Renton Hill, and by adding six more stores in Seattle's southern neighborhoods. Promoting discounted groceries generated a lot of customers during the Great Depression, and eventually the chain had fifty-two outlets throughout the state.

Eba's survived the Depression with just one store closure. In 1932, Eba's Cut Rate Grocery & Markets merged with Mutual Markets to form Eba's Mutual, a new fifty-two-store chain with stores across Washington State. The Mutual Markets chain had been established in 1931 with ninety-four statewide stores by joining Pay'n Save, Jones Piggly Wiggly, and United Groceries & Markets, but fifty stores had closed earlier because of the Depression. Debt finally did snare the chain and its owner Earl Eba in 1939. That year, his chain was taken over by a distributor, eventually becoming part of Tradewell Stores, a new Seattle-based grocery chain formed in 1939 by joining Eba's Mutual Markets in Seattle with Eba's Mutual Piggly Wiggly stores located around the state. (The first Piggly Wiggly stores were opened in 1921 in downtown Seattle by William Lewis Avery after the Tennessee company founder, Clarence Saunders, lost control of his self-service grocery company.)

Another pioneering grocery chain in Seattle was founded and operated by Carl Gotfried Anderson. A Swedish immigrant and entrepreneur who made his way from Michigan to Portland, Oregon, he opened his first grocery store in Portland in 1905 and built the chain to thirty-nine stores by 1926. Selling his Portland business that year, Anderson moved to Seattle and founded Anderson Food Stores in downtown Seattle in the Mann Building (today the location of the Triple Door Theatre and Wild Ginger restaurant) on Third Avenue and Union Street, where there was also a public market. In less than two years, Anderson's Seattle chain included nineteen stores spread around the city from Madison Park to Ballard.

In 1928, Anderson sold his grocery business to Seattle-based United Groceries and returned to Portland. United Groceries (also called United Grocers), formally known as United Groceries & Markets with a food distribution business named United Foods, was formed in 1927 under the direction of Clifford M. Schumacher and had offices in the lower Queen Anne neighborhood. At the time of United Grocers' 1928 merger with Anderson Groceries, the business represented five stores. Through several mergers and acquisitions, United soon owned eighteen stores in greater Seattle, along with ten in nearby cities, and eventually expanded statewide for a total of forty-two stores. United soon became part of the Mutual Markets chain mentioned earlier in relation to the 1932 merger between Mutual Markets and Eba Groceries. This grocery group was consolidated into Tradewell Stores, founded in 1939 by Monte L. Bean, a Seattle-based company operating stores along the West Coast. When the chain folded in the 1980s, it became part of Safeway Stores, the grocery chain based in southern California. Safeway had established its Seattle presence in 1932 by taking over Seattle's Piggly Wiggly stores.

SEATTLE'S SELF-SERVICE GROCERY SHOPPING PIONEERS

As mentioned earlier, the early twentieth century witnessed a significant change in how people shopped for groceries—from having orders filled and delivered to self-service. While Piggly Wiggly, the grocery chain founded in Tennessee in 1916, is credited with initiating the self-service grocery model, Groceteria Stores was first in Seattle to promote the discount, self-service food-shopping model. Two brothers, Alvin and Walter Monson, sons of a Swedish immigrant and grocery merchant in Nebraska, moved to Seattle seeking financial opportunities and opened Groceteria in 1915 on the corner of Fifth Avenue and Pine Street. The retail self-serve concept was simple: If you can carry a basket, come and help yourself—and save money because there are no telephone bills, no clerks' salaries, and no delivery costs.

After two years, the brothers' Groceteria enterprise numbered thirty stores, reaching a maximum of forty stores in Seattle and in neighboring towns. However, as the cost of leasing space increased, the stores eventually closed and were history by 1928. It was also a time when national discount chains such as Piggly Wiggly and Idaho-based O. P. Skaggs United Stores were establishing themselves in the Seattle market. (Skaggs merged with Safeway Stores in 1926, launching its entry into the Puget Sound region.)

Smaller, family-owned grocery stores also existed to fulfill neighborhood needs, and their owners often made them stand out. In Columbia City, William Phalen arrived from the Midwest and established a grocery store in 1903 on Rainier Avenue, eventually becoming mayor of Columbia City and also establishing the local baseball team. Also in Rainier Valley, in 1901, the Hausler family opened the Hausler Grocery and Meat Market to specialize in meats and dry goods. Its location beside the Rainier Avenue streetcar line made it accessible to customers as well as facilitated grocery deliveries. Running a successful small business enabled the Hausler family to expand and, in 1922, build a sizable two-story brick building to house their grocery business, now called the Atlantic Market & Grocery. The building still stands today on Rainier Avenue, although without a grocery store.

S & M Market, on the top of Queen Anne hill, is another example of a successful family-owned grocery enterprise. The store was founded by Morris Mezistrano, an immigrant from Gallipoli, Turkey, who arrived with his mother and four brothers after World War I fighting killed his father and simultaneously destroyed the family's mercantile business. Familiar with selling fresh fruit from his boyhood days, Mezistrano opened S & M Market in the 1920s on Queen Anne Avenue specializing in produce, which he sold for less than other local grocers. His business survived the Great Depression because he had bought the building that housed the grocery. As Jan Hadley wrote in her article for the Queen Anne Historical Society, Mezistrano (or Morris, as he was usually called) was engaged in community activities and is remembered for providing bags of leftover groceries to Hooverville residents and trading office space for weekly ads in the *Queen Anne News*. His son Jerry maintained the grocery for a few years after his father retired in 1985 but finally closed it in 1989.

A JAPANESE IMMIGRANT ESTABLISHES
A LEGACY GROCERY CHAIN

In a similar way, the Uwajimaya grocery store in Seattle's International District (or "ID") around South Jackson Street is based on personality and community involvement. Today the ID is a bustling neighborhood hub of shops and grocery stores, just as it was in past decades, and as described in chapter 4 in this book. A residential destination for Asian immigrants in earlier eras, as a source of authentic ingredients unique to South Asian cooking, the neighborhood is still a destination for present-day shoppers. Viet-Wah, established in 1981, is an emporium for all things edible and Asian. With a second store in Renton, Washington, the company also manages a distribution center. The owners of Lam's Seafood Market in Little Saigon, an enclave on the edge of the ID, are from Vietnam, which seasons the international offerings of their grocery store. There are aquariums of fish and shellfish, from tilapia to lobsters and clams. Anyone seeking tamarind paste, fresh rice noodles, jackfruit, or durian, or simply craving lunch with a different flavor, should know that this grocery store is a treasure chest (and an affordable one at that).

Without question the most famous Asian grocery store in the International District is Uwajimaya. It could even be considered the first brick-and-mortar store inspired by a food truck. In 1928, a young Japanese immigrant named Fujimatsu Moriguchi started a business selling homemade fish cakes and various authentic dishes from his truck to other Japanese immigrants working in lumber and fishing camps in the area around Tacoma, Washington. That was until 1942, when Moriguchi and his family were interned in a California camp. After the family's release at the end of the war, he and his wife Sadako bought a small building on South Main Street in Seattle's prewar Japantown. The building housed a small retail store named Uwajimaya and a commercial fish-cake production company. The grocery store's name was based on the town of "Uwajima," where he first learned the grocery trade, and the word "ya," which, translated from Japanese, means "store." The shop served the Japanese American community with an inventory of local and imported Japanese gift items and food, from fish ready for sushi rolls to mushrooms by every name, plus an extensive line of live shellfish, including sea urchins, clams, and lobsters. In 1962, the Moriguchis were also proprietors of a successful gift shop at the Seattle World's Fair.

Following Fujimatsu Moriguchi's death in 1962, his four sons took over management of Uwajimaya. Tomio Moriguchi, who had been a mechanical engineer with Boeing Company, moved into the CEO position, where he served for forty years. The current CEO is Tomoko Moriguchi-Matsuno. Between 1970 and 2017, Uwajimaya expanded geographically in the Seattle area and in Oregon, opening five additional stores. The most recent store opening in the chain was Kai Market, which opened in 2017 in the Hall, a new retail space in the South Lake Union neighborhood.

The company's largest footprint remains in Seattle, where, in 2000, Uwajimaya opened as the cornerstone in a huge new retail and apartment complex in the International District named Uwajimaya Village. This space also features Kinokuniya Bookstore (Japan's largest bookstore chain), a bank, a hair salon and cosmetic shop, an optical shop, and a large Asian food court with twelve shops offering everything from sushi to tempura and more. A highlight of the flagship Uwajimaya is its huge tanks brimming with live fish and shellfish. From seafood to hard candies, numerous varieties of soy sauce, and exotic Asian vegetables, what started small is now a huge influence and a resource for multiple generations and ethnic groups seeking foods from all parts of Asia. As these cuisines become mainstream in today's Seattle, Uwajimaya is the premier destination.

These are highlights of significant beginnings, mergers, and consolidations among Seattle's grocers in the first decades of the twentieth century. More changes were brewing in how and where Seattle's residents shopped for food, both during and after World War II.

A NEW SEASON OF SUPERMARKETS
AND PRODUCE PURVEYORS

When World War II started, thousands of newcomers arrived in Seattle from other parts of the United States to take jobs in federal shipbuilding enterprises and

Boeing's aircraft manufacturing factories. Pike Place Market provided a dynamic link between nearby farmland and farmers, but with the surge of industry beginning in the 1940s, the area surrounding Seattle changed.

At the beginning of this decade and following the world war, land value soared in the verdant valleys south of the city, the result of zoning changes and the trend away from small farms to consolidated operations. Farms once supplying food grown locally were no longer essential because produce could now be trucked in relatively quickly from California's massive industrial farms. Many farmers left their farms to find better-paying jobs in war-related manufacturing industries. As a result, farmland in the Kent and Duwamish Valleys was rapidly converted to manufacturing and warehouse facilities, and agricultural communities in areas surrounding Seattle faded. Jeffrey Craig Sanders reports in his book, *Seattle & the Roots of Urban Sustainability*, that "King County farms began to vanish, falling from 6,495 farms in 1944 to only 1,825 farms by 1964." This shift from local farms providing food to nearby cities followed the national pattern. Driving the change, Seattle's population soared during this period (many tag 1945–1970 as the Boeing era), from 368,302 in 1940 to 557,087 in 1960, according to US Census data.

With the source of food products changing, shopping for food also changed dramatically by the time World War II ended. As the economy gathered momentum in the 1950s, consumers' shopping behaviors changed with the influx of refrigerators with freezers, frozen meals ready to heat and serve, cars, and suburban neighborhoods where supermarkets were the norm. No longer was a daily trip to the grocery store required. Seattle followed this national trend, its neighborhoods expanding north, east, and south with more supermarkets, and with State Route 99 and Interstate 5 streamlining north–south access.

If Seattle was a hotbed of activity for grocery chain entrepreneurs with numerous acquisitions, mergers, and consolidations before World War II, this pursuit continued from the 1950s into the 1970s, only with different players. The large, national retailer Safeway Stores maintained its presence, and Boise, Idaho–based Albertsons arrived, but new local grocery chains also opened. What makes Seattle's grocery scene different and unusual from the rest of the country is that several independent retailers still exist and thrive here. That's even with the recent invasions by Whole Foods Markets and Trader Joe's. Add the country's largest natural, organic foods retailer—Puget Consumers Co-op—and dinnertime choices are available to please every appetite.

Early on, Quality Food Centers was one of the first new local groceries established after World War II. Although part of Kroger Corporation since 1999, the original chain came about through a merger in 1960 between Jack Croco's grocery store in Bellevue and Vern Fortin, who is credited with opening the first Quality Food Center store in 1955 on Roosevelt Way Northeast. Croco had arrived in the Seattle area as northwest district manager for Albertsons Supermarkets, but in 1955 he opened Lake Hills Thriftway, his own independent grocery store, in Bellevue. In 1963, the new grocery group was renamed Quality Food Centers, or QFC, and expanded rapidly to thirty Puget Sound–area stores through acquisitions of small, independent retailers and by taking over A&P Supermarket stores in 1974 when the East Coast–based company left Seattle. In 1986, QFC was sold to a Seattle investment group, which took the company public. In 1997, QFC bought the grocery company managing Thriftway and Stock Market stores; later that same year, QFC was sold to Fred Meyer. In May 1999, Kroger acquired Fred Meyer, which added a big-picture spin to local grocery shopping.

Although based on a different structure—a warehouse club store for members, established initially in San Diego—Costco Wholesale's presence on Seattle's food scene is notable. The concept of club stores was entirely new in the 1970s. The mega-retailing company was founded in 1976 in San Diego under the name Price Club. Costco and Price Club merged in 1993, operating side-by-side with 206 locations. In 1997, Price Club and Costco split apart, and Costco returned to a single-word name. The company's first warehouse location opened in Seattle in 1983. Today, there are two Costco stores within Seattle city limits, with eight additional locations in the greater Seattle area, and the company's corporate headquarters is in Issaquah just east of Seattle.

National supermarket chains and club warehouses may be the grocery shopping norm for most Americans, but Seattle has always been a bit different. Call it progressive or "forward-thinking," but the following shopping options invented here have proven to be very successful.

INNOVATION AND ALTERNATIVE THINKING INSPIRE A COOPERATIVE GROCERY CHAIN

With Seattle's progressive mindset, it's not surprising that an alternative retail option would take hold here. That happened in 1953, when John Affolter founded a food-buying club with fifteen families as a cost-savings option. For a time, when its founder moved to Renton, Washington, the co-op was named the May Valley Food Club, but in 1961 the group officially became the Puget Consumers Co-op (PCC). Member purchases were made collectively through Affolter, who also set up a network of pick-up and delivery points around the city. A board of trustees managed the cooperative following prescribed bylaws, and members paid monthly dues.

Fast-forward to 1967, when PCC opened its first retail store in the Madrona neighborhood and membership totaled 340 households. A discussion opened in the early 1970s among members about whether the co-op should focus on natural foods or cost savings. Growth was not appealing to everyone, and some members withdrew to form the Capitol Hill Co-op (later becoming the Central Co-op). PCC's employees also took over more tasks, using the democratic management system to centralize store functions; by 1972, employees were fully running day-to-day retail operations. To further professionalize store functions, a general manager was hired in 1982, and a contract was negotiated in 1983 with the retail clerks union.

From its first location, which quickly proved to be too small, PCC moved to a larger store in the Ravenna neighborhood and purchased Co-op East in Kirkland, Washington, as its second location. By 1978, PCC membership included 11,200 families, and the cooperative's focus was on natural, organic foods. Demand from consumers prompted more expansion, and the PCC Greenlake neighborhood store opened in 1980. To enhance appeal, stores added deli counters, cooking classes, dry goods, an extensive wine section, a meat service counter, and monthly member discounts on designated days, along with a nutrition and education program. The co-op also established its own natural foods wholesaler to facilitate large-scale orders. In 1998, PCC's board of trustees renamed the company PCC Natural Markets. Paying attention to big-picture food issues, the nonprofit PCC Farmland Trust was founded in 1999 to help secure and preserve farmland in Washington State.

These measured beginnings set the stage for the community-based cooperative's growth in both members and retail locations. By 2015, PCC listed eleven stores on its roster, easily making it the largest consumer-owned natural foods retail cooperative in the United States, with more than fifty-six thousand members. Recognizing the need to differentiate itself in Seattle's competitive grocery market, where almost every store now carries organic produce and products, in 2017 the cooperative changed its name to PCC Community Markets to underscore its local, member-owned difference. In 2018, the cooperative will have an even dozen stores, opening its newest location in Burien, just south of Seattle, and another is scheduled to open in 2019 in Seattle's Madison Valley neighborhood. In a move to keep up with today's online shopping environment, the company has partnered with Amazon and Instacart for delivery services.

HOME-GROWN INDEPENDENT SUPERMARKETS THRIVE

If innovation is a key to success in the retail grocery world, Seattle's independent, locally owned markets are prime examples. Both Town & Country Markets and Metropolitan Markets have legacies that make them distinctly Seattle and attractive to hungry customers.

Town & Country Markets, a chain of six stores in the Puget Sound area, has one store, Town & Country Ballard Market, serving the Ballard neighborhood twenty-four hours a day. The chain started in 1957 on Bainbridge Island when two immigrant families joined forces: Jitsuzo Nakata from Japan, and Tom Loverich from Austria. Both families were involved in grocery businesses before World War II. After the war, three brothers from both families linked up to open the Bainbridge Island Town & Country Market.

Today, the business operates three stores under the Town & Country name, and three as Central Markets. On the mainland, the group opened the Ballard Market in 1985, and two Central Markets north of Seattle—one in Shoreline in 1990, and the other in Mill Creek in 2004. All are noted for offering an abundance of fresh produce, both conventionally grown and organic. Full-service meat and fish counters also distinguish the stores, as do their extensive bulk ingredient areas, ethnic food offerings, and large deli and take-out sections. The staff is always helpful, guaranteeing that no one leaves without finding what they came for. (If you arrive in the late evening, you may even hear the Ballard crew singing along to the overhead music track.) An innovative renovation of the Ballard Market launched in 2017 added more in-store seating space, a larger deli, and a cooking demo area—all guaranteeing the store's parking lot will continue to be full to the max.

The Metropolitan Market group also offers a prime example of successful innovation at the retail level. From its sparkling fish and meat cases to extensive deli and cheese selections, plus welcoming front door flower boutiques and food samplings, MetMarket, as it's fondly called, is a mecca for hungry Seattle shoppers.

Back in 2003, the company founded by Terry Halverson as Food Markets Northwest, Inc., started out with three stores offering upscale food products in Queen Anne, West Seattle, and Tacoma under the Thriftway name. (At the time, there were twenty-three stores with the Thriftway name, all with different owners and part of a wholesale cooperative run by Associated Grocers.) That year, Halverson, a Seattle native who started working in the grocery business as a teenage bagger, renamed the stores Metropolitan Markets to distinguish them from other Thriftway stores and added three more stores to make it a six-store chain. In 2006, the company acquired and remodeled Larry's Market in the Lower Queen Anne neighborhood when Larry's went bankrupt, turning the huge space into a shopping experience with eat-in or take-out food options as well as extensive retail and dry goods offerings. The new store replaced the small original Thriftway store at the top of Queen Anne hill that was displaced by a six-story residential building and a Trader Joe's.

With its upscale and widespread offerings of food and wine, Metropolitan Markets stands out on Seattle's food scene, but over the years it also earned a distinct advantage because of its collaboration with the late Jon Rowley, a local consultant about all things seafood and fresh peaches. As a result, the stores are known for their top-quality fish selection and the annual August Peach-O-Rama celebration. It's a summer event that MetMarket customers drool over!

Now part of a Seattle-based private equity fund named Endeavor, which specializes in mid-sized businesses, most with a food focus, Metropolitan Markets is stable by all accounts.

SEATTLE'S PIONEERING FOOD IMPRESARIO

Think of Copper River salmon and Metropolitan Market's Peach-O-Rama peaches or Olympia oysters: Seattle's food fans have MetMarket and Jon Rowley to thank for introducing these delights to our kitchens and palates. The collaboration started some twenty years ago when Rowley, a self-described "professional dreamer," but obviously one who enjoyed eating and was immensely curious about flavors, first proposed bringing Alaskan Copper River salmon to the Seattle market.

Rowley, who was born in Astoria, Oregon, and grew up in Valdez, Alaska, is considered the instigator behind introducing many foods now considered integral to Pacific Northwest and Seattle cuisine. He also influenced food professionals across the country. He first followed his food fascinations to France, where he learned all he could about the mystique of oysters. Next, he traveled to Spain, Portugal, and Norway to discover how commercial fisheries operated. Rowley eventually returned to the States, entered Reed College in Portland, Oregon, and then dropped out in a quest to fish Alaskan waters, a ten-year routine giving him winters back in Europe. A chance interaction with Robert Rosellini, son of Seattle's legendary restaurateur Victor Rosellini, discussing the ideal way to preserve raw seafood quality based on Rowley's travel observations, led to a lucrative fish-selling business named R&R Seafood (for Rowley and Rosellini). The quality difference was based on immediately cleaning, bleeding, and icing fish to preserve firmness and flavor. Money difficulties based on overwhelming demand eventually ended the fishing business, but Rowley went on to other projects, including learning all he could about Copper River salmon. He knew it was a richly flavored fish given the length of the river—the longest in Alaska—requiring returning salmon to pack on a delicious amount of fat to survive the journey. (Salmon returning to their home habitats to spawn do not eat during their trip.)

In spring 1983, Rowley air-shipped the first catch of Copper River King salmon processed to his standards and introduced the salmon in person to chefs at Rosellini's Other Place, Triplese (Restaurants Unlimited), Ray's Boathouse, and McCormick's Fish House. The Copper River salmon arrival turned into a media event, but the appearance, flavor, and satisfaction difference of the mighty fish were unmistakable. It was the beginning of the Copper River cult. Metropolitan Market also caught the wave, and its fish counters are now regularly stocked in mid-May with fresh Copper River kings (or frozen in the following months).

Regarding the juicy orange globes known as peaches, Rowley was equally knowledgeable. Aware that the sugar content and sweet taste of peaches builds as they ripen, he used a refractometer gauge to measure "brix," or the index of fruit sugar—the same tool used by winemakers to determine the ideal harvest time for grapes used in winemaking. Traditionally, farmers would ship peaches when still hard to ensure that they'd arrive in the market without dents or dings. Working with Frog Hollow Farms in Brentwood, California, and Pence Orchards in the Yakima Valley, Rowley introduced the brix approach. He also collaborated with Metropolitan Market to promote the concept as a point of distinction for its annual Peach-O-Rama peach promotion, which was launched in the mid-1980s.

Given his passion for oysters, Rowley also reintroduced Olympia oysters in 1983. The native Puget Sound oyster had almost vanished from Seattle's dining tables, except at Canlis Restaurant. After Rowley's introduction at Ray's Boathouse, oysters, in all their local glory, returned as a fixture on many restaurant menus. As a consultant for several years with Taylor Shellfish Farms, which started in Totten Inlet in south Puget Sound and now has three shellfish tasting bars in Seattle, Rowley expanded his role, making oysters available and fashionable again. He also launched the West Coast Oyster Wine Championships, an annual pairing contest to promote ideal wines for enjoying with oysters.

As a measure of his impact and contributions to the local food scene, in 2006 Rowley was awarded *Seattle Weekly*'s inaugural Pellegrini Award, established to recognize individuals who have a significant impact on the city's food culture. The award, named after UW professor Angelo Pellegrini, recognizes the winemaker, gardener, and author writing about food culture who inspired many local cooks. In the same way, any attempt to define Seattle's culinary traditions has to mention Jon Rowley. Despite his passing in late 2017, Rowley will always be a legendary food evangelist.

Jon Rowley's Skillet-Roasted King Salmon Recipe for Home Cooks

In this recipe, Jon Rowley shared his approach to cooking salmon, an approach he recounted in a personal interview, that "came about when attempting to replicate, in a skillet in a home kitchen, the succulent bronzed King or Sockeye fillets slow-roasted Makah-style on a vertical latticework of cedar sticks next to a bed of coals from neutral bleached out driftwood fire." He also commented that, in his humble opinion, the Makah tribe from Neah Bay cooks the best salmon.

Based on the method of cooking salmon by placing it at the side of the fire, the fish cooks by radiant heat. Rowley noted that the slow, even heat produces a bronze pellicle that seals the juices inside. If juices or albumin run out of the fish during cooking, it is cooking too fast. Adding more imagery to his description, he said:

It took me awhile to figure out why the grandmothers who tended the cooking fire kept moving the sticks closer or farther from the fire. By putting my hand next to the cooking salmon fillet, I could count 13 seconds before my hand got too hot. Holding an oven thermometer next to the fillet, I determined the salmon was cooking at 200 degrees Fahrenheit to 220 degrees Fahrenheit.

Skillet-Roasted King Salmon

INGREDIENTS

1½ pounds King salmon steak at least 1⅛-inch thick (or 1½ pounds center cut, skin-on King salmon fillet)

1 tablespoon extra-virgin olive oil
Salt and black pepper, to taste

DIRECTIONS

1. Start by preheating the oven to 200 degrees Fahrenheit. Heat a dry skillet to medium hot on top of the stove.
2. Brush both sides of the steak or fillet with olive oil, and then season the flesh side of the fillet or one side of the steak with salt and pepper.
3. Place the fish in the medium-hot skillet, flesh-side down, and cook for one to two minutes until the surface is bronzed.
4. Turn the fish over, and transfer the skillet to the preheated oven. Roast the fish for ten minutes or so until it is cooked through (the flesh should look opaque and not transparent, but still tender and juicy).

NEW PATHS FROM FARM TO TABLE

Pike Place Market's legacy as a primary source for locally grown produce naturally created expectations about freshness and accessibility for many Seattle residents. Although weekly trips to grocery stores are the norm for modern lifestyles, there is still room for alternatives on both commercial and consumer levels. Innovators in Seattle have seized the opportunity in several areas to offer shopping options ranging from delivery alternatives and neighborhood farmers' markets, to "grow-it-yourself" gardening possibilities through the city's network of community gardens called P-Patches and urban farms. Because Seattle is the home of Amazon, the shopping revolution promoted by online grocery ordering must also be mentioned.

Looking first at the commercial level, yes, there really is a Charlie behind the colorful logo for "Charlie's Produce" embossed on the sides of many big white trailer trucks trundling through town. Founded in 1978 by Ray Bowen, Charlie Billow, and Terry Bagley, Charlie's Produce is employee owned and has remained the largest independent produce company on the West Coast since its early days. The company's warehouse facility in south Seattle receives more than four hundred loads of produce weekly, which are then delivered to local retailers, restaurants, hospitals, wholesalers, marine industry customers, and others. The company's four additional distribution centers receive and deliver goods from Alaska to Los Angeles. Produce ranges from conventionally raised products to organic and specialty produce and new fruits such as dragon fruit and citrus hybrids such as yuzu.

From the grand scale food distribution represented by Charlie's Produce, to the personal, backyard variety harvested from a container garden or raised beds, several ideas over the decades have given Seattle residents innovative options for finding local food. These include the many P-Patch community gardens and organized neighborhood farmers' markets.

In a logical connection, PCC member Darlyn Rundberg Del Boca started Seattle's P-Patch gardens in 1973 with management help from the cooperative. Her mission was to teach children to grow food and contribute produce to the "Neighbors in Need" program, a precedent of today's food banks. The first gardens were located on a truck farm in the Wedgewood neighborhood that the city first leased and then bought from the Picardo family. It was the decade of layoffs related to the "Boeing Bust," meaning hard times for Seattleites, with many residents anxious to cut food costs. The idea of community gardens also linked to the Victory Gardens of World War II.

For the first garden on the Picardo Farm, children from the nearby Wedgewood Elementary School turned into part-time farmers. Any families who helped out were rewarded with small plots to cultivate. The activity created the idea of formally establishing community gardens, an idea the city council approved in 1974. By 1984, there were ten P-Patch gardens around Seattle, and an advisory council formed to ensure the gardens would continue under the supervision of Seattle's Department of Neighborhoods. In a recent count, there were ninety P-Patch community gardens spread across the city.

The convivial spirit and back-to-the-land awareness behind community gardens has also inspired other community gardens. The Seattle Tilth garden, a learning garden in the twelve-acre park at the Good Shepherd Center in the Wallingford neighborhood, is one of the oldest. Complete with solar-powered greenhouses, drought-tolerant plantings, a green roof, and a rain garden, it was started in 1974 as an outgrowth of the Tilth movement in the Pacific Northwest, a spirit still active and reaching the next generation. As evidence, in 2016, community garden activists established a new seven-acre Food Forest site on city property in the Beacon Hill neighborhood, also operating under the Department of Neighborhoods. The goal of this site staffed by volunteers is to teach a land management system based on edible plants, from trees to shrubs and flowers.

As the success of Seattle's community gardens illustrates, fresh and local food still ranks tops among food choices for many city residents. It's a desire Seattle farmers' market groups also perceived and have worked to fulfill.

A VISION LINKING FARMERS AND CUSTOMERS

As farms disappeared from King County in the face of development in the second half of the twentieth century, cravings for local farm-fresh produce rose. Call it the locavore movement or simply an inverse reaction to the widespread prevalence of processed food, but more and more home cooks wanted to know where their food came from. Knowing it was from a local source was a selling point. Finding that local source wasn't impossible. While the number was lower than it was ten years earlier, in 1993, there were still 1,800 farms in King County spread over fifty thousand acres. Many farmers were curious about the farmers' market idea and were eager to test it.

Seattle's original farmers' market group, the Seattle Farmers Market Association (SFMA) made the connection between farmer and customer in 1990 when it launched as a spinoff of the Fremont Sunday Market. Recognized as the first neighborhood farmers' market since the 1950s to involve only Washington farmers, the market became a local focus point with a key goal—as described on its website, sfmamarkets.com—of promoting the "town square" concept, where "local small farmers sell their products in a setting bringing rural and urban entrepreneurs together." Overall, the market is described as "an exciting meeting place for neighbors to meet, commune, and enjoy the great bounty of our state."

The group next started the Ballard Sunday Market in 2000, also a hugely popular, year-round enterprise—Seattle's first year-round farmers' market—with as many as one hundred vendors lining Ballard Avenue between twentieth-century brick buildings. One visit is all it takes to experience the Market's sense of community and vitality. As of 2017, SFMA also managed seasonal farmers' markets in the Wallingford and Madrona neighborhoods.

Aware of customer dissatisfaction with many food shopping choices, Chris Curtis also envisioned an option: smaller neighborhood farmers' markets where local farmers and consumers could engage in direct sales—and conversation—about seasonal produce as well as meats, poultry, fish, dairy, and eggs. It was not an impossible idea, and, ever inventive, she initiated it working from an office in her garage.

To implement her idea, in 1993, Curtis organized the first University District Farmers Market, achieving a positive community response. Participating farmers sold freshly picked everything—from tomatoes and corn on the cob to lettuces, basil, beets, carrots, cabbage, cucumbers, peaches, apples, pears, plums, nectarines, and dozens more seasonal items—plus, shoppers could enjoy prepared dishes such as tacos, tamales, and crêpes to ward off shopping hunger pangs.

A few years later, in 1998, Curtis advised Karen Kinney about starting the Columbia City Farmers Market, and she organized the new West Seattle farmers' market herself in 1999. In 2000, Curtis and Kinney petitioned the city of Seattle to support a new, nonprofit farmers' market alliance, and their petition was accepted. The Neighborhood Farmers Market Alliance (NFMA) was established as a sanctioned 501(c)(3) nonprofit organization.

Between 2002 and 2007, four more markets in the NFMA group were opened in Lake City, Magnolia, Broadway (Capitol Hill), and Phinney Ridge, bringing the total number of weekly markets to seven. While most markets operate seasonally, the University District and West Seattle markets started year-round operations in 2007 and 2008, respectively, followed by Capitol Hill in 2014. Along with farmers selling seasonal produce, entrepreneurs promoting local wines, baked goods, cider, gluten-free baked goods, and other food products have found customer interaction at the markets to be an excellent "testing ground" for their products before they are marketed to mainstream outlets. A genuine pioneer in the landscape of neighborhood farmers' markets, Chris Curtis announced in early 2018 that she would retire from day-to-day NFMA management.

ONLINE GROCERY SHOPPING COMES OF AGE

When comparing past with present, many changes are happening in how consumers approach grocery stores and what they want from food products. Leave it to Seattle-based Amazon.com, the largest internet retailer in the world, to instigate more changes and rethink the standard grocery shopping model. The company may have started by selling books, but someone, somewhere along the line, realized the value of selling something people can't live without—food—and started rethinking how this task is accomplished.

With this mission, in 2008, Amazon started rolling out the AmazonFresh grocery system to Amazon Prime members in limited geographical bites. It was positioned as a system to make shopping for groceries while sitting at a computer a total snap. Products available range from standard everyday dairy and cheese to deli choices, beverages, snack foods, cooking and baking needs, frozen foods, baby foods, beer, breads and bakery items, and so on, covering the standard grocery list.

Add the seduction of free home delivery, with everything delivered direct to your doorstep within a designated time on the same day or the next day, and the new system has naturally proven hugely appealing. Another delivery option is to cruise by one of Amazon's grocery pick-up spots (two in Seattle) and your bags will be rolled out and loaded into your car. Since the launch, cities have been added annually; as of 2017, there were thirteen US cities being served by AmazonFresh.

Amazon.com is also pushing its literal shopping cart into Texas, where it purchased Austin-based Whole Foods Market in 2017. Moving quickly to make changes in the upscale supermarket chain's pricing structure, Amazon decidedly has a finger in the pie, determining how consumers will shop for food in coming decades in Whole Foods stores across the United States.

A CITY OF FOOD ENTREPRENEURS

Any recounting of what travels from the grocery store, bakery, specialty food store, or farmers' market into the kitchen, and then onto the stove or oven, and at last onto the dining table, would be negligent if it did not mention the vibrant entrepreneurial spirit of Seattle's culinary universe. Food connoisseur and writer Ronald Holden, in an effort to describe the various business personalities and their food products, has written entire books on this topic. The list is long and the food products are eclectic and delicious, but here is a short list (apologetically so) of a few of Seattle's most unusual food entrepreneurs.

In the area of food staples, Josh Schroeter and Edmond Sanctis launched Sahale Snacks to fill the gap for wholesome munchies. Both outdoorsmen, the Sahale brand of nut and fruit snack packs was created in 2003 as the better-than-trail-mix snack for hikes, bike rides, and more. Sold through warehouse club stores, convenience stores, and supermarkets, the company was acquired by the J. M. Smucker Company in 2014.

Beekeeper Corkey Luster grew his Ballard Bees business from one beehive in 2011 to more than one hundred today, all stashed in backyards around town. As an urban beekeeping business, it's been hugely successful, with individuals and restaurants clamoring to pay him for their hives and a share of the liquid gold results.

In the category of fermented foods and must-have pantry items, Seattle's entrepreneurs are quick to catch a national trend. Naturally fermented foods are hot, hot, hot. Julie O'Brien and Richard Climenhage launched Firefly Kitchens in 2010 to produce everything pickled. Working with local ingredients, their sauerkraut and kimchi are hard to beat. At Pike Place Market, Britt's pickles has a stand selling practically homemade pickles, sauerkraut (try the curry sauerkraut to be seriously wowed), kimchi, and more. The topic of pickles must include chef Renee Erickson's Boat Street brand of pickled vegetables and fruits used in her Provençal dishes.

On the protein side, Uli Lengenberg's sausages are tops, a status guaranteed given his German Master Butcher certification. Awakened to the power of flavorings and spices while living in Taiwan, Uli is now a master of combining flavoring ingredients. Sausages may be purchased at his shop in Pike Place Market, which he established in 2000, or in local grocery stores. Along the same lines, but with Italian flair, Frank Isernio and Art Oberto manage a big-boys sausage company founded in 1918 by Oberto's parents. A Seattle original and staple, Oberto's in any of its forms, from beef jerky to salami, is "a win."

Another revered destination for Italian artisan cured meats is Salumi, a tiny shop just east of Pioneer Square featuring both a *salumeria* and a restaurant. Founded by Armandino Batali in 1999 as a retirement dream, shop ownership and management was transferred in 2014 to his daughter and son-in-law, Gina Batali and Brian D'Amato. The brand is still producing the same outstanding and authentic meats.

With meat, so goes bread. As a staple in almost every culture, Seattle is fortunate to have Macrina Bakery raise the bar for this everyday food. From hearty artisan loaves and muffins to coffee cakes, pastries, rolls, and more, Leslie Mackie, a transplant from Portland, pursued her vision and, in 1993, opened the first Macrina Bakery & Café in Belltown. The bakery served a full array of bakery products from sweet to savory, plus coffee beverages, and was an instant hit. The fanfare hasn't stopped. In 2001, Macrina expanded to the Queen Anne neighborhood, and in 2008, Mackie opened a third café, moving the bread kitchen, wholesale production, and the main office to a historic brick building in the SoDo district. Today, production facilities are in Kent, just south of Seattle, but bakery choices remain tantalizing year-round at Macrina cafés and in grocery stores.

Chocolate provides a sweet finale to any list of food entrepreneurs, and Seattle has more than its share of chocolate merchants. Fran's Chocolates dates to 1982 when master chocolatier Fran Bigelow founded the company following a trip to Paris, where she became intrigued by the confection. The company's Georgetown manufacturing facility turns out gray-salted and smoked-salted caramels, truffles, and more chocolate enticements that may be purchased in the company's three retail shops in Seattle.

Theo's Chocolate is another stand-out artisanal company focused entirely on chocolate. It was established in 2006 in Seattle's Fremont neighborhood by Jeff Fairhall (a founder of the Essential Baking Company in Seattle) and Joe Whinney, along with Debra Music. Theo's earned attention even then as the first organic fair-trade cocoa producer in the United States. Its product line includes caramels, chocolate bars, butter cups, and crunchy chocolate clusters combining fanciful and trendy flavors such as turmeric and coconut, raspberry and dark chocolate.

Altogether, Seattle's legacy of local foods anchored by Pike Place Market and its many years of community enrichment give the city a rich and colorful food history few other locations can match. It's a legacy still inspiring today's food visionaries and entrepreneurs and a role the Market is guaranteed to continue playing far into the future.

6

Cooking at Home, the Seattle Way

The American housewife—man or woman—is potentially the best of all possible cooks; for even in times of scarcity . . . she has in shameful abundance all the necessary ingredients. She lives in a veritable paradise of flesh, fish, and fowl, of fruits, vegetables, and dairy products; while the great transoceanic airliners bring to her market all the condiments and ingredients not indigenous to the region in which she lives.

—Angelo Pellegrini, *The Unprejudiced Palate:*
Classic Thoughts on Food and the Good Life (1948)

What's for dinner? The age-old question and how home cooks answer it can be a cornerstone for defining a local and regional cooking style. Preparing dishes using indigenous and homegrown ingredients to nourish and please family and friends, passing on cherished personal recipes, and sharing food and drink experiences are time-tested, serendipitous ways local cooking patterns become established. There may not be a defined and agreed-upon "Seattle cuisine," but diverse and delicious Pacific Northwest ingredients are easily and seasonally accessible here, found today at Pike Place Market, a neighborhood farmers' market, in a backyard garden, in supermarkets, or in a secret blackberry patch. Added together, these ingredients and their place on home dining tables go a long way to explain which foods are distinctly "Seattle." The fact that they have been celebrated since humans first inhabited the Pacific Northwest and the Salish Sea region makes Seattle's food story even more striking.

Other factors can also determine what is genuinely local cuisine. Within a historical context, investigating how and what the first pioneers stirred together in their kitchens as the city was established in 1853, and then grew over decades, is enlightening. Restaurants and chefs also play a role in defining what foods are local, showcasing—and sometimes reviving—their value. From this angle, cookbooks from local chefs and restaurateurs can be important in expanding appreciation for local foods. Add twentieth- and twenty-first-century technology innovations for home cooks, and Seattle has a surplus of resources to complement what's stirred on the stove and served at dinner tables.

Investigating the history of home cooking in Seattle must acknowledge that Native American cooking rituals and demonstrations by Salish cooks showing early settlers how to prepare local edibles also influenced regional home cooking practices and helped define local culinary traditions. Outlined in chapter 2, Native American food traditions won't be re-examined here, but their spirit and vibrant legacy underlie any narrative about home cooking in the Pacific Northwest.

Reflecting this range of perspectives and influences, cooking traditions in the Pacific Northwest are rich and sustainable. Highlights describing how these different angles affect home cooking follow.

THE EVOLUTION OF PACIFIC NORTHWEST KITCHENS

During early pioneer days, fire pits, fireplaces, cast-iron stoves, and skillets defined the cooking world for most home cooks. The majority of the Puget Sound region's first settlers in the mid-1850s had journeyed west via the Oregon Trail, which meant transporting a limited quantity of household items in covered wagons. Even if a positive mindset prompted loading a cast-iron stove for the journey west, the odds of it being tossed overboard at some point before reaching the end of the trail were high—simply based on weight. The picture changed somewhat later, when settlers arrived in the 1880s aboard trains from the Midwest and California, and commercially manufactured cooking equipment also arrived via the railroad. But for the first arriving settlers—the Arthur Denny party in 1851, for example—cooking tools and food supplies were rudimentary and often invented on the spot in their new surroundings. Discovering the foodways of the area's Native Americans also helped new arrivals stave off hunger. While the familiar foods of home were most appealing to settlers, home cooks arriving in the area learned to merge their cooking traditions with local ingredients.

In her book *The Way We Ate: Pacific Northwest Cooking, 1843–1900*, Jacqueline B. Williams shares in-depth descriptions about what and how the first settlers cooked and ate based on her research and study of numerous period letters outlining early settlers' food and cooking priorities. Evaluating these resources, Williams notes the challenges of organizing a kitchen in a rustic new home site. Understandably, the priority of early settlers was constructing secure places to live, typically one-story log cabins with one or two rooms. Having a roof over the family was imperative; inclement weather was guaranteed around Puget Sound in fall and winter. Locating the cabin close to a reliable water source—an indisputable kitchen (and survival) essential—was also imperative.

Until cabins were completed, cooking happened over campfires and dirt fire pits. Once a cabin was constructed, it might have an attached lean-to or a separate structure for cooking. More sophisticated log cabins built by more industrious, prosperous, or experienced craftsmen often had an interior fireplace in the main room for warmth and light as well as to serve as the kitchen focal point. Inventive carpenters would complete the kitchen area by constructing benches for seating and tables for eating and food preparation, often adding open wall shelves. The same room would also serve as the bedroom, the dining room, and the storage room for barrels and bags of flour, corn, potatoes, sugar, and cured meats. Families traveled west with nonperishable (as much as possible) food supplies ranging from flour and dried fruit to coffee. Once established in Seattle, the first settlers relied on regular stops by commercial ships to replenish perishable food supplies that weren't yet locally available. Many families also kept a home garden, a cow for milk, maybe a pig, and a flock of chickens to supply both eggs and poultry, which could also be an income resource.

Pioneer housewives in this early era welcomed cooking inside on a fireplace hearth, but preparing daily meals over an open fire meant using sturdy, yet primitive, cooking tools. Cast-iron Dutch ovens, skillets, hand-carved wooden spoons and whisks, a coffee pot, wooden buckets for carrying water used for meal preparation and washing up (dry sinks constructed from sheets of tin arrived in the 1880s), a kettle for boiling water, and a standing metal "reflector oven" directing heat from hot coals to a cooking pot, were standard equipment in most early kitchens.

Early settlers also knew the importance of keeping food cold. Early on, they accomplished this by storing perishables in barrels in cold streams or wells, or stashing boxes and bags in cold cellars. Some families attempted homemade iceboxes using winter or summer ice transported from caves northeast of Seattle, but this method was unreliable. (Manufactured ice was being produced in Washington State by 1889.) By 1913, electric home refrigerators started replacing iceboxes.

Reviewing kitchen history, separate rooms designated as "kitchens" did not come into existence until the 1870s. As Williams describes the evolving kitchen, Seattle's settlers picked up on "modern" design trends popular in the rest of the country, including separate kitchen areas. Pattern book floor plans for houses in this period show the kitchen as its own room at the back of the house, the rear location being ideal for keeping cooking odors from disturbing living spaces. A nearby pantry room expanded kitchen storage for dishes, cookware, and storable food. Most kitchens in this era also had running water.

Many of these changes, Williams says, resulted from the campaign by sisters Catharine Esther Beecher and Harriet Beecher Stowe "advising American women how to maintain a traditional home in a modern context," a campaign complete with detailed instructions. Williams goes on to note that mass production of many household items also started in the 1860s after the Civil War, including "processed canned goods, commercial yeast, baking powder, ground coffee, mechanical cooking implements, and factory-made kitchen furniture." Add the completion of railroads to Seattle in the 1880s, and now retail merchants could order and then sell commercially produced cooking stoves and sinks, along with plumbing equipment. Practical, freestanding kitchen cabinets known as the Baker's Table (1879) and the Hoosier Kitchen Cabinet (1899) also became popular, valued for their expanded "work space" features.

Manufacturing production in the East and railroad connection also converged to bring cook stoves to many pioneer home cooks in the late 1800s, although for some families they arrived earlier due to ship delivery. With the advent of the kitchen as a separate room, cook stoves fit right in. Their advantages over fireplace cooking (including stove-top cooking and baking) were immediately apparent, even with the learning curve required to use them successfully. Aware of regional demand, Oregon Iron Works in Portland started a Pacific Northwest stove manufacturing facility with patented designs in 1871. Wood-fueled, the cast-iron stoves also had reservoirs for hot water and warming ovens. By the 1900s, many cook stoves could be heated using wood, gas, or electricity. The first electric stoves came on the market in 1925 with surface cooking units, a broiler oven, and a warming oven. The "modern kitchen" had arrived and home cooks in the faraway corner of the Pacific Northwest experienced the changes and new conveniences as fast as cooks in the rest of the country.

With Seattle's surrounding farms in verdant valleys south of the city and many on the San Juan Islands, food to prepare in home kitchens from the late 1890s up to the start of World War II was generally accessible and local. There were notable downturns, of course, for World War I, the Great Depression in the 1930s, and World War II rationing. In these periods, home cooks learned to be inventive and relied on home gardens. For the most part, fresh produce, meats, and grains were transported daily to markets ranging from neighborhood grocery and produce stores to Pike Place Market. Many families also had backyard gardens. For more information about how food reached Seattle's markets and then arrived in the kitchens of home cooks, refer to chapter 5.

Signs of progress in a 1940s-era Seattle kitchen: a freestanding sink and a separate electric cooking range. Standard for many years, by the 1990s, built-in appliances, stove tops, and sinks set into continuous counters were the new, updated kitchen style. *Courtesy of MOHAI, [Museum of History & Industry Photograph Collection], [1983.10.16798].*

COMMUNITY COOKBOOKS AND RECIPES

Learning how to cook using evolving kitchen technology requires direction, even for experienced home cooks. Add to this situation the challenges of venturing into new surroundings and cooking unfamiliar ingredients, and the learning curve is set. People usually yearn for familiar foods, not necessarily new foods, even if they arrive in a land of plenty. This was true for the first settlers arriving in the Puget Sound region. The foods eaten by these pioneers are outlined in chapter 3, but suffice it to say here that learning to adjust to new ingredients and new food preparations required basic instructions. Word of mouth was one way of learning new procedures for home maintenance and cooking, but cookbooks provided another credible resource. As women's roles evolved, two cookbooks from the mid-1800s offering lifestyle advice for a national audience were also popular in Seattle. Also, a few immigrants brought cookbooks from their home countries with them.

Beginning during the Civil War, many community service organizations published charity cookbooks to share favorite recipes, serve as organizational fundraisers, promote a cause, clarify how to prepare local foods, and share homemaking advice. This cookbook type is still popular in the twenty-first century.

In the category of cookbooks written for a general audience of American women, one of the most comprehensive early resources was *Miss Beecher's Domestic Receipt Book*. Written by Catharine Esther Beecher in 1846, the cookbook gave detailed directions for every sort of dish. Home cooks could read up on how to prepare fried and boiled meats, gravies, and sauces, numerous vegetables, and even yeast, a required ingredient for bread baking. This last recipe was essential to every home cook in Seattle. Having flour to bake bread was important for most families. By the 1860s, wheat farmers around Puget Sound were growing high-protein wheat, and grist mills had adapted their stone grinding equipment to the steel rollers used to process high-gluten grain. The result made home bread baking a successful endeavor, but learning to make homemade yeast, an indispensable ingredient, was a skill requiring guidance and practice. The instructions in Miss Beecher's cookbook proved invaluable for mastering this task and made a household staple more affordable than bakery loaves.

Mrs. Hale's New Cook Book: A Practical System for Private Families in Town and Country (1857; reproductions are still available today) by Mrs. Sara Josepha Buell also falls in the category of broad subject cookbooks. Well known as a prolific writer in her era, and editor of *Godey's Lady's Book*, a magazine considered the most influential of the nineteenth century, Mrs. Buell's mission was to teach women the connection between good health and a simple diet combined with a frugal approach to housekeeping. It was a quest that reached women in all parts of the country. Along with how to smoke meats, make sweet potato stew, and pickle salmon, the cookbook offers remedies for common ailments and cleaning household items.

Along with these popular cookbooks written for a national audience, a search of Seattle's early cookbook archives identified a few with distinct local connections. One is related to a women-organized church group, while another is in the Nordic Museum's collection. In the immigrant category, a simple hardcover *kokbok* came with Agnes Hakala Englund, who arrived in Seattle in 1911 from Finland by way of Canada. The book's traditional Finnish recipes, written in Swedish, the country's primary language at the time, include everyday dishes such as berry soup to more elaborate concoctions like pork roast for special occasions.

In the category of community cookbooks, which served as fundraisers for local organizations by selling advertisements, as well as camaraderie boosters for members producing the cookbooks, *Clever Cooking* is a Seattle original. Originally published in 1896 by the Women's Guild of St. Mark's Church, it is accessible today, amazingly, in a digitized, archived version. Covering an extensive list of recipe topics, including "A Cold Lunch for a Hot Day," the cookbook's table of contents reflects its era with chapters about "Household Economy" and "How to Keep House with One Servant." Certain directions were not specific in early cookbooks; authors assumed home cooks knew how much dry wood was required to raise a cook stove's heat to medium hot, or how much sugar a teacup held.

Moving further into the twentieth century, community cookbooks often reflected societal trends as well as kitchen changes. One significant cookbook of this genre is the *Washington Women's Cook Book*. Published in 1908, the cookbook was created as a fundraiser promoting women's right to vote with recipes collected from suffragists throughout the state. It followed the advocacy idea behind the *Women's Suffrage Cook Book*, a first of this genre published in Boston in 1886. The Washington suffrage cookbook was sold statewide and in Seattle at the Alaska-Yukon-Pacific Exposition. Its message was subtle—or maybe not so subtle—to reassure men that women would not neglect their domestic responsibilities if and when they gained the right to vote.

Recipes in the *Washington Women's Cook Book* even included several for mountaineering—"How to Build a Campfire," "Cooking in Camp"—described by Paula Becker in her *HistoryLink* essay as the result of a collaboration with the Mountaineers Club, which was founded in Seattle in 1906. The Junior Equal Suffrage League Recipes contributed recipes for sweets and desserts, including chocolate caramels and homemade marshmallows. Vegetarian recipes, plus a section titled "Household Economy and Helpful Hints," along with a review of the Pure Food Movement and national food safety regulations, were also featured. As history documents, the November 1910 Washington State ballot included a referendum for an equal suffrage amendment, which was passed.

Another theme of early twentieth-century cookbooks was promoting standardizations for oven temperatures and ingredient measurements. This was the mission Fannie Farmer initiated with her *Boston Cooking School Cookbook* (1896), a cookbook noted as the first to use cups and teaspoons as uniform measurement devices. While not a community cookbook sponsored by a civic group, the *Seattle Brides Cook Book* (1912) also reflects its era (and is now available in digital form). Along with recipes ranging from canned fruits and pickles to éclairs, the cookbook offers practical tips for dealing with basic household chores and challenges, as well as multiple ads and a complete directory of home-related businesses. Every new bride would appreciate reading assurances and remedies for ivy poisoning and sore throats. The book was reprinted often in the same format and with new advertisers.

As Seattle grew after World War II, additional opportunities and themes presented themselves for cookbooks. A favorite from this period is the *Seafair Cook Book*. It was published in 1951, a year after Seattle's Seafair Festival launched, with five hundred recipes collected by the women's committee of the St. Andrew's By-the-Lake Episcopal Church in the Greenlake neighborhood. Containing convenient dinnertime dishes of the mid-century period (think tuna-noodle casserole), a copy of the cookbook is worth tracking down because it includes many historical recipes. As Paula Becker notes in her blog post, "Seafair Cook Book," from March 20, 2015, the recipes were contributed by members of the Daughters of the Pioneers of Washington, an organization founded in 1911 to honor Washington State's first women settlers. A typical recipe from this historic era, Feather Cake, is included here, along with a note at the end about its family heritage.

Feather Cake

This recipe, from the blog of Paula Becker, Seattle historian and author, is included with her permission. The ingredient list has been slightly rearranged to follow the sequence in the recipe directions.

INGREDIENTS

Butter half the size of an egg
1 cup sugar
1 teaspoon vanilla
1 egg

1 cup sifted flour
Pinch of salt
1 teaspoon baking powder
½ cup hot water or milk

DIRECTIONS

Beat butter, sugar, and vanilla; stir in egg and beat. Add dry ingredients sifted together, and mix. Add hot liquid. Bake in greased and floured pan about 35 minutes at 350° Fahrenheit.

Recipe of Mrs. James Willis Law (Mary Gorloch) (grandmother of Mrs. Hugh E. McTague). Mrs. Law came to Stellacoom in 1854 with her mother and sisters to join her father who was a tailor with the Army at the Fort. Mr. Law came to Stellacoom in 1855 and had a wagon factory at Chamber's Creek. Later he engaged in hop raising at Puyallup and then moved to a farm on the Nooksack.

Mrs. Hugh E. McTague, Daughters of the Pioneers

This tradition of sharing home recipes is still vibrant today. Seattle's enthusiastic, upscale home cooks have shared recipes in three cookbooks published by the Seattle chapter of the Junior League, and in 2002, the Rainier Valley Historical Society published a book of stories and recipes documenting the neighborhood's multiethnic history along with its cooking and eating trends. The first Junior League cookbook, *The Seattle Classic Cookbook*, dates to 1983 and features recipes with local ingredients, plus general family favorites. As local cooks became more aware of regional distinctions in Seattle's seasonal cooking style, the League's cookbooks promoted this concept. *Simply Classic: A New Collection of Recipes to Celebrate the Northwest* (2002) and *Celebrate the Rain: Cooking with the Fresh and Abundant Flavors of the Pacific Northwest* (2004) both featured seasonal recipes as a cooking theme to rejoice about.

A look at other factors influencing Seattle's home cooks takes the story back to the World War II period and another era of change.

SEATTLE'S VICTORY GARDENS

The idea of "make do or do without" may date to the Great Depression of the 1930s, but the saying resurfaced during World War II. Seattle's population soared by 25 percent in the 1940s. The huge influx of people moving to the city from the South and Midwest for wartime jobs in shipyards and plane factories, plus food rationing because of feeding overseas troops and European refugees, quickly constricted food supplies. Add the fact that trucks, trains, and ships were engaged with moving troops and equipment instead of food, and food shortages were common. A federal rationing program with coupon books was established to ensure even food distribution for purchased commodities such as sugar, flour, and butter. Home cooks learned to substitute or do without. Canning fruits and vegetables became a priority, and finding substitutes for meat—how about Spam?—or learning to stretch small amounts was also important. Of course, Seattle's abundance of accessible native foods also proved to be a valuable resource. Digging for clams, fishing, picking berries and foraging for mushrooms were all necessary pursuits in this period.

As one solution to wartime food shortages, the federal government promoted planting "Victory Gardens" or "War Gardens." The idea first originated in 1917 during World War I when starting gardens on unused land was a way to grow more food to send to famished, war-torn Europe. The idea reappeared in 1942, and by 1943, there were more than twenty million Victory Gardens growing in both large and small cities throughout the United States, planted at private residences and on public land. Seattle residents joined the cause, especially in the Rainier Valley, a city neighborhood with a sizable influx of newcomers and families with ethnic heritage. Being self-sufficient for food resources was considered patriotic, eased food shortages, and took pressure off commercial farmers whose produce was primarily sent to feed troops. After World War II ended and Victory Gardens were no longer critical, the idea of P-Patch gardens took hold in Seattle. For details about the P-Patch program, refer to chapter 5.

The following recipe from Seattle's Victory Garden period is shared from *The Rainier Valley Food Stories Cookbook* and features a native ingredient that grows lavishly everywhere in the city: blackberries.

Blackberry Pie

This recipe for blackberry pie, originally from Mrs. Skowronek's *The Victory Binding of the American Woman's Cookbook*, published in 1943, is related here in *The Rainier Valley Food Stories Cookbook* with gusto by her daughter, Theo Nassar. It uses the native blackberries that have delighted Rainier Valley residents for millennia.

> Our favorite dessert: we had the little [native] blackberries on our property—the little tiny ones that are native to the area, and it takes a long time to pick enough. They're more intense, more sour [than the usual blackberry], but more blackberry. They're really not so much water. The big Himalayas that we have now, they're really watery. My mother made the best pies in, really, in the world. You want me to give you the recipe? It's from the Wartime Cookbook that we used, the Victory Cookbook. It's very simple, very easy, and I have got a couple of good tips.

The Crust
Two cups flour, about a half teaspoon salt, four to six tablespoons of very cold water—very, very cold water. Because it makes a flakier [crust]. And then, two-thirds cup of shortening. Mother used half butter, half lard. I use half margarine, half Crisco. How you do it is you fork the flour and the shortening together, get it all pea size, you know so it's all little crumbles. Then, you've got this very cold ice water, and you gradually add it, but barely, barely mix, barely. You don't want to do hardly anything to that dough. Then, when you got the dough, you're gonna barely roll it with your rolling pin. Or you can even almost pat it. Do not over do it—handle it as quickly as possible. Get it into that pie tin.

The Filling
Then, on top of [the crust], you pour the blackberries—about three cups of these little [native blackberries]. I just put like about a half cup of sugar sprinkled over it, and a teaspoon or more of corn starch or flour, to thicken it. And then a little bit of lemon to keep the berries bright and nice. And then you can put a shell over it, another piece of dough, or you can leave it un-topped, as you wish. And then you bake it in a very hot oven, about 400 degrees [Fahrenheit], for about half an hour. And let it cool afterwards, of course. And have it à la mode—with a big ball of vanilla ice cream on top, which we get at the Columbia City ice creamery, which was hand-packed ice cream. Oh, to die for!

If anyone needs persuading to decide whether preparing this simple blackberry pie recipe is worth the effort, Theo Nassar's final comment should be the answer.

Following World War II and through the 1950s and 1960s, home cooks across the country were swept up in changes in how food was produced and prepared.

Commercialization, convenience, and consolidation were leading factors in many areas of food preparation. The dinnertime spotlight sparkled on frozen foods, TV dinners, canned soups, and ready-to-eat meals, all seductive with their convenience quality. Also, the post-war economic boom and the return of military men pushed women away from their wartime jobs and back to the kitchen full time as home-makers. These changes became the norm, but they were not always welcome. One person in Seattle protested loudly and, through his efforts, inspired a revolt and a renaissance in local cooking that still resonates today.

ANGELO PELLEGRINI—THE GODFATHER INSPIRING SEATTLE'S CULINARY RENAISSANCE

A man [or woman] who loves good food has a way of making it gravitate toward his kitchen.

—Angelo Pellegrini, *The Unprejudiced Palate:*
Classic Thoughts on Food and the Good Life (1948)

One voice and personality stands out on Seattle's mid-century food stage: Angelo Pellegrini. Many would agree few individuals have had such a deep and lasting effect on the city's culinary values and dining tables as Dr. Pellegrini, even decades later. Described as unpretentious and passionate, Angelo Pellegrini, a professor of English at the University of Washington, loved good food and cherished its contribution to a well-balanced, rich life. Starting in the late 1940s and into the 1960s, he promoted the idea of "soil to table," even ripping out the lawn at his own house to plant a vegetable garden, at a time when mainstream food news showcased convenience and commercially prepared foods. Instead, Angelo Pellegrini linked homemade dishes prepared with simple, fresh, and seasonal ingredients to nourishment for body and soul. As an example, he was first to share a recipe for pesto sauce with American home cooks. The year was 1946, and the story was in *Sunset Magazine*. He also was an avid wine maker, bottling his own vintages each fall in his basement with grapes sent north by Robert Mondavi, a friend and compatriot in the food world. With these perspectives and food passions, he presented articulate arguments about what he viewed as the perils of contemporary mainstream food culture. Ruth Reichl, the former editor-in-chief of *Gourmet Magazine*, described him as "a slow-food voice in a fast-food nation" in her *Seattle Weekly* article on April 13, 2010. Connecting these diverse angles, it's easy to understand why Angelo Pellegrini is considered the instigator and conscience behind the flourishing local and seasonal food scene happening today on many restaurant and home dining tables.

Angelo Pellegrini's biography offers clues to his fascination with food and its role in creating a good life. He was an Italian immigrant born in a small village near Florence, where his Italian cooking heritage provided a foundation for his culinary values. He arrived in America at age ten, traveling from Ellis Island to the Pacific Northwest with his mother and three sisters to join his father who was working in a lumber camp in McCleary, Washington. The family lived simply and frugally with a vegetable garden and farm animals. Pursuing an academic path, he became a professor of English at the University of Washington specializing in Shakespeare and retiring in 1973. It was his first book in 1948, *The Unprejudiced Palate* (reissued twice), not intended as a cookbook, but rather a thoughtful manifesto describing his philosophy and principles connecting food and the good life, that brought him attention.

Building on *The Unprejudiced Palate*, Pellegrini published ten books in his lifetime (he died in 1991), several relating to his philosophy about the role of food in creating a harmonious life, including *Wine and the Good Life*; *The Food Lover's Garden*; *Lean Years, Happy Years*; and *Vintage Pellegrini: The Collected Wisdom of an American Buongustaio*. For many in the contemporary food world, from M. F. K. Fisher to Alice Waters, Ruth Reichl, and Mario Batali, Pellegrini's thoughts were groundbreaking. Overall, his forthright expression and promotion of eating locally and celebrating basic culinary principles are anchors underlying Seattle's present-day food scene as well as in other areas of the country.

RETAIL, ONLINE, AND CLASSROOM RESOURCES

Along with Dr. Pellegrini's thought-provoking words about cooking and eating fundamentals, Seattle's home cooks have also been fortunate to have easy access to basic ingredients, cooking equipment, and cooking schools. From retail specialty stores selling the latest French cast-iron Dutch oven to a neighborhood fish market noted for freshness and variety, to several cooking schools, opportunities for trying and tasting new dishes are numerous. In the past decade, online retailers have added another option for finding ingredients and food products. Following is an overview of these resources, some now disappeared, but others alive and thriving.

A tour of Seattle's retail resources for home cooks has to start with Sur La Table. This local business, now a national brand with an international owner, was described in chapter 5 as one of Pike Place Market's cornerstone stores. Other independent retail options exist for kitchen tools. Once upon a time there was City Kitchens in downtown Seattle on Fourth Avenue. Started in 1988 by Robert Hammond and subsequently owned by his manager, Kerry Niesen, the store was once considered the largest in dollar value of any stand-alone cookware store in the United States. With two large and long rooms packed floor-to-ceiling with cookware and every sort of cooking utensil, glassware, state-of-the-art knives, and small appliances, the store was nirvana for home cooks in Seattle and beyond. An expert, trained staff was always ready to answer questions and demonstrate products. Unfortunately, past tense must be used, because the store closed in 2013.

For cooks in the University, Laurelhurst, and Ravenna neighborhoods, Mrs. Cook's in the University Village Shopping Center is recognized as an exceptional and abundant resource for cookware, tools, and kitchen accessories. Founded in 1976 by Carol Bromel and her husband to honor his grandmother, Hylie Cook, and her idea that "cooks cook to have fun," the store offers classic tools as well as what's new and hot.

When shopping for seafood, home cooks have an established and respected resource in Mutual Fish Company, located in the Rainier Valley neighborhood. A retail/wholesale outlet founded in 1947 by Dick Yoshimura, the store is acclaimed as one of Seattle's best seafood markets and renowned for quality; it was one of the first anywhere to feature live seafood tanks. Today, owned and operated by second- and third-generation family members, Dick's son Harry and grandson Kevin Yoshimura, the store continues to be a valuable resource for home cooks and many restaurant chefs offering seasonal catches, which can include Copper River salmon, oysters from Tottenham Inlet, or sushi-grade tuna.

When home cooks want inspiration for baked goods, but convenient preparation is preferred, they only need to look for Krusteaz products on the grocery shelf. From scones to muffins, the line is produced by Continental Mills, a family-owned business located just south of Seattle in Kent. The company started in 1932 with an easy-to-make, quick-mix piecrust product inspired by ladies in a Seattle bridge club who had invented a "just add water" pie crust. While the bulk of Continental Mills' products are prepared for food-service industry use, the company also has its own brands, which include Krusteaz, Wild Roots, Kretschmer, Alpine, and Albers. In addition, the company produces licensed products for Ghirardelli, Red Lobster, Snoqualmie Falls Lodge, and Old Country Store.

Along with Krusteaz, Carnation evaporated and condensed milks are pantry staples with Pacific Northwest origins. Easily found by home cooks in every grocery store, the original manufacturer, the Pacific Coast Condensed Milk Company, was founded in 1899 by E. A. Stuart in Kent, Washington. Various companies through the 1950s and into the 1980s, including Nestlé S. A. in 1985, acquired it. With a management buyout in 1986, the Carnation brand became part of Milk Products, a company privately held since 1992. Most Pacific Northwest home cooks would agree that using evaporated milk makes a difference in preparing flavorful New England–style clam chowder.

Two decades ago, home cooks encountered a new shopping landscape for cooking ingredients. The new era began with ChefShop.com and MarxFoods. Co-founded in 1997 by Mauny Kaseburg (who earned acclaim in the 1980s as Seattle's "Radio Gourmet") and Tim Mar, ChefShop.com offers Seattle's home cooks a brick-and-mortar Interbay-neighborhood retail location on Fifteenth Avenue West and an online store for specialty foods shopping. As outlined on the ChefShop.com website, the retailer's mission is "supporting family owned artisan food producers and growers who both preserve old and create new food traditions, and create and preserve flavorful foods." Products available are both prepared and fresh, with hard-to-find ingredients featured as the shop's specialty. What home cook wouldn't be intrigued by olive oil from Marrakesh or chocolate "pearls" with crispy cereal centers from France?

MarxFoods specializes in meat, seafood, poultry, produce, and cheese, but all transactions are online or over the phone, with free shipping on orders. A family business specializing in meats and originating in New Jersey in the 1900s, MarxFoods now operates from locations in Uplands, New Jersey, and Seattle. Its business model is based on a direct-to-consumer distribution model. The company's website describes its business as "a network of farmers, ranchers, artisans, fishermen, and foragers, [meaning] the company can eliminate the middleman with a direct-to-consumer distribution model, which means customers are assured a higher level of value and freshness."

When it's time to learn something new or add to basic skills, heading for a cooking class can be the answer. Seattle's home cooks have multiple choices in this area. Sur La Table's Kirkland store features a large classroom, and the Columbia City, Issaquah, and Redmond stores in the PCC Community Markets group also schedule hands-on classes, a feature of the markets for twenty-five years. Downtown is the Hot Stove Society operated by Tom Douglas Restaurants and managed by chef and instructor Bridget Charters. Offering public classes (private corporate team-building classes may also be scheduled) since 2014, classes may feature guest chefs or focus on "how to" lessons such as how to prepare gnocchi or unravel the charcuterie virtues of bacon and pancetta. Not too far away in Ballard is the Pantry, which owner Brandi Henderson opened in 2011; it also offers hands-on classes on topics ranging from heirloom tomatoes to Southern biscuits and mushrooms of the Pacific Northwest.

Another Seattle original, the Blue Ribbon Cooking School was founded in 1995 in a former residence on the edge of Lake Union. Cooking classes here are structured like dinner parties, with students enjoying a complete dinner featuring Pacific Northwest wine and microbrews while they practice new cooking skills. Classes feature seasonal topics and can range from knife skills to autumn comfort food classics and holiday buffet favorites. The space is also available for special events such as weddings and team-building activities.

All things considered, with the abundance of resources available in so many areas, it's easy to understand why Seattle has so many passionate cooks, both past and present.

COOKBOOKS TO INSPIRE MODERN HOME COOKS

So you want to learn to throw a halibut? Or find out how to properly bake a whole wild salmon, the iconic fish of the Pacific Northwest? Both of these objectives can be met at Pike Place Market. This is the place where Pacific Northwest culinary traditions come alive. For starters, there are daily demonstrations as the crew of Pike Place Fish (the Pike Place Fish Guys) leap into action at their retail seafood stand. You can watch as one worker tosses a huge whole fish across the counter in a seamless movement to a colleague who catches the slippery, silver-finned creature, wraps it securely in paper for its ride home, and then delivers the package to a pleased customer. The flying fish, along with the agility and teamwork of "the guys," attract daily crowds of sightseers.

When it comes to instructions for cooking flying fish, the Pike Place Fish crew has customers covered there, too. The answer is their cookbook: *In the Kitchen with the Pike Place Fish Guys: 100 Recipes and Tips from the World-Famous Crew of Pike Place Fish*, available in hardcover and digital versions. Along with one-hundred-plus mouthwatering recipes, which range from Thai curry mussels to coconut maple salmon and are ideal for everyday meals and party gatherings, the cookbook is a primer for anyone learning the basics of cooking seafood. It shares recommendations about how to choose fish from a local fishmonger and offers preparation advice, lessons about sustainability, and storage tips.

The Pike Place Fish Guys' cookbook is just one current example of how cookbooks support and encourage eating locally and seasonally, Seattle-style, and make the concepts accessible to home cooks. (Overall, surveys show that cookbooks are still an indispensable resource that most home cooks continue to rely on.) It follows the trail of several cookbooks from the 1970s into the 1990s, rediscovering local foods in light of the "eat local, slow food" movement percolating northward from California—along with Seattle's frugal economic turn in the 1970s. Cookbook authors in this period understood there was something remarkable in the bounty of available ingredients outside their front and back doors and felt they needed to be noticed and used.

A significant cookbook taking a first step to promote the Seattle way of cooking and eating is *The Northwest Kitchen: A Seasonal Cookbook*, published in 1978. Author Judie Geise recognizes the potential of seasonal feasts to link people and offers home cooks a month-by-month breakdown of recipes. There is seafood in

March, fresh herbs in May, buffet food in September, and so forth, to capitalize on freshness and promote seasonal cooking. Geise also recognizes the conflicts in the modern food landscape:

> The twentieth century has seen some strange and paradoxical developments in the realm of food, cooking, and eating. Technology, plus high-speed transportation and communications, have made more food accessible more of the time to more people than ever before. At the same time, it has become much harder to procure foods that are not processed into anonymity, that are ripe and flavorful, untainted by chemicals and additives. We have easy access to cookbooks featuring cuisines from Armenia to Zulu, but meanwhile most of us have lost touch with the family traditions—the day-to-day practices, the attitudes towards ingredients and their combinations—that created those cuisines in the first place.

This awareness of the Pacific Northwest's abundant food resources is also the roadmap for Schuyler Ingle and Sharon Kramis's 1988 cookbook, *Northwest Bounty: The Extraordinary Foods and Wonderful Cooking of the Pacific Northwest*. Writing about food and farmers in both Oregon and Washington, Ingle's essays celebrate the region's harvests and the personalities driving local food businesses, while Kramer shares personal recipes, plus others from area chefs using local seafood and shellfish, berries, tree fruit, baked goods, and, of course, wines and spirits.

In the next decade, Braiden Rex-Johnson's best-selling *Pike Place Market Cookbook*, published in 1992, stands out as a landmark, a catalyst for reviving home cooks' awareness about the relevancy and resources of the Market. As new residents of Seattle, Rex-Johnson and her husband were inspired by living downtown on the Market's edge and explored its offerings almost daily. Her cookbook outlines her yearlong exploration getting to know various vendors, their products, and their personalities. While not all participated, she invited every vendor to submit a recipe for the cookbook, which created an expansive and inventive recipe assortment. The end result, compiled with an enthusiastic insider's food knowledge, makes savoring and cooking from the pages of Rex-Johnson's cookbook pure pleasure and another reason to explore Pike Place Market.

Translating restaurant fare into a cookbook format with recipes designed for home cooks is another proven and popular channel for promoting local foodways. If the chef has "celebrity status," home cooks are even more eager to explore the recipes. Although Seattle's chefs are comparatively low-key, and even collaborate with each other for special projects, several have cookbooks featuring their interpretations of the region's distinctive dishes. A classic in this category is Chef Kathy Casey's *Pacific Northwest: The Beautiful Cookbook*. First published in 1993 as a companion to the PBS television regional cooking series, the cookbook covers

Washington State, along with Oregon, Idaho, and British Columbia, and outlines culinary influences from European and Asian immigrants, plus Native Americans. It features a generous helping of two hundred recipes, all using indigenous ingredients spanning seafood, meat, poultry, and game, while full-color photographs convey the region's geography and residents.

Seattle's star chefs are noted in chapter 7. In the cookbook category, the chefs first noted for their Pacific Northwest affinity are Tom Douglas, Jerry Traunfeld, Greg Atkinson, and John Sundstrom. All have produced cookbooks—more than one, in some cases—with a Pacific Northwest focus and recipes adapted to express their own personal cooking style. For example, the signature recipes in Chef Tom Douglas's first cookbook, *Tom Douglas' Seattle Kitchen*, a James Beard Award winner, combine local ingredients with Asian influences to create inventive dishes. Curious cooks will find Chef Douglas's recipes for classics such as Dungeness crab cakes and roast duck with huckleberry sauce, along with lobster potstickers and saké-cured hot smoked salmon with inventive ingredient twists.

Also inventive, Chef Jerry Traunfeld's tenure in the kitchen at the Herbfarm Restaurant inspired the content of his cookbook, *The Herbfarm Cookbook*. Between its covers are two hundred herb-inspired recipes producing the sophisticated, inventive dishes that distinguished the restaurant in its early days.

For Chef Greg Atkinson, who starred as executive chef at Canlis Restaurant for seven years and now heads his own kitchen at Restaurant Marché on Bainbridge Island, Pacific Northwest cuisine was an early fascination. His first cookbook, *Northwest Essentials Cookbook: Cooking with Ingredients That Define a Regional Cuisine*, promotes the concept of starting with the best ingredients, which he defines as "the ones grown nearby, harvested at their peak, and eaten within a reasonable distance of their source." This statement is a prelude to the recipes in the book, which are arranged by ingredient type, from apples and pears to hazelnuts, with oysters, berries, and "other fish in the sea" in between. Accessible deliciousness is guaranteed.

Adding his personal cooking style to Pacific Northwest ingredients, Chef John Sundstrom acknowledges three seasons in his photograph-infused cookbook *Lark: Cooking against the Grain*. Arranged within three seasons—Mist, Evergreen, and Bounty—his recipes celebrate available ingredients in a format he describes as "a picture of life in the Pacific Northwest and the rhythm of the seasons." From mussels and razor clams to rabbit and mustard-roasted chicken, home cooks will be intrigued.

While not regional in its content, the six-volume set pubished in 2011, *Modernist Cuisine: The Art and Science of Cooking*, coauthored by Nathan Myhrvold, Chris Young, and Maxime Biletand, added a singular experience to Seattle's culinary world—and for cooks beyond. Produced by an interdisciplinary group founded by Dr. Nathan Myhrvold, former chief technology officer at Microsoft, a team of scientists, chefs, and writers broke ground by offering a fascinating scientific look at what happens physically and chemically to ingredients in the cooking process. In the Modernist Cuisine research kitchen, dubbed the Food Lab, the team enlisted laser cutters, evaporators, a freeze dryer, an autoclave, a pizza oven, and other equipment to determine how the cooking process transforms various ingredients from raw to cooked, and then captures the process through exquisite step-by-step photographs. Other books (and e-books) followed, including *Modernist Cuisine at Home* in 2012 and *Modernist Bread: The Art and Science* in 2017, each work serving as a testament to Myhrvold and his team's intellectual curiosity and financial ability to instigate the project.

One outcome of the *Modernist Cuisine* collaboration was another called Chef Steps.com. Alumni of the innovative *Modernist Cuisine* group working on this project—Chris Young, Ryan Matthew Smith, and Chef Grant Lee Crilly—founded their own workshop kitchen in 2012, called Delve Kitchen in Pike Place Market. The trio and their team built a website for home cooks, ChefSteps.com, explaining the techniques and science of cooking to everyone, regardless of their cooking experience. Recipes and techniques explained on the site are accessible, with high-quality instructions intentionally educational.

From screens as a resource for home cooks to the printed page, any conversation about cookbooks has to mention the Book Larder, Seattle's community cookbook store. Located in the Fremont-Wallingford neighborhood, the shop boasts floor-to-ceiling bookshelves brimming with collectible, imported, and brand-new cookbooks. Lara Hamilton opened the shop in 2011, connecting her passions for books and food. Along with tables of cookbooks, there is a demonstration kitchen adaptable for regular cooking classes and author talks.

With this background on predictable resources for home cooks in Seattle, the home of so much e-commerce, one has to wonder: How has the internet age expanded the horizons and cooking adventures of home chefs?

HOME COOKING, FROM SCREEN TO SOUP POT

Invention and innovation are hallmarks of many Seattle companies. Speculating about the reason, perhaps Seattle's location, far from established East Coast business models, makes it easier to ignore business conventions and focus on experimentation. Regardless, in the decades since Microsoft launched in 1975 in Redmond just east of Seattle, the city has proven itself an epicenter for internet businesses and a northern outpost of Silicon Valley, with Google, Facebook, and Apple all in residence. Amazon reigns as the current force behind Seattle's high-tech employment and residency surges. In 2017, the mega online retailer also became a significant player in the retail grocery trade with its acquisition of Whole Foods Market, the Austin, Texas–based supermarket chain renowned for exclusively stocking natural and organic grocery products.

This climate of internet obsession paired with a passion for all things edible has serendipitously inspired numerous food-related websites and apps to launch here since the 1990s. The long list includes UrbanSpoon.com. BigOven.com, Foodista .com, Barn2Door.com, CowTipping.com, SeattleDining.com, KitchenBowl.com, RecipeZaar.com, and, as already mentioned, ChefShop.com. The titan among all of these sites is Allrecipes.com, which celebrated its twentieth anniversary in 2017.

Key mover-and-shaker companies on Seattle's internet-plus-food scene include sites with appeal for home cooks and restaurateurs. Some, such as UrbanSpoon .com were initially desktop-only sites. Adam Doppelt and his fellow Jobster colleagues founded UrbanSpoon in 2006 to offer restaurant information and recommendations. In 2015, the India-based restaurant-search-and-discovery internet service company Zomato bought UrbanSpoon as its entry into the US market. As often happens in the land of mergers and acquisitions, Zomato was unable to jump-start the site to a higher level of engagement and consequently shut it down, also ending its app development. What has continued are Eater.com and SeattleDining .com, sites founded to share peer-to-peer feedback about restaurants. Eater.com is part of a national group with local Seattle writers, while SeattleDining.com started in 1999 as the brainstorm of Connie Adams and Tom Mehren to highlight peer-to-peer restaurant reviews.

Among internet recipe sites with Seattle roots, BigOven.com, Foodista.com, Food.com, and Allrecipes.com stand out. BigOven is a free recipe app launched in 2003 by Steve Murch with a searchable database of 350,000 linked recipes and features enabling followers to create meal plans and grocery lists. The company's offices are in the Fremont neighborhood.

In a similar yet different setup, Foodista.com offers a collection of free recipes contributed by its community of food writers and bloggers. Founded in 2008 by Barnaby Dorfman, Sheri Wetherell, and John Chase, all former Amazon staff members, the free site features recipes and cooking instructions for various techniques from select participating food bloggers. In 2009, Foodista sponsored the first International Food Bloggers Conference (IFBC), and in 2010 it published *The Foodista Best of Food Blogs Cookbook.*

RecipeZaar.com (briefly named Cookpoint.com) was founded in 1999 by two former Microsoft technologists living on Vashon Island, across from Seattle, and purchased in 2007 by Scripps Network Interactive. The site evolved into Food.com with user-generated recipes, photos, and videos. In September 2017, Food.com was relaunched as Genius Kitchen, a multi-platform digital brand featuring migrated content including recipes from home cooks and celebrity chefs, plus videos, photos, articles, and licensed food shows from Food Network and Cooking Channel.

Allrecipes.com is built around a highly engaged community of home cooks. Founded as Cookierecipe.com in July 1997, the site was conceived by University of Washington graduate students who knew about the practice of exchanging recipes on index cards. If handwritten cards worked to share recipes, they thought, why not create a collection of sharable online recipes based on user-generated content? The result: Cookierecipe.com arrived first on the screen through the efforts of Tim Hunt, Dan Shepherd, Mark Madsen, Carl Lipo, Michael Pfeffer, and David Quinn. Following this came Cakerecipe.com, Chickenrecipe.com, and Thanksgivingrecipe.com. By 1998, these early sites were rolled into Allrecipes.com.

Today, the site is the world's largest digital food brand, ranking in the top five hundred sites worldwide and receiving 1.5 billion annual visits with nineteen websites around the world serving home cooks in twelve languages and twenty-four countries. Membership is free, and once signed in, visitors can rate, review, save recipes to personal collections, watch videos, post photos, and try more than sixty thousand recipes in an engaging, supportive online environment. With offices at Westlake Park in downtown Seattle, the company was owned from 2006 to 2011 by *Reader's Digest* and sold in 2012 to become part of the Meredith Corporation based in Des Moines, Iowa. Under this national publisher, Allrecipes launched its name-brand magazine in 2014, featuring themed content exclusively using user-submitted recipes from the site. Aware of new trends, in 2017, Allrecipes teamed with Amazon to launch a new Alexa Skill offering home cooks a convenient, voice-activated option for connecting with the site's recipes.

As a forward-thinking, data-driven organization, Allrecipes follows cooking trends closely and can slice and dice site traffic numbers to determine what's hot and what's not on American dining tables. For example, its business intelligence statisticians analyzed site traffic for Seattle and determined that the following ten recipes are the most uniquely popular among Seattle's home cooks:

1. Authentic Phở
2. Pad Thai
3. Mom's Zucchini Bread
4. All Day Apple Butter
5. Dutch Babies
6. One Dish Rock Fish
7. Blackberry Pie
8. Salmon Chowder
9. Sarah's Applesauce
10. Heavenly Halibut

With Allrecipes available on their smartphone screens, laptops, or desktops, home cooks will always find an answer to "What's for dinner?" and know that they will be successful preparing their selected recipe.

Digital interactions with hungry consumers are certain to continue, and Seattle is guaranteed to remain a tech leader driving future changes and innovations in the food industry. An obvious dominating influence is Amazon's drive to be a leader initiating change in the online retail food sector. Its 2017 purchase of Austin-based Whole Foods Market, plus online shopping innovations involving its fee-based membership for Amazon Prime and Amazon Fresh delivery services, are significant.

In addition, Amazon's agreements in late 2017 with Fexy Media and Allrecipes .com stand out as nimble efforts to integrate online meal planning and food purchases—and be ahead of the curve. These relationships aim to make it extra easy for hungry e-commerce shoppers to push the "Buy" key and—for Fexy Media—add ingredients from sponsored recipes featured on SeriousEats.com and SimplyRecipes.com, two of Fexy Media's top food sites, directly to their Amazon Prime Now cart for speedy home delivery.

As background, Fexy Media was founded in 2014 by the husband-and-wife team of Cliff and Lisa Sharples (formerly president of Allrecipes.com) and their partner Ben Sternberg, and it is based on Mercer Island, just east of Seattle. Its group of digital food and lifestyle brands includes previously mentioned Simply Recipes and Serious Eats; Road Food, the radio food show created by Jane and Michael Stern; Food Lab; Relish; and Daily Parent. The arrangement between Fexy Media and Amazon Prime Now propels both parties into significant leadership roles in the developing online grocery-retail world.

Another example of the inventive minds inhabiting all levels of Seattle's culinary landscape is the AmazonFresh Now (a subsidiary of Amazon.com) liaison with Allrecipes.com. Announced in late 2017, the agreement makes it easy for online shoppers in select metropolitan areas to find mealtime inspiration and plan inventive, convenient meals by clicking on the digital food site's sixty-thousand-plus recipes. They can then go shopping to order the required recipe ingredients for delivery directly to their front door. Both Allrecipes and Fexy Media's associations with Amazon illustrate how the space is narrowing between online content and the point of purchase.

Considering the bounty of culinary creativity and the abundance of local ingredients so readily available in the greater Seattle region, along with the fundamental wisdom behind Angelo Pellegrini's philosophy linking food to a healthful, well-balanced life, home cooks in Seattle are rich in reasons to celebrate preparing everyday dishes as well as special meals.

Selected Seattle and Pacific Northwest Cookbooks

Happily for home cooks ready to explore local culinary favorites, an abundance of cookbooks exists celebrating Seattle and the Pacific Northwest's bountiful indigenous ingredients. For anyone wishing to investigate more deeply, a selected list follows with titles of cookbooks ranging from several classics published in the 1970s and 1980s, when Northwest cuisine first earned attention beyond its geographical boundaries, to those published recently.

Atkinson, Greg. 1999. *Northwest Essentials Cookbook: Cooking with Ingredients That Define a Regional Cuisine*. Seattle: Sasquatch Books.

——. 2011. *At the Kitchen Table: The Craft of Cooking at Home*. Seattle: Sasquatch Books.

Berger, David. 2017. *Razor Clams: Buried Treasure of the Pacific Northwest*. Seattle: University of Washington.

Brewer, Karen G. 2014. *Seafood Lover's Pacific Northwest: Restaurants, Markets, Recipes & Traditions*. Guilford, CT: Globe Pequot.

Brown, Dale. 1970. *American Cooking: The Northwest*. New York: Time-Life Books.

Casey, Kathy, ed. 1993. *Pacific Northwest: The Beautiful Cookbook*. San Francisco: Collins.

Cook, Langdon. 2013. *The Mushroom Hunters*. New York: Ballantine Books.

Crew at Ivar's. 2013. *Ivar's Seafood Cookbook: The O-fish-al Guide to Cooking the Northwest Catch*. Seattle: Ivar's Inc.

Crew of Pike Place Fish, with Leslie Miller and Bryan Jarr. 2013. *In the Kitchen with the Pike Place Fish Guys: 100 Recipes and Tips from the World-Famous Crew of Pike Place Fish*. London: Penguin Group.

Dammeier, Kurt Beecher. 2007. *Pure Flavor: 125 Fresh, All-American Recipes from the Pacific Northwest*. New York: Clarkson Potter.

——. 2016. *Pure Food: A Chef's Handbook for Eating Clean with Healthy, Delicious Recipes*. Dallas: BenBella Books.

Dern, Judith H. 2006. *Sensational Smoke: Simple, Delicious Recipes Celebrating Wood Plank Cooking*. Seattle: Nature's Cuisine.

Douglas, Tom, Duskie Estes, and Denis Kelly. 2000. *Tom Douglas' Seattle Kitchen: A Food Lover's Cookbook and Guide*. New York: HarperCollins.

——. 2003. *Tom's Big Dinners Big Time Home Cooking for Family and Friends*. New York: HarperCollins.

Douglas, Tom, and Shelley Lance. 2011. *I Love Crab Cakes: 50 Recipes for an American Classic*. New York: HarperCollins.

——. 2012. *The Dahlia Bakery Cookbook: Sweetness in Seattle*. New York: William Morrow.

Erickson, Renee. 2014. *A Boat, a Whale & a Walrus: Menus and Stories*. Seattle: Sasquatch Books.

Geise, Judie. 1978. *The Northwest Kitchen: A Seasonal Cookbook*. Seattle: B. Wright & Company.

Gouldthorpe, Ken. 2003. *Ray's Boathouse: Seafood Secrets of the Pacific Northwest*. Seattle: Documentary Media, LLC.

Henderson, Josh. 2012. *The Skillet Cookbook: A Street Food Manifesto*. Seattle: Sasquatch Books.

Hibler, Janie. 1994. *Dungeness Crab and Blackberry Cobblers: The Northwest Heritage Cookbook*. New York: Alfred A. Knopf.

Howell, Makini. 2013. *Plum: Gratifying Vegan Dishes from Seattle's Plum Bistro*. Seattle: Sasquatch Books.

Ingle, Schuyler, and Sharon Kramis. 1988. *Northwest Bounty: The Extraordinary Foods and Wonderful Cooking of the Pacific Northwest*. New York: Simon & Schuster.

Junior League of Seattle. 1983. *The Seattle Classic Cookbook*. Seattle: Junior League of Seattle.

———. 2002. *Simply Classic: A New Collection of Recipes to Celebrate the Northwest*. Edited by Kay Baxter. Seattle: Junior League of Seattle.

———. 2004. *Celebrate the Rain: Cooking with the Fresh and Abundant Flavors of the Pacific Northwest*. Edited by Cynthia Nims. Seattle: Junior League of Seattle.

Klebeck, Mark. 2011. *Top Pot Hand Forged Doughnuts: Secrets and Recipes for the Home Baker*. San Francisco: Chronicle Books.

Lightner, Jill. 2012. *Edible Seattle: The Cookbook*. New York: Sterling Epicure.

Mackie, Leslie, and Andrew Cleary. 2003. *Macrina Bakery & Café Cookbook: Favorite Breads, Pastries, Sweets & Savories*. Seattle: Sasquatch Books.

Mackie, Leslie, and Lisa Gordanier. 2012. *More from Macrina: New Favorites from Seattle's Popular Neighborhood Bakery*. Seattle: Sasquatch Books.

Moon-Neitzel, Molly, and Christina Spittier. 2012. *Molly Moon's Homemade Ice Cream: Sweet Seasonal Recipes for Ice Creams, Sorbets, and Toppings Made with Local Ingredients*. Seattle: Sasquatch Books.

Moscrip, Duke, and Chef "Wild" Bill Ranger. 2016. *As Wild as It Gets: Duke's Secret Sustainable Seafood Recipes*. Lake Placid, NY: Aviva.

Music, Deborah, and Joe Whinney. 2015. *Theo Chocolate: Recipes & Sweet Secrets from Seattle's Favorite Chocolate Maker*. Seattle: Sasquatch Books.

Nims, Cynthia. 2002. *Crab*. Northwest Homegrown Cookbook Series. Portland, OR: Westwinds Press.

———. 2016. *Crab: 50 Recipes with the Fresh Taste of the Sea from the Pacific, Atlantic & Gulf Coasts*. Seattle: Sasquatch Books.

———. 2016. *Oysters: Recipes That Bring Home a Taste of the Sea*. Seattle: Sasquatch Books.

O'Donnel, Kim. 2017. *PNWVeg: 100 Vegetable Recipes Inspired by the Local Bounty of the Pacific Northwest*. Seattle: Sasquatch Books.

Rautureau, Thierry, and Cynthia Nims. 2005. *Rover's: Recipes from Seattle's Chef in the Hat*. Berkeley, CA: Ten Speed Press.

Rex-Johnson, Braiden. 1992. *Pike Place Market Cookbook: Recipes, Anecdotes, and Personalities from Seattle's Renowned Public Market*. Seattle: Sasquatch Books.

——. 2005. *Pike Place Public Market Seafood Cookbook.* Berkeley, CA: Ten Speed Press.

——. 2007. *Pacific Northwest Wining & Dining: The People, Places, Food, and Drink of Washington, Oregon, Idaho, and British Columbia.* Hoboken, NJ: John Wiley & Sons, Inc.

Shea, Jennifer, and Rina Jordan. 2013. *Trophy Cupcakes and Parties!* Seattle: Sasquatch Books.

Stowell, Ethan, and Leslie Miller. 2010. *Ethan Stowell's New Italian Kitchen.* Berkeley, CA: Ten Speed Press.

Sundstrom, John. 2012. *Lark: Cooking against the Grain.* Seattle: Community Supported Cookbooks.

Thomson, Jess. 2012. *Dishing Up Washington: 150 Recipes That Capture Authentic Regional Flavors.* North Adams, MA: Storey.

Traunfeld, Jerry. 2000. *The Herbfarm Cookbook.* New York: Scribner.

Wetzel, Blaine, and Joe Ray. 2015. *Sea and Smoke: Flavors from the Untamed Pacific Northwest.* Philadelphia: Running Press.

7

Dining Out

100+ Years of Seattle's Restaurants

Our greatest regional blessing, food fresh from the seas, is offered by our restaurants in bountiful array: Dungeness crab—the most delicate, delightful crab meat in the world; our great sport fish, the salmon and its delicious kin, the rainbow trout; tiny Olympia oysters . . . clams . . . cod . . . red snapper . . . all served within a day of the "catch." We're a land of ripe juicy berries . . . fresh vegetables . . . eggs and chickens. The great cornucopia is right at the chef's kitchen door, and they're making the most of it. Our restaurant industry—for the most part—is young . . . robust . . . progressive . . . competitive.

—William C. Speidel Jr., *You Can't Eat Mt. Rainier!* (1955)

Compared to other major cities in the United States, Seattle's restaurant history has a relatively short life span. To put things into perspective: San Francisco's Tadich Grill—the oldest restaurant on the West Coast—opened its doors in 1849, two years before the Denny Party even set foot on Washington Territory. Or consider that Delmonico's in New York, which is often identified as the first fine-dining restaurant in the United States, began serving elegant dinners in 1857, thirty-two years before Washington became a state in 1889. Despite this late start, Seattle is now an internationally recognized dining destination. World-class chefs here continue to be inspired by the region's plentiful resources that inspire a sophisticated, evolving cuisine infused with culinary styles and global ingredients introduced by immigrants.

143

Exploring Seattle's history through its restaurants not only tells us what was on their menus but also reveals who was eating in the dining rooms, cooking in the kitchens, and washing dishes. Reflecting local economics, politics, and culture, restaurants mirror Seattle's development as a city and illuminate the evolution of contemporary dining.

In reviewing this history, decades don't neatly define dining trends, and, although political and economic milestones influence what we eat, they tell only part of any story. This chapter, therefore, offers a casually curated chronological look at some of Seattle's most significant, iconic, and influential restaurants, as well as the men and women behind them. The story begins right before the Great Fire of 1889 and follows the evolution of "modern" restaurant dining up to 2017. Descriptions of the restaurants over the decades will also reveal the notable, colorful, creative chefs and restaurant owners who influenced Seattle's culinary landscape and defined the city's interpretation of Pacific Northwest cuisine.

Seattle's earliest public eating spaces would hardly be defined as restaurants by modern standards. That's because the first was a combination barbershop/restaurant opened in 1853 by the city's first African American resident, Manuel Lopes. The second was a mess hall established by Henry Yesler to feed workers at his lumber mill. At the turn of the century, most residents ate at home, while others took their meals in boarding houses and cheap hotels where there were no menus and food was served family-style. Numerous saloons and taverns focused primarily on serving beer and whiskey to quench the thirst of hardworking, hard-drinking lumberjacks, miners, and sailors.

Another restaurant with cultural meaning in this nascent city opened in 1876: Our House restaurant at First Avenue and today's Yesler Way. Owned and operated by black entrepreneur William Gross (sometimes spelled "Grose"), Gross could be counted on to generously welcome and feed newcomers, even those with empty pockets. Although his building burned in 1889, Gross went on to establish other successful businesses in Seattle's first African American neighborhood in the East Madison area.

RISING FROM THE ASHES AFTER SEATTLE'S GREAT FIRE

The Great Seattle Fire of 1889, which burned Seattle's business district, was a defining milestone in the development of the city's restaurants. Because the entire fifty-eight-square-block (116 acres) Pioneer Square area had to be rebuilt all the way to the waterfront, Seattle quickly transformed from a Wild West frontier town into a prosperous city with permanent stone buildings and carefully planned streets. In the year following the fire, the city's population more than doubled, climbing from twenty thousand to almost forty-three thousand inhabitants. This surge created a demand for a variety of dining establishments, from taverns for laborers rebuilding the city to restaurants for affluent merchants and politicians.

Among the new establishments in the rapidly growing city were numerous oyster houses. The abundance of oysters in Puget Sound, typically harvested by local tribes, also inspired the construction of new restaurants. One of the first, the Haines Oyster House, started serving seafood on the waterfront in 1890 and became famous for its cream of oyster stew made with small, succulent Olympia oysters. Successful for decades with residents and eventually tourists, the San Francisco Oyster House served bivalves in Seattle for sixty years, while the American Oyster House operated until 1952.

Maison Riche, which opened in 1893 at Second Avenue and James Street, is considered Seattle's first official high-end restaurant. It served French cuisine, which could be ordered à la carte or from a table d'hôte menu (fixed price and set dishes), and also offered a selection of fine imported wines. The sophisticated fare, however, was not the only reason Maison Riche was significant. An article titled "What Seattle Needs," in the August 18, 1893, edition of the *Seattle Press Times*—as cited by Robert S. Fisher in his essay "Mirror of Taste" in *More Voices, New Stories*—described Maison Riche as

> the only first class place in the city where a gentleman can take his wife, sister, or sweetheart with that feeling that everything connected with the place is beyond suspicion, is thoroughly respectable, and that proper service be given them.

Fisher goes on to say the restaurant later changed its menu to Italian fare and its name to Maison Tortini, and then it became Maison Barbeis, which was famous for both its steaks and its "private rooms." Unfortunately, the private rooms housed prostitutes, which spurred a quick demise of reputation and forced the once reputable restaurant to close in 1906.

Victor Manca, a restaurateur from Salt Lake City, opened his family-run restaurant, Manca, in 1899 in the heart of Pioneer Square on Cherry Street between Second and Third Avenues. Offering an eclectic menu of sophisticated American fare, the family-run restaurant is credited with introducing the Dutch Baby—a fluffy German-style pancake—to American households. According to Victor Manca's great-granddaughter in an online posting, her family believes Dutch Babies became famous when *Sunset Magazine* featured the recipe.

Manca also was famous for its "poached eggs Vienna," a dish of grilled crab legs, razor clam hash, and braised ox joints. It was a popular lunch spot for local bankers and brokerage executives, who ate in dark oak booths or at a massive counter with twelve bar stools. Manca's moved to several different locations, closed for a period, was reopened by family members in Madison Park, and finally closed for good in 1998.

Not surprisingly, given the abundance of fresh seafood available and reflecting the food desires of the era's Japanese immigrants, the first sushi restaurant opened in 1904 in a pristine white three-story building at Sixth Avenue and Main Street, the heart of Seattle's *Nihonmachi*, or Japantown. It lasted, even in a shabbier location, until the mid-1940s.

At the turn of the twentieth century, Seattle's business directory boasted ninety-two restaurants, which paralleled culinary trends across the country. This group included inexpensive lunchrooms catering to growing ranks of white-collar workers, cafeterias, tea rooms, and vegetarian cafés. Concerns about food safety and cleanliness launched restaurant inspections, while cooks and waiters unionized. High-end restaurants in Seattle proliferated, often adding entertainment, such as live orchestras and organ music, to entice affluent diners.

Two of Seattle's most notable restaurant entrepreneurs in this early era were Chauncey Wright (1871–1917) and Charles Blanc (1881–1955). Wright was ten years old when he came to Seattle from Minneapolis in 1881 with his parents. According to Hattie Graham Horrocks, the great-granddaughter of Judge Thomas Mercer, one of Seattle's first settlers, in her unpublished memoir *Restaurants of Seattle: 1853–1960*, Chauncey Wright's father started a restaurant on Front Street (now First Avenue), which at that time was close to the water's edge. Chauncey fished from the back of the building while customers were served in front. After the restaurant was destroyed in 1889 by the Great Seattle Fire, Chauncey, at age nineteen, opened his own restaurant at Second Avenue and Yesler Street. At age twenty-seven, he journeyed north to the Klondike, where he made more "gold" than the prospectors by selling cups of coffee for fifty cents each and inexpensive meals. Back in Seattle, in 1905, he opened a steak house on Washington Street that led to a string of restaurants and bakeries. Following a dispute with a business partner, in 1912, he opened a lavish restaurant on Occidental Avenue, the Chauncey Wright Restaurant, which served up to three thousand people per day.

French-born Charles Joseph Ernest Blanc, who came to Seattle in 1906 from San Francisco, worked as a chef at several high-end hotels until 1916, when he and his wife opened Café Blanc at 315 Marion Street. January 1916 was the same month and year that Prohibition went into effect in Washington State—an auspicious coincidence, perhaps—but, in addition to being a talented chef, Blanc was a savvy businessman known for his pithy slogans. As also recounted by Robert Fisher in *More Voices, New Stories*, Blanc described another of his restaurants, the Chantecler Cafeteria, as offering "An Aristocratic Meal at a Democratic Price," and he attracted a different segment of diners at night by transforming his restaurant into a ballroom with a live orchestra.

After moving Café Blanc to the elegant, historic Stacy Mansion in 1925, he re-named it Maison Blanc, advertising it with the slogan "Where Epicureans Meet," and painted the Victorian mansion in pristine white. The extensive menu focused on international cuisine (Blanc was a founder of the Chefs de Cuisine organization), offering sophisticated dishes such as escargot, schnitzel, and "Chinese Pheasant on Toast." Its interior was decorated in high style with paintings, art objects, and marble statues. Blanc later opened a German beer garden, the Rathskeller, in the basement of the mansion's lower level. Despite its German theme, it served a wide range of international dishes in rooms with names and decor from places both near and far, ranging from England and France to Louisiana and the Alki area of West Seattle.

A menu cover from 1950 for Charles Blanc's legendary Maison Blanc Restaurant. *Courtesy of MOHAI, [Ephemera Collection], [2009.71].*

Another legendary turn-of-the-century restaurant was Rippe's Cafe, opened in 1910 by Frank Rippe at 315 Pike Street, moving later to 1423 Fourth Avenue. With its elegant decor featuring mahogany and brass booths, white tablecloths, heavy silver, and sophisticated menu (including cracked crab and oysters Rockefeller), Rippe's attracted Seattle's elite as well as visiting celebrities such as President Calvin Coolidge and Hollywood actress Jean Harlow.

After Mr. Rippe's death in 1934, the restaurant was sold to John Von Herberg, a theater and motion picture magnate who renamed it Von's Café. Open twenty-four hours and popular in the 1940s with the martini-loving after-theater crowd, the menu offered seven hundred items, all served twenty-four hours a day. Despite its distinguished history, the restaurant closed in early 2013. Its namesake (under different ownership) moved and opened later that year as Von's 1000 Spirits Gusto-bistro on First Avenue, just south of Pike Place Market. The legacy of Rippe's and Von's continues, today with an Italian spin of pizzas, salads, seafood, and more.

HAVE TRAY, WILL EAT—EVERYDAY DINING OPTIONS

While Seattle's luxury restaurants flourished from the late 1890s and into the early twentieth century, other eating options also appeared in this time period, many with appeal for hungry blue- and white-collar workers. Cafeterias, named after the Spanish word for "coffee shop," became popular after their introduction at the 1893 World's Fair in Chicago and the concept spread quickly across the country. Several popped up in downtown Seattle in the early 1900s, offering the city's growing middle class an opportunity to eat out for less money than dining at a restaurant.

In this early era, Seattle's cafeterias ranged from simple to elegant. Wings Cafeteria, founded in 1910 at 1409 First Avenue, was the first cafeteria in town, according to history chronicler Hattie Horricks. A main attraction: large picture windows on the second floor paired a pleasant seating area with views of boating activity on Elliott Bay. Both the Spiers Cafeteria, established in 1910 in the Norton Building at Second Avenue and Columbia Street, and the Good Eats Cafeteria, located at Second and Seneca Streets, featured fancy decor and white linen tablecloths.

Tea rooms and department store restaurants were other popular dining destinations in many US cities during the first half of the twentieth century, including Seattle, where tea room culture is steeped with history. In addition to tea, despite the name, these restaurants actually served lunch, and many evolved into special destinations to enjoy Sunday dinner. Tea rooms were primarily owned or managed by women. One of these was Eva Dove, the owner of the Red Candle gift shop on Pine Street. Dove earned her degree from the University of Washington in home economics, with a specialty in tea room and institutional management. As Robert Fisher wrote in a 1935 article for the *Seattle Post-Intelligencer*, Dove reportedly said, "Tea room management is a happy career for a woman to undertake." More specifically, "She earns a living. She earns a living in a pleasant way, works in pleasant surroundings, and meets nice people."

However, not all tea rooms were women-managed or male-focused. The Dolly-Madison, owned by Arthur Gabler, offered Southern-style dishes served in an elegant dining room filled with chandeliers and antiques. The attractions of Gabler's tea room included the artistic designs of his vegetable plates and the baked ham with corn pone. Although Seattle's tea rooms typically catered to women, men were not excluded, and several tea rooms even had separate "men's grills."

While the majority of tea rooms were independently operated, the major department stores held the most elaborate rooms, including the elegant Rhodes Department Store, a spin-off of a Tacoma coffee shop founded in 1852. Opened in 1907, ladies who lunched in the Rhodes Mezzanine Tea Room listened to live organ music performed by staff organists. But despite the luxury of Rhodes, the tea room and restaurants of the legendary Frederick & Nelson department store surpassed almost every lunchroom in the city, including the lunch counter and dining and tea rooms of Seattle's other locally owned department store, the Bon Marché, a grand, eight-story building, which in 1928 filled the entire block at Third Avenue and Pine Street (its third location).

Founded in 1891 by partners Nels Nelson and Donald J. Frederick as a new- and used-furniture store on Second Avenue in Seattle's downtown hub, Frederick & Nelson added a tea room to the dry goods department in 1906. Tea was just the beginning. In 1918, Frederick & Nelson moved to larger, more lavish quarters at Fifth Avenue and Pine Street, where the massive store established a small restaurant empire with five dining options. As described on the back of a Frederick & Nelson menu from this early period, the department store's restaurants included the Tea Room and Continental Buffet, which specialized in "fine food and excellent service presented in a luxurious atmosphere." The tea room was touted as the place where "Seattle's fashionable women meet daily to enjoy creamed chicken on toast and assorted salad plates." In a nod to culinary history, William C. Speidel Jr. included a mouth-watering description of a favorite Frederick & Nelson salad in his charming directory of the city's restaurants, *You Can't Eat Mount Rainier!*

Frederick & Nelson's Crab Ravessant

A salad distinguished for its piquant combination of flavors.

On each individual plate (use a generous dinner size), place a base of lettuce. On this, alternate grapefruit segments, slices of avocado, and extra-large legs of our superlative native Dungeness crab, placing them in a beautiful fan shape. With this, Frederick's serves their Chiffonade Dressing, a blending of mayonnaise, chili sauce, tomato catsup, pickle relish, and chopped olives that is similar to a Thousand Island dressing.

The hungry lineup for Frederick & Nelson's in-store Continental buffet in 1939. *Courtesy of MOHAI, [Seattle Post-Intelligencer Collection], [P121069].*

Other Frederick & Nelson restaurants kept the male gender happy and families well fed. Men were invited to dine in the clubby, oak-paneled Men's Grill. Closed to women during the week, the grill offered a special menu "prepared for a man's taste," which included prime rib and broiled crabmeat among its selections. The casual Paul Bunyan Kitchen, located on the store's Budget Floor, focused on families with meal options such as sandwiches, salads, and famous beef and chicken pies also available to take home. Speidel also mentions that Frederick & Nelson fed an average of 2,300 people each day and ordered fresh vegetables, fruit, and eggs from the same local farms and gardens for forty years.

Although the famed department store closed in 1992, its food legacy continues today in the form of Frango Mints. According to US trademark documents, the name Frango was first used in 1918 for a frozen dessert served in the tea room. Ray Alden, who ran Frederick's in-store candy kitchen, is credited with developing the Frango chocolate mint truffle. In his 1993 book *The Legend of Frango Chocolate*, retail historian Robert Spector suggests the name Frango may derive from linking "Fran" from Frederick & Nelson and "go" from the period's tango dance craze. The chocolates were prepared on the tenth floor of the company's flagship Pine Street store (today the headquarters of Nordstrom) and sold in distinctive hexagon-shaped boxes.

As a footnote to this Seattle chocolate story, in 1929, Chicago-based department chain store Marshall Field and Company, another venerable American department store chain, acquired the Frango candy line and trademark when it purchased the Frederick & Nelson Company that same year. A Northwest versus Midwest tug-of-war ensued over the candy's packaging style and recipe, including recipe modifications made by Marshall Field's candy makers. Despite this, Frango mints (plus additional flavors) remained popular and continued to be sold at the Bon Marché, Seattle's other venerable department store chain, after Frederick & Nelson's closure in 1992. Although the Bon Marché has now vanished into Macy's Northwest, through its corporate owner, Federated Department Stores, Frango Chocolates are still produced locally by Seattle Chocolates using the original Frederick & Nelson recipe and are sold only in Macy's Northwest outlets.

DEPRESSION, RECESSION, PROHIBITION RESTRICTIONS, AND CAR CULTURE

During the Prohibition era in Washington State, which took effect four years *before* the national mandate (1916–1933), many Seattle restaurants were forced to close. Surviving restaurants worked hard and found creative ways to attract diners, often with special events and entertainment. A few illegally offered alcohol under the table, since booze was easy to procure and slip across the Canadian border, thanks to elaborate bootlegging operations and limited Coast Guard supervision on sea routes. Private clubs (for example, the Rainier Club and the University Club) were exempt during the state's various pre-Prohibition experiments in managing alcohol sales. During the Great Depression, for obvious economic reasons, few people ate outside home, and little capital was invested in restaurant development. Once Prohibition was repealed and a state-run Liquor Control Board was established in 1933 to be the sole distributor and retailer controlling sales and consumption, alcohol began to be available in limited capacities; beer and wine were served at restaurants and taverns, but hard alcohol was only sold in state stores. A bill passed in 1948 finally allowed restaurants to serve "liquor by the drink" with some restrictions. In 2011, Washington State voters approved privatizing liquor sales throughout the state, making wine, beer, and hard liquor sales possible everywhere, from grocery stores to drug stores.

From the restaurant history perspective, back in the late 1930s, as the economic pinch receded, the affordability of automobiles played a role in launching a different type of dining and drinking culture, most often in underground speakeasies, typically located outside Seattle's city limits.

In this era, roadside restaurants with eye-catching signs began popping up on highways, attracting affluent customers motoring for pleasure. The Old Bothell Highway was a major destination, especially because of its location outside Seattle city limits. One destination, the Coon Chicken Inn, opened in 1930 and was a family-owned fried chicken chain featuring a twelve-foot-high caricature of a grinning African American man's head at the entrance to each restaurant. The chain later became notorious because of its racist logo, although this didn't seem to bother white patrons coming to the basement Cotton Club to dance and drink. Other minstrel-themed fried chicken restaurants such as Mammy's Shack and My Southern Inn were famous for frying chicken in the window to entice customers.

In 1930, the NAACP filed a complaint against the racist logo and offensive advertising of the Coon Chicken Inn. To avoid prosecution, owners Maxon Lester Graham and Adelaide Graham repainted the grotesque black faces blue and covered up the words "Coon Chicken Inn" painted on the figures' teeth. But they didn't change anything else. Orders of "piping hot, crisp delicious chicken," according to one advertisement, were still delivered in a car plastered with the Coon Chicken Inn logo, sending the racist imagery across the city day and night.

Ironically, Uncle Tom's Cabin, at Eleventh Avenue NE and Fifteenth Avenue NE in today's Pinehurst neighborhood, was popular because of the automobile. Opened in the mid-1920s by Mr. and Mrs. Thomas Meeker, the roadside restaurant located on the Lake Forest Park–bound Pacific Highway is described by William Speidel in *You Can't Eat Mt. Rainier!* as set in a "picturesque setting among firs and cedars in a rustic log cabin" and serving Southern fried chicken dinners and T-bone steaks, along with mouth-watering pies (baked by Mrs. Tom) for thirty-plus years. Meals were cooked to order while guests wandered the woodsy grounds. The restaurant turned out to be a forerunner of other roadside restaurants that arrived later in the northern parts of Seattle.

SEATTLE'S FIRST FOREIGN AND ECCENTRIC RESTAURANTS

Seattle, like many other cities in the 1930s, lured diners to restaurants with exotic themes and foreign cuisines. From traditional Russian and Scandinavian fare to authentic Italian dishes, the choices were varied. Among the standouts was Moscow Restaurant, sometimes referred to as "A Little Bit of Old Russia," which opened in this era at 763 Lakeview Avenue near Eastlake and Mercer. The exterior was a replica of a candy house from a Russian fairy tale, and the Russian proprietor and his mother wore traditional folk dress. As Ms. Horrocks noted in her manuscript, the signature dark Russian bread was always fresh from the oven.

Although Ballard, a hub for Seattle's Scandinavian immigrants, had few neighborhood restaurants, the upscale King Oscar's Smörgåsbord opened in 1938—the only one in the country with a copyrighted name—in the vintage 1890s home of Captain Frank Winslow on Aurora Avenue and NW Forty-Third Street. Proprietor Bill Jensen welcomed guests into the many intimate rooms of an interior resembling a Scandinavian mountain chalet complete with dark wooden beams and touches of red, yellow, and blue, the colors of Scandinavia's national flags. While buffets and cafeterias were not new to Seattle, nor the *smörgåsbord*-themed restaurant, this was a lavish version with dishes spanning the hot and cold culinary spectrum from fish and meats to cold cuts, sausages, cheeses, salads, and various breads and crackers. One specialty, Swedish pancakes, was served tableside and filled with chicken and mushrooms in a rich, wine-enhanced cream sauce.

Two classic restaurants offered tastes of Italy's culinary legacy. Casa Villa, an Italian-style villa at 1823 Eastlake Avenue, was one of Seattle's first Italian restaurants outside of the Central District's Garlic Gulch. Opened in 1936, the peach-colored stucco Italian "villa" featured dark woodwork and maroon draperies, as described in Speidel's guide to Seattle restaurants, *You Can't Eat Mount Rainier!* When it first opened, the menu offered as many main courses as you wanted to eat for a total of one dollar.

Another popular Italian restaurant of this era was Gasperetti's Roma Café located on Fourth Avenue and Main Street. William Gasperetti (1919–2002) was born in South Seattle, the son of Italian immigrants from Florence. The café's claim to fame was its status as Seattle's first sports bar because Mr. Gasperetti displayed signed baseballs and hung pictures of athletes who came to dine at his restaurant, including baseball greats Yogi Berra, Elston Howard, and Carl Yastrzemski. Among its distinguishing features, the restaurant also had a special Squad Room reserved solely for police officers and served green ravioli on March 17 to celebrate Saint Patrick's Day.

One of the most eccentric restaurants in the 1930s was Ben Paris, a combination restaurant and lounge, pool hall, pull-tab parlor, barbershop, and sporting goods establishment at Fourth Avenue and Westlake. Paris, a sportsman, conservationist, and restaurateur, created a macho haven for fishermen and other sportsmen. The restaurant's star attraction was a stand-alone trout pool, plus its large glass tank stocked with live bass. Intent on protecting the area's natural resources, Paris was elected president of the Washington Conservation League. His primary cause: commercial salmon traps that he claimed were snaring fish before they could reach Puget Sound or its tributaries. The state legislature took notice and, in 1935, outlawed the traps in Puget Sound.

POST-PROHIBITION AND POST–WORLD WAR II

The national repeal of Prohibition in 1933 and the end of World War II in 1945 changed restaurant dining across the United States. This was especially significant in Seattle, which until then had a relatively modest restaurant community. With the strong post–World War II economy, Seattle's restaurant scene surged and offered diners a host of new eating adventures. The options spanned inexpensive fast food at drive-ins along new highways and quirky themed restaurants to upscale "foreign" restaurants such as Trader Vic's. The Northern California–based chain with a Polynesian theme, whose owner, Victor Bergeron, invented the mai-tai, opened its first franchise in Seattle in 1940 at the Westin Hotel. At the opposite, sophisticated end of the spectrum, the post-war years marked the start of refined gourmet restaurants in Seattle.

Following national trends in the post–World War II decade, Seattle's restaurants reflected consumers' interest in experiencing "foreign" cuisines. If you were dining out, you wanted to experience something completely different from what you ate every day at home—"adventures in eating" was how a restaurant advertising slogan tagged this experience, as William Speidel described in *You Can't Eat Mount Rainier!*

Scandinavian cuisine fit the definition of "exotic" foreign cuisines, which may be a surprise considering one of Seattle's largest immigrant groups hailed from the Nordic countries and lived clustered in Ballard. However, historically limited by income and climate, frugal Nordics tended to eat at home, making their type of ethnic restaurant rare. But the deliciousness of Scandinavian food inspired the opening in 1948 of Selandia at 711 Elliott Avenue, which served an elaborate Danish *smörgåsbord*. More than sixty items were offered in a lavish buffet, including traditional foods such as pickled, marinated, and smoked herring, steamed and smoked salmon, barbecued sablefish, fried codfish, Norwegian fish cakes, and Swedish meatballs. A few years later, another Scandinavian restaurant, the Norslander, opened on the third floor of an imposing stone building known as the Norway Center, located on Third Avenue West and Thomas Street. Its menu offered Norwegian fish cakes as well as Olympia oysters, lobster, and cuts of meat from manager Roy Peterson's own butcher shop. To represent the Swedish version of *smörgåsbord*, the appropriately named restaurant A Little Bit of Sweden opened on Sixth Avenue and served both traditional Swedish and American dishes.

For a dining experience on the opposite side of the globe from Scandinavia, Seattleites had two choices. One was the Outrigger at the Benjamin Franklin Hotel, which transported diners to the South Seas for a Tahitian-themed experience. A series of rooms from the Turtle Room to the Garden Room or the Captain's Cabin offered seating choices. The Tiki Room showcased round Chinese ovens—one of

Authentic Swedish *smörgåsbord* table with servers in traditional Swedish folk dress at the Little Bit of Sweden Restaurant. *Courtesy of the Nordic Museum.*

three sets in the country—fed by alder wood. Appetizers and curries spiced the menu with heat levels matching personal tastes, and dishes were served tableside by an Asian serving staff. In the context of Seattle's restaurant history, the Outrigger is significant because it became the first franchise of the national chain Trader Vic's. This put Seattle on the map and confirmed the city's status.

The second tropical dining option featured the inspired South Seas decor and menu of the Kalua Room in the Hotel Windsor. Here, guests entered a Polynesian paradise complete with an orchid waterfall, waitresses in native costumes, and two ring-tailed monkeys in a plate glass, air-conditioned cage to entertain diners. The restaurant served tropical drinks and Hawaiian appetizers such as rumaki (spiced chicken livers with water chestnuts wrapped in bacon), barbecued spareribs marinated in Kahlua sauce, and jumbo fried shrimp.

Off in a different direction, Scottish dishes intersected with Pacific Northwest ingredients at the Plaid Piper, which was distinguished by wooden hobby horses on top of its building and a small waterfall inside its garden entrance on East Olive Street in the First Hill neighborhood. Once inside, diners discovered a cocktail lounge displaying one-hundred-plus Scottish tartans and featuring live organ music, but the restaurant kept its Pacific Northwest connection by specializing in grilled crab legs.

For a taste of favorite foods from this era, the following recipe from the Plaid Piper for Dungeness crab legs is adapted from the recipe William Speidel shares in his description of the restaurant in *You Can't Eat Mt. Rainier!*

Crab Legs au Fromage aux Sourbise from the Plaid Piper

Sauté ten to twelve jumbo Dungeness crab legs, and arrange on split and toasted English muffins. Top with melted Cheddar cheese and a drizzle of melted butter, and then sprinkle with paprika and finely chopped green onions. Garnish with lettuce, tomato slices, and chopped ripe olives.

Closer to home, Western themes were also popular and attracted a crowd. The Ranch, located on Sixth Avenue just south of Pike Street, re-created the ambiance of an Old West ranch with an interior combining brick and rough board walls, rodeo photos, saddles, and horseshoes, along with checkered tablecloths. Waitresses wore gingham dresses to complement the theme. Chefs worked in full view and, as Speidel describes the action, used a "JucyRay" light that was advertised as "cooking steaks from inside out, putting flavor on the customer's plate instead of leaving it behind in the pan."

Other Western spots around town included Roosevelt Hotel's Rough Rider Room at Seventh Avenue and Pine Street, where large murals of former US president Theodore Roosevelt in action illustrated the theme, along with decor that included cactus, sand effects, and pony-hide patterns on seats and barstools. Western-style chicken potpie was a popular dish. At the Legend Room in the now defunct Bon Marché department store (wrapped into Macy's Federated Department Stores in 2003), the Western theme was given a Pacific Northwest twist by featuring Native American art and was accompanied by a Western buffet on Thursday nights featuring barbecued beef, steamed salmon, deviled clams, kidney beans, hot potato salad, and more.

Despite its name and racist logo, Pancho's was not a Mexican restaurant, although waitresses dressed in Mexican costumes and served Mexican-inspired cocktails. Opened in 1949, Pancho's claim to fame was having Seattle's first open-pit broiler and a menu of shish kebabs, hickory-barbecued spareribs, double-loin lamb chops, and beef.

Two quirky restaurants, both with transportation themes, also attracted adventurous Seattle diners in the post–World War II era. Bill Moultray, a former math teacher, and his wife Chris transformed a retired ferryboat, once part of the Mosquito Fleet that had zipped across Puget Sound, into a floating restaurant. Named Moultray's Four Winds, the New Orleans pirate-themed restaurant docked at the southwest end of South Lake Union and featured waiters dressed as pirates. The eclectic menu offered Caesar salads prepared tableside, New Orleans "Po" Boy sandwiches, whole broiled Cornish game hens, frogs' legs, oysters Rockefeller, and broiled salmon following the "Orcas Island method." The restaurant's Cannon Ball cocktail was touted as a drink for "a real he-man" that would "shiver your timbers."

Back on land, hungry drivers on Fourth Avenue South headed for Andy's Diner, comprising two historic railroad banquet cars—including one used by President Franklin Delano Roosevelt—lined up in 1949 by Andrew Nagy. Together, they formed a bar and dining room, seating two hundred people in the restaurant's heyday. Serving burgers, sandwiches, salads, and soups for lunch, the "old-school Seattle" menu expanded at dinnertime to include prime rib and steaks cooked on a charcoal broiler, all with "workingman appeal." Plenty of railroad history was on display, with framed photos on the walls along with bowling memorabilia. In its later years, Andy Yurkanin, a nephew of the founder, ran the restaurant. Andy's chugged along until 2008, when it was sold and reincarnated as the Orient Express, a tacky karaoke lounge and Chinese restaurant.

CAR CULTURE TAKES OFF AND DRIVE-INS ARRIVE

New roads, bridges spanning waterways, and more automobiles dramatically changed the face of Seattle from the late 1940s into the 1950s. The resulting mobility also influenced residents' dining out patterns, and their embrace of fast, inexpensive food inspired the launch of several locally owned burger chains and distinctive drive-in restaurants.

Dick's Drive-In is the perfect example of a then-and-now restaurant chain with roots in 1950s car culture. It still flourishes today, a favorite with high schoolers, as well as their parents and grandparents, and a Seattle landmark with a roof sign spelling out its name in cursive red neon script. The namesake of one of its three founders, Dick Spady (who later bought out his partners), Dick's opened its first location in 1954 in the Wallingford neighborhood. Its iconic menu (unchanged even today) features American fast-food staples: 100 percent, never-frozen beef burgers—cooked to well done, with no substitutions allowed unless you hold the cheese—real, hand-cut French fries, shakes made to order, and ice cream cones. In 1954, burgers cost nineteen cents; today, the price of a basic burger is still affordable at two dollars.

Over the years, Dick's expanded to four more locations in Seattle: Capitol Hill (1956), Crown Hill (1957), Lake City (1963), and its only sit-down restaurant in lower Queen Anne (1974). Dick Spady also "gave back" significantly to his community by supporting homeless relief charities and public policy engagement efforts; guests may also "round up" their bill, with the difference becoming a charitable donation. In a historic move in a new century, in 2011 Dick's opened a franchise north of Seattle in Edmonds, a location based on a customer poll. By fall 2018, Dick's plans to open another "outside Seattle" location in the south end, with the specific location again determined by customer votes.

The signboard for Dag's Drive-In, a hamburger joint at the 800 block of Aurora Avenue between Aloha and Valley Streets, amused and attracted drivers cruising by with witty slogans as much as its juicy burgers satisfied their hunger pangs. A business owned and operated by brothers Ed and Boe Messet and named for their father, the drive-in opened in 1955 with a classic menu of fries, shakes, and nineteen-cent burgers. Their "Beefy Boy" reader board added humor to a drive with lines such as "Good Meat but Humble Attitude" and "This Is Dag's, Canlis Is Ten Blocks North." The family business survived until 1993, when competition caught up with it and forced a closure.

A short way down the road, the Dog House was another favorite highway haven that both survived the Depression and thrived with the new car culture. Constructed in the mid-1930s on the north side of Denny Way between Aurora Avenue and Dexter Street, the boozy twenty-four-hour cocktail lounge serving comfort food and known as a working man's and a working woman's bar was an easy detour once the new Aurora Bridge crossed above the ship canal.

Only in the 1950s, when the Battery Street tunnel changed traffic patterns, did business dwindle. In 1954, the Dog House closed (according to anecdotes, on closing day, no one could find the key to the main door—because the restaurant never

A fabled dining and drinking destination from the 1930s until 1994, Bob Murray's Dog House was open twenty-four hours and provided nonstop food, booze, music, and fellowship. *Courtesy of MOHAI, [Museum of History & Industry Photograph Collection], [MP940102-29]; photographer: Howard Giske.*

closed), but then-owner Laurie Gulbransen moved it to Seventh Avenue and Bell Street, where it lasted until 1994. Today, its legacy lives on in name and spirit at the Dog House Bar & Grill on Fourth Avenue South in Seattle's SoDo district.

Along with basic restaurant building blocks, Seattle's restaurant history includes kitschy cool cafés with odd and unusual shapes. Some were constructed as antidotes to the Great Depression and were festooned end-to-end in neon lights, while others were designed to grab the attention of passing motorists as car traffic picked up around the city after World War II. All have now vanished, but they ranged from the architectural whimsy of the Igloo's twin domed buildings to the Jolly Roger's pink stucco tower topped by a skull-and-bones flag and the two teepee-shaped towers appropriately named Twin T-Ps.

Northbound drivers would encounter the Igloo Restaurant when accessing on-ramps for Aurora Avenue, Seattle's principal north–south highway in the 1940s. Established by entrepreneurs Ralph Grossman and Ernie Hughes, the diner and drive-in restaurant on the southeast corner of Sixth Avenue and Denny Way was a metal-clad, twin-domed building topped by a neon sign with a smiling Eskimo and the slogan "Good Food." It operated from 1940 to 1954 with seating for seventy, and with a drive-in staffed by perky female car-hops in short skirts serving a mostly male clientele. Deluxe cheeseburgers, double malts, and crisp onion rings lured hungry customers. Alas, the Igloo was demolished in 1960.

In the same wacky category, anyone driving north on Pacific Highway to the new community of Lake Forest Park or taking a weekend excursion to Bothell couldn't miss the Jolly Roger. Opened in 1933, just after Prohibition ended, the Jolly Roger was originally a Chinese-themed dining and drinks roadhouse called Chinese Castle. When its original Asian owner hit a monetary hard spot, Nellie and Oroville Cleveland took ownership of the pink stucco building and raised a pirate's skull-and-bones flag from the main tower. The husband-and-wife team served specials for forty-plus years, offering everything from soup, nuts, meat, and potatoes, all for fifty cents, with dancing and jukebox music included. The building earned landmark status in 1979 but, unfortunately, burned to the ground in 1989.

Perhaps the most unexpected sight from the highway was the Twin T-Ps Restaurant. Opened in 1937 on Aurora Avenue (State Route 99), the Twin T-Ps (named Power's Pancake House between 1959 and 1967, and later renamed Twin Teepees) was a classic Americana roadside restaurant housed in an unusual structure: two side-by-side pavilions resembling teepees of the Plains Native American tribes. Both featured kitschy decor inspired by Native American designs, with the main room of one focusing on a huge, open-pit fireplace and the other a cocktail lounge and kitchen. For hungry guests, the menu featured classic American road food such as burgers, fries, milkshakes, and frappes. On Friday nights in the 1980s and 1990s, prime rib was a popular draw.

The distinctive architecture of Walter Clark's Twin T-Ps Restaurant was unmistakable driving north along Aurora Avenue (State Route 99) in the 1930s, and the family-friendly menu ensured a stop. *Courtesy of MOHAI, [Museum of History & Industry Photograph Collection], [1986.5.11405].*

As stories go, the Twin T-Ps may have made a contribution to American fast-food history. First operated by Herman E. Olson, it passed between several owners before Walter Clark acquired it in 1942. Clark, who went on to build a restaurant empire in Seattle (see page 166), employed a former war buddy, Colonel Harland Sanders, to staff this restaurant. According to an unproven legend, Sanders worked on his famous "Kentucky Fried Chicken" recipe in the Twin T-Ps' kitchen as the first step to establishing his own fast-food empire. A long-standing favorite landmark, Twin T-Ps closed in 2001 following a kitchen fire, and the buildings were soon demolished, a sad end for one of Seattle's favorite quirky restaurants.

SEATTLE'S FINE-DINING RENAISSANCE

From its rough-and-tumble beginnings and boarding house mess halls to fine hotel and early restaurants, Seattle has evolved into a sophisticated city with

white-tablecloth, fine-dining tastes combining regional ingredients with ethnic flavors and foods. This path wasn't evident to most native residents and, as William
Speidel points out in *You Can't Eat Mount Rainier!*, most locals had an inferiority
complex when asked to name the best places to eat in town. In fact, according to
Speidel, it was better not to ask a native Seattleite where to dine. The complex was
no doubt the result of Prohibition restrictions, the 1930s Great Depression, and
two world wars, not to mention Seattle's faroff location on the other side of the
continent, away from East Coast cities at the "back door" of European cuisine. In
reality, by the 1950s, as Speidel reports, national restaurant critics "rated Seattle up
in the top ten best restaurant cities and at least second-best on the Pacific Coast."

Along with significant movers and shakers behind Seattle's restaurant renaissance in the 1950s, a change in the state's liquor law was driving transformation.
Selling hard liquor by the drink became legal in 1948 at any establishment serving
full meals, which took drinking exclusivity out of private clubs and illegal venues
and enabled restaurants to become full-service locations. The Cloud Room restaurant on the top floor of the Camlin Hotel in downtown Seattle was first to expand
its alcohol offerings. Others followed, as the attraction of an additional income
source was enormously motivating.

Stepping into this modern restaurant environment were several top restaurateurs—also accurately described as entrepreneurs—Victor Rosellini, Peter Canlis,
Walter Clark, Morrie Buckley (El Gaucho), Jim Ward (13 Coins), and John Franco
(Franco's Hidden Harbor). All were super savvy and influential in creating a thriving restaurant community. What follows is a recap of the most influential personalities whose visions and legacies still resonate today in Seattle's restaurant world.

Also not to be discounted in this era was the power of the press. Although initially a sports writer, Emmett Watson's weekly "This, Our Town" column, which
he started writing in 1956 for the *Seattle Post-Intelligencer*, publicized happenings
on the restaurant scene. Partially financed by a group of restaurant owners as a way
to encourage dining out, the advertising format evolved into a legitimate restaurant
review column, encouraging residents to explore. (A footnote: In 1979, Watson
and a business partner, Sam Bryant, opened Seattle's first exclusive oyster bar in
Pike Place Market, which survives today. Despite its "old-school Seattle" history,
Emmett Watson's Oyster Bar was named "one of the best oyster bars in Seattle" in
a review by Allison Austin Scheff in the January 2014 issue of *Seattle Magazine*.)

A key leader on the Seattle restaurant scene by all accounts—some even consider him the father of the city's modern restaurant era—Victor Rosellini was a
child of Italian American immigrants who grew up in Tacoma. After his father's
early death and his mother's move to San Francisco, he assisted her in running her
small Italian restaurant in the late 1920s. (His older brother had migrated first to
America during the Klondike Gold Rush.) After returning to the Pacific Northwest

in 1932, in Seattle, Rosellini gained experience in the restaurant trade, holding a series of front-of-the-house and back-of-the-house jobs.

Moving into his own in 1950, in partnership with his brother-in-law, John Pogetti, he opened Rosellini's 610 on the corner of Sixth Avenue and Pine Street, and in 1956, Rosellini's Four-10 opened in the White-Henry-Stuart Building. Both restaurants were notable for their formal and luxurious white-tablecloth style, not to mention "flaming table-side cookery." Rosellini's ebullient welcoming style, plus his emphasis on service, ambience, food, and wine, set his restaurants apart and kept patrons returning.

The restaurants were also non-partisan hubs for politicos and city business leaders of the era, with a roster of influential regulars. However, as downtown Seattle expanded in the 1970s and 1980s, Rosellini's original restaurant locations were lost to new skyscrapers; Rosellini's Four-10 moved to Belltown, but the building there was also eventually demolished. Notwithstanding these setbacks, Rosellini's legacy among Seattle's restaurateurs remains monumental.

The ultimate host, in this photo from 1959, Victor Rosellini presents a menu to guests seated in front of the distinctive wine rack at his acclaimed Rosellini's Four-10 Restaurant. *Courtesy of MOHAI, [Museum of History & Industry Photograph Collection], [1986.5.11398.1].*

A measure of his influence, Rosellini also served as the first president of the Washington State Restaurant Association and the National Restaurant Association. On the local scene, he was vice-chair of the Century 21 Commission for the 1962 Seattle World's Fair, and he served on boards of numerous Seattle charitable institutions. Extending the family influence into the next generation, Rosellini's son, Robert, followed his father into Seattle's restaurant universe and opened Rosellini's Other Place, which was acclaimed for its French cuisine. Its star opening chef was Dominique Place, who would go on to open his own Dominique's Place and founded Gerard & Dominique Seafood. Many considered Rosellini's Other Place to be Seattle's first world-class restaurant, and some call Robert Rosellini the Northwest's Alice Waters. His restaurant's legacy extended to Chef Bruce Naftaly, who started there as well.

The same year Rosellini opened his first restaurant, another Seattle restaurant legacy opened on a bluff three miles north of downtown on land owned by restaurateur Walter Clark. Built in 1949, on the east side of Queen Anne hill, right off Aurora Boulevard (State Route 99) before it crossed the Aurora Bridge, and overlooking Lake Union, the new restaurant was a knockout from day one. The restaurant's partly cantilevered, mid-century modern building designed by Seattle architect Roland Terry celebrated the Pacific Northwest landscape from expansive windows with sweeping views looking east to Mt. Baker, the Cascade Range, and across Lake Washington. Its mastermind? Peter Canlis. But Canlis's restaurant vision wasn't only about views.

Canlis hailed from an immigrant family whose patriarch, Nikolais Peter Kanlis, came to America by way of Greece, Turkey, and Egypt; while in Cairo, he cooked at a famous hotel. After landing a job cooking for Teddy Roosevelt while Roosevelt was on safari after his two terms as US president, Peter's father came to America, settling in California's Central Valley and opening a diner. Canlis (the spelling of the family name changed at Ellis Island) assisted in the family restaurant, but, with an adventurer's spirit, he moved to Hawaii, where he opened the Canlis Charcoal Broiler in Honolulu. His arrival in Seattle and interactions with the city's other entrepreneurial restaurateurs led to his namesake restaurant.

Elegance was—and still is—a cornerstone of the Canlis philosophy, along with an innovative seasonal menu showcasing its head chef's creativity, a stellar wine selection, and intimate tables in a spacious room. Originally, the service staff was dressed in lovely Japanese kimonos, and although this tradition was discontinued, today's wait staff are friendly and top-notch professionals. Dishes served have always been both exotic and familiar, from Hawaiian mahi-mahi to robust grilled steaks, moving subtly from expected classic restaurant dishes to more modernist cuisine. Star chefs in the recent past have included Greg Atkinson, Jason Franey, and Brady Williams.

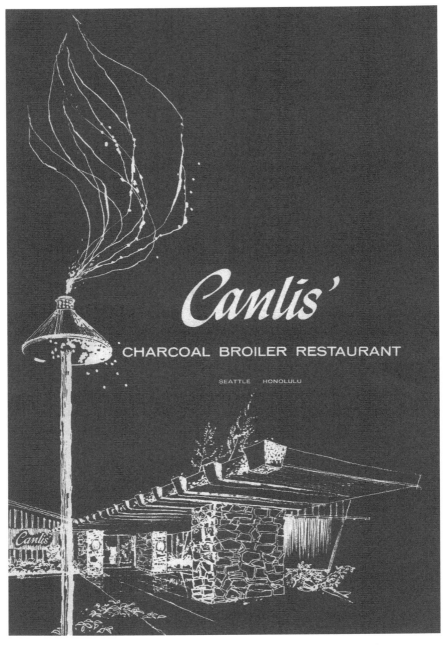

A 1964 menu cover from Canlis's Charcoal Broiler Restaurant shows the restaurant's elegant midcentury modern building, a clue to the special occasion dining experience waiting inside. *Courtesy of MOHAI, [Museum of History & Industry Photograph Collection], [2007.51.13].*

After Peter Canlis passed in 1977, his son Chris Canlis, with his wife Alice, took over the restaurant, managing it with grace and warm hospitality for thirty-plus years. In 2005, their two sons, Mark and Brian, took over the family restaurant as co-owners. Renowned for its inspired menu and serene setting, Canlis has maintained its reputation as *the* place in Seattle for celebrating family milestones and special events. In 2017, Canlis earned its first James Beard Award for its "Outstanding Wine Program." And although it might seem like a classic steakhouse offering, the fresh herbs and made-for-the-moment dressing of the Canlis Salad make it a perennial favorite. The recipe for Canlis Salad is shared below with permission from Canlis Restaurant.

The Canlis Salad

INGREDIENTS

2 heads of Romaine lettuce, washed, dried, and chopped
4 slices of bacon, cut into pieces
1 cup of cubed Italian bread
1 large egg
¼ cup fresh lemon juice
½ cup extra virgin olive oil
1 garlic clove, peeled and crushed

Kosher salt and freshly ground black pepper, to taste
½ cup thinly sliced green onions
¼ cup roughly chopped fresh mint leaves
1 tablespoon roughly chopped fresh oregano leaves
12 cherry tomatoes, cut into halves
¾ cup freshly grated Romano cheese

DIRECTIONS

Place the prepared Romaine lettuce into the refrigerator to chill until the salad is assembled.

In a large skillet set over medium-high heat, cook the bacon pieces until almost crisp and set to drain on paper towels. Leave 1 tablespoon of bacon fat in the skillet and drain off the rest. Turn the heat on low, toss in the bread cubes, and stir until they turn crisp and golden brown. Place in a separate bowl to cool.

Prepare the dressing by heating 2 cups of boiling water. Place the whole egg—still in its shell—into a coffee cup and pour the boiling water over the egg. Let the egg "cook" for 1 minute, and then pour out the water and rinse the egg under cool water. In a mixing bowl, whisk the lemon juice and olive oil together until thoroughly blended. Stir in the crushed garlic. Crack the coddled egg into the mixture and whisk again fiercely to thoroughly blend all the ingredients. Add the desired amount of salt and pepper and set aside.

Choose a salad bowl, place the cold lettuce, green onions, mint, oregano, and cooked bacon into it, and then toss all the ingredients together with the dressing until thoroughly coated. Top the salad with the tomatoes, croutons, and a heaping shower of Romano cheese. (Serves 4.)

WALTER F. CLARK—MR. ACE BUSINESSMAN RESTAURATEUR

Along with Rosellini and Canlis, another giant on Seattle's restaurant landscape was Walter F. Clark. In a remarkable fifty-five-year career, Clark established and managed restaurants in Seattle, along with Tacoma, Portland, and Yakima, opening a record fifty-three restaurants. Dig behind the scenes, and it becomes evident that Clark's influence and high standards influenced all of Seattle's post–World War II restaurateurs, along with many investments. In fact, Victor Rosellini is quoted in an article by Don Duncan in the *Seattle Times* as having once called Clark "the father of the restaurant industry in Seattle."

Although he grew up in Portland, Oregon, and found his first job in Manning's Cafeterias in that city, Clark moved north to open a new cafeteria in Seattle, making an acquaintance with the city that kept bringing him back. His career progressed, and he became the West Coast manager for Manning's until the 1929 stock market crash. Losing his Manning's job because of the crash, Clark went to work for Adolph Schmidt, an Olympia brewer building the Puget Sound Hotel Company (a chain that eventually became Westin Hotels). With an independent bent, Clark went out on his own back in Seattle and, in 1930, bought his first restaurant, Marie's Barbecue, in the University District. It was just the beginning.

In his heyday, Clark's restaurant chain included the Salad Bowl, the Red Carpet, Village Chef, Round the Clock, Twin T-Ps, Little Chef, the Crabapple, Clark's Northgate, Clark's Third Avenue, Minute Chef, Clark's Corner, two Windjammers, Dublin House, Big Top, and Plaza 5—all different with a special concept and menu. For his menu selections, Clark's early restaurants served familiar, lighter, and simpler fare at Depression-era affordable prices. While all offered oysters, a "must" in this time period, other items ranged from grilled steaks and veal and pork chops to spaghetti and chili con carne. His first full-service, tablecloth restaurant was Clark's Salad Bowl, a standout with its focus on quality over quantity and a clean, quiet tea-room-like environment appealing to women customers.

Clark is also credited with opening the first restaurant in the first indoor shopping mall in the United States, Seattle's Northgate Mall. Astute enough to realize that hungry shoppers needed a convenient food source, in 1951 he opened Clark's Northgate, along with the Feather Duster Cocktail Lounge. Five years later, he opened a restaurant in Bellevue Square Shopping Center and, in 1957, the 178-seat Clark's Village Chef at University Village, which even served dinner with candles on blue-and-white checked tablecloths. His last major impresario project was in 1967, when he opened the Irish-themed Dublin House. Ever a businessman restaurateur in the right place at the right time, Clark also had the concessions contract on the Washington State Ferry System for thirty-two years.

In 1970, Clark sold Seattle's largest restaurant chain to the Campbell Soup Company, with mixed results for the new owners. Clark was able to buy back his Red Carpet Restaurant in the Medical Dental Building on Olive Way, which had long been a favorite of Frederick & Nelson shoppers and downtown theater buffs. Although by contract he wasn't able to name the restaurant after himself, his son became manager and it was called Eugene's Red Carpet Restaurant until it closed in 1983.

At the time of the 1962 World's Fair, Clark chaired a group of eight local restaurateurs in a partnership, Century Concessions, Inc., which operated a significant percentage of the fair's food services. Clark's influence was felt nationwide as he also served on the board of the National Restaurant Association.

THE 1960s—DESTINATION: SEATTLE WORLD'S FAIR

The "Century 21" World's Fair held in Seattle in 1962 brought the city into the spotlight for the rest of the country. The fair's food legacy also proved instrumental in reshaping local dining habits, a welcome side effect noted by Seattle historian and journalist Knute Berger in his article in *Crosscut* on April 12, 2012. It wasn't only the revolving restaurant atop the Space Needle; the fair also showcased local foods from salmon to Washington State apples. According to Berger, the most popular food encountered at the fair was Belgian waffles. He speculated that the sale of "500,000 thick airy waffles, piled with strawberries and whipped cream . . . if put into a single stack, would have been the height of 70 Space Needles."

The World's Fair also introduced Seattleites to a new world of international culinary traditions. The old armory (built in 1939) was converted into a vertical shopping mall called the Food Circus (which later became Center House at Seattle Center—and recently reclaimed its almost original name, the Seattle Center Armory). At the Food Circus, traditional dishes were served from cuisines around the world, including Thailand, Japan, Mongolia, Korea, Mexico, Denmark, Germany, Creole, and Native American, among others. Along with these tastes, the revolving Eye of the Needle Restaurant (now the Space Needle Restaurant and Seattle's top grossing restaurant) had long lines of eager diners waiting up to three hours for their elevator ride to dinner. The locally focused menu atop the landmark tower featured fresh salmon, Dungeness crab, local apples and berries, and seasonal fiddlehead ferns.

The restaurant business group Century 21's influence extended beyond Seattle Center and was the catalyst for turning Piers 50 and 51 on Seattle's working waterfront into a dining destination with several seafood restaurants. The group also launched the Argosy tour to Tillicum Village on Blake Island to showcase the Coast Salish tribe's culture and culinary traditions. Overall, as a national event, the World's Fair opened Seattle's horizons and made residents value their own culinary heritage even more.

LOCAL RESTAURANT GROUPS THRIVE

As described, over the decades individual restaurateurs in Seattle have successfully owned and operated multiple restaurants. Behind the scenes, many of Seattle's seemingly independent restaurants are actually part of larger umbrella groups that are not chef-driven. In this category, Seattle's oldest surviving local restaurant group is Consolidated Restaurants, established in 1951 by David Cohn as Barb Enterprises and later renamed. Although most restaurants under the Consolidated label no longer exist (including the Barb, Polynesia, Select Grill, Pescatore, Hiram's, Union Square Grill, and DC's Grill), the group's current roster includes Elliott's Oyster House (originally Elliott Bay Fish and Oyster Company), the Metropolitan Grill, and several fast-food chains such as the Wing Dome, Steamers, and Quincy's (the last two with branches on Microsoft's campus).

Another Seattle-based company owning multiple restaurants is Restaurants Unlimited, started in 1969 by Rich Komen and partners. Its first restaurant was the Red Baron, a steak and lobster house serving fine food in a casual setting. The company established itself with the national restaurant chain Palomino, plus the individual restaurants of Stanley & Seafort's, Kincaid's Fish, Chop & Steak House, and Palisade. This latter was, and is, a multimillion-dollar building with vast windows overlooking sailboats and yachts docked at the Elliott Bay Marina in the Magnolia neighborhood. The company was also the original promoter of the fast-food chains of Cinnabon Bakery and Zoopa. While owned by various firms over the years, in 2007 it was purchased by Sun Capital Partners.

Add Schwartz Brothers, started by John and Bill Schwartz, to the list of firms that are in the background but own full-service restaurants. Started in 1973 as a bakery, the business expanded to the Sandwich Shop and Pie Place, but when the brothers couldn't find anyone making cheesecakes and pies to their standards, they expanded their own bakery. From baked goods to restaurants, Schwartz Brothers Restaurants owns and operates Daniel's Broiler and Chandler's Crabhouse Restaurant, both on south Lake Union, as well as Spazzo Restaurant, a casual restaurant serving contemporary American cuisine on the Eastside in Redmond.

TWO NATIONAL CHAINS LAUNCH FROM SEATTLE

Enhancing Seattle's restaurant profile, two well-known restaurant chains—Black Angus and Red Robin—started in the city. Both focus on beef instead of seafood, which is surprising given the Pacific Northwest's abundant aquatic resources.

People referred to the founder of Black Angus, Stuart Anderson (1923–2016) as "a rancher," but Anderson was actually raised in Seattle. After returning from the army following World War II, he opened his first restaurant and called it the French Quarter. In 1964, Anderson, who by then had moved to a 2,400-acre ranch in Eastern Washington, opened the first Black Angus Restaurant in the Caledonia Hotel on Elliott Avenue near Western Avenue. The original dinner cost for one person was $2.95 and included a choice of steak, green salad served in a wooden bowl, plus a baked potato. From this location, he launched a national chain that grew to 121 restaurants in eighteen states. The chain was acquired by the food service giant Sage in 1972 and has since changed hands several times. As of 2017, there were forty-five Black Angus steakhouses, including four in Puget Sound.

The second Seattle-based chain is Red Robin. The first Red Robin started as a tavern at the south end of the University Bridge on the edge of the University of Washington campus. Originally called Sam's Tavern, the restaurant's name changed because its owner, Sam, who sang in a barbershop quartet, liked the song "When the Red, Red Robin (Comes Bob, Bob, Bobbin' Along)" written by Harry Woods in 1926. The new name, Sam's Red Robin, lasted until 1969, when Gerry Kingen, a Seattle restaurant entrepreneur, bought the tavern and dropped "Sam's." Under Kingen's direction and the eating pleasure of patrons, a variety of gourmet hamburger options were added to the menu. In 1979, the restaurant expanded from its local base with headquarters in downtown Seattle to become a national franchise chain. Two customers, Michael and Steve Snyder, established the first franchise in Yakima, Washington, in 1979. By 1985, the chain had grown to 175 locations. After various managing companies and buyouts, not all of which were successful, Kingen and Snyder re-entered to take back the company and regain its profitability. At last count, there were 538 Red Robin restaurants, plus a quick-service, simplified version called Red Robin's Burger Works. (The original Red Robin closed in 2010, and the building was torn down in 2014.)

SEAFOOD RESTAURANTS SET SEATTLE APART

If seafood is a cornerstone of Seattle's fundamental culinary being, it follows that restaurants in the city would celebrate seafood—and many do. Whether they are seafood palaces with sweeping waterfront vistas or sushi-and-chips concession stands at baseball and soccer stadiums, restaurateurs and chefs have long bowed down with reverence before the bounty of Pacific Northwest seafood. This section shares details about notable leaders and their restaurants in this seafood worship.

As outlined in detail in chapter 1, Seattle's geographic location blesses it with a bounty of seafood, from shellfish such as native and new species of oysters, mussels, Pacific razor clams, spot prawns, Dungeness crab, sea urchins, and geoducks, to marvelous finned fish. Leading the finned fish category are the five species of iconic wild salmon, followed by Pacific halibut, steelhead trout, black cod or sable-fish, ling cod, petrale sole, and Pacific lamprey.

Seafood may have appeared first on the menu of the Haines Oyster House, dating to 1890. Hattie Graham Horrocks writes in *Restaurants of Seattle: 1853–1960* that the Oyster House was an excellent place to stop and enjoy a bowl of creamy oyster stew "using only small succulent Olympic oysters." Other seafood-focused establishments soon followed, including Don's Oyster House, started by Don Ehle and his father in 1898 in Pioneer Square. Their menu offered a small selection of seafood—Eastern oysters, Eastern oyster stew, and Alaskan black cod—along with a sizable assortment of steaks, chops, sandwiches, eggs, omelets, soups, and salads.

The 1920s through the 1940s saw the first wave of modern seafood restaurants. No question that the opening of Fishermen's Terminal in 1914 on Salmon Bay, a freshwater home for the North Pacific Fishing Fleet during off-season, made seafood more readily accessible and affordable. This proximity went a long way toward prompting more local restaurateurs to feature seafood on their menus.

Among Seattle's first seafood restaurants were the Marine Room, which opened in 1925 in the posh Olympic Hotel (now the Fairmount Olympic), and Ocean House, considered the first waterfront seafood restaurant with its 1931 opening on Elliott Avenue. In 1936, Marvin and Dorothy Rosand opened a modest seafood restaurant that expanded to two floors and was later called the Breakwater. The same year, Rosand's Seafood opened on Ray's Wharf at the end of the Ship Canal and on the way to Shilshole Marina, a destination for diners seeking seafood dishes professionally prepared. Rosand's would later become the acclaimed Ray's Boathouse specializing in local seafood.

In 1939, Skippers opened its first Seattle location featuring a nautical theme inside and out, complete with ship models and sea charts. The restaurant offered a traditional seafood menu showcasing oysters, especially tiny native Olympia, Quilcene, and Cove oysters. A chain of independently licensed Skippers Seafood & Chowder House restaurants, founded in 1969 in Bellevue under the management of Starway Restaurants, LLC, today has thirty locations throughout Washington, Oregon, Idaho, and Utah.

The opening of Crawford's Sea Grill by C. C. Crawford on Elliott Avenue in 1940 turned into a godsend for seafood fans. Alaskan shrimp were flown in regularly by plane, its menu showcased a "Catch of the Day," and the restaurant invented a "Puget Sound Crab-Meat-Burger," a forerunner to crab cakes. In his essay "Mirror of Taste," Robert Fisher describes how a glass-enclosed dining room offered unobstructed views of Puget Sound, and the restaurant's stated mission was "to serve the widest possible variety of sea foods all prepared in a specially designed broiler with olive oil used exclusively in preparation." Outside of clam chowder, salmon, and halibut, this meant that the menu featured seafood hailing from other parts of the United States. After Crawford's untimely death in 1942, J. E. Meaker owned and managed the popular restaurant until Nick Zanides took it over around 1948. As Chuck Flood recounts in *Lost Restaurants of Seattle*, the waterfront location was ideal for a seafood restaurant. Given this prized setting, in 1965 Ivar Haglund bought the property and turned it into his Captain's Table restaurant.

The legacy of Ray's Boathouse must also be included in Seattle's seafood restaurant saga. What began as a dockside fish-and-chips and coffee café in 1945 opened by Ray Lichtenberger to complement his boat rental and bait house business on Shilshole Bay, by the 1970s had turned into a nationally acclaimed seafood restaurant. At the helm of the transformation for both building and menu were Russ Wohlers, Earl Lasher, and Duke Moscrip. (Read more about Moscrip below.) The food focus was on fresh seafood, locally grown produce, and seasonal dishes. Ray's was also a pioneer in reintroducing tiny Olympia oysters, the only species native to the Pacific Northwest, and in celebrating Bruce Gore's flash-frozen-at-sea salmon, along with rich and flavorful Copper River salmon. Under Chef Wayne Ludvisen, in 1983, Ray's was one of the four Seattle restaurants to be first in serving Copper River salmon.

Despite fires in 1987 and 1997, Ray's Boathouse & Café continues to flourish, with both its menu and the spectacular views of the Olympic Mountain range to the west making it a top destination for seafood lovers.

When the Port of Seattle constructed buildings in 1952 at Fishermen's Terminal, restaurant space was included. The first food service resident was the Wharf Restaurant, filling a spacious area with a wall of windows overlooking docked fishing boats. An adjacent coffee shop added local flavor catering to local fishermen. In 1969, the space was renamed Chinook's at Salmon Bay and became part of Anthony's Restaurants, a privately held company with local investors managing a chain of twenty seafood restaurants in Washington, Idaho, and Oregon. From fish tacos to seasonal specials starring salmon and a signature blackberry shortcake, Chinook's has huge appeal for hungry families living nearby. A separate grab-and-go seafood booth was also set up for quick bites.

Anthony's roots date to 1969 when Budd Gould opened a steak and lobster restaurant in the Bellevue area. From this beginning, successive restaurants were established in marina locations with waterfront views. To ensure top-quality seafood, in 1984, Anthony's started a wholesale seafood company that sources the freshest seafood from the Pacific Northwest, Alaska, and Hawaii, a measure of its commitment and high standards for serving fresh, local seafood at its restaurants. Along with its roster of highly qualified chefs managed by executive chef Pat Donahue, Anthony's enlisted Sharon Kramis, a food writer and top culinary consultant, to develop seasonal recipes for Northwest produce ranging from blackberries and strawberries to tomatoes and corn. No wonder following a seafood entrée at an Anthony's Homeport restaurant with blackberry cobbler in July is a must.

BIG FISH IN SEATTLE'S SEAFOOD RESTAURANT POND

It takes a chef to prepare seafood without fuss or fear. That's the opposite of most home cooks, who shy away from cooking fish because they're apprehensive about messing up the results. Even though the quality and freshness of fish purchased in every Seattle grocery store and retail outlet is top quality (particularly when compared to other parts of the country), ordering fish at a restaurant, especially one specializing in seafood, is a welcome treat. Happily, Seattle has a lengthy roster of chefs and astute entrepreneurs with specialty restaurants that have made perfectly prepared seafood accessible to diners. Among them are chefs Christine Keff and John Howie, along with seafood restaurateurs Duke Moscrip and Ivar Haglund, and seafood expert Jon Rowley.

Chef Christine Keff, a 1999 James Beard winner, opened her Flying Fish Restaurant in 1995 on First Avenue in Belltown, serving fish exclusively in preparations often with international flavor twists. Keff moved her restaurant in 2010 to the South Lake Union neighborhood. In 2013, needing a break, she sold it to a Chinese company, Fortune Garden Group, which owns several high-end restaurants in China. No longer headed for the restaurant kitchen every day, Keff has consulted with the group managing the Tillicum Village Native American attraction on Blake Island to update and improve its traditional salmon-focused menu.

Although on the Bellevue side of Lake Washington, Chef John Howie's Seastar Restaurant and Raw Bar, which opened in 2002, is also a standout. Over the intervening years it has consistently received accolades for its superb and creative presentations of Pacific Northwest seafood. (Howie's South Lake Union branch of Seastar was open from 2009 to 2014.)

Three individuals with long legacies add a special sauce to any story about Seattle's seafood restaurants. With color, wit, and perseverance, not to mention good taste and successful businesses with multiple locations, restaurateur Ivar Haglund and Chef Duke Moscrip are genuine Seattle originals. Each in their own way has enriched the city on many levels. Jon Rowley also fits this profile, influencing awareness about seafood quality, sourcing, and preparation techniques for both chefs and home cooks.

From a historical perspective, one who is still remarkable today, thirty-plus years after his passing in 1985, is Ivar Haglund, who stands out as Seattle's most famous seafood restaurant maverick. The son of Swedish immigrants living in West Seattle, Haglund was both a University of Washington graduate and a musician singing and playing guitar on local radio shows. In 1938, Haglund set up Seattle's first aquarium on Pier 3 (now Pier 54) with his personal collection of sea creatures. The pier, owned by Washington Fish and Oyster Company (now part of Ocean Beauty Seafoods), had numerous fishing vessels unloading every day. Motivated by hungry aquarium visitors, Haglund opened a tiny fish-and-chips spot on the pier. Financial challenges and luck combined in 1946, when he sold the aquarium and opened Ivar's Acres of Clams, a fine-dining restaurant on the south side of the pier. The restaurant's name is linked to a song called "Acres of Clams," which Haglund also used as the theme song for his radio show, and which Pete Seeger sang under the title of "The Old Settler's Song."

> No longer a slave of ambition
> I laugh at the world and its shams,
> As I think of my happy condition—
> Surrounded by acres of clam-m-m-m-s!

(The song is attributed to Francis D. Henry and was first recorded in April 1877.)

Ivar's Acres of Clams attracted patrons with its seafood menu and gracious service, and it entertained them with Haglund's eclectic gathering of collectibles, including a "clam gun" and his grandmother's china set. The restaurant's slogan, "Keep clam," is a measure of Haglund's irrepressible wit and showman's style, as was the annual clam-eating contest pitting West Coast against East Coast contestants.

Restaurateur Ivar Haglund's mischievous side is unmistakable in this portrait. *Courtesy of the Nordic Museum.*

The success of Ivar's Acres of Clams spurred Haglund to open more spots around the city. A drive-in Ivar's opened on Broadway in 1951 in the Capitol Hill neighborhood, where it was a favorite until 1970. In 1956, Ivar's Fifth Avenue opened downtown, evolving into the Captain's Table and moving to Elliott Avenue. In 1966, Haglund purchased Pier 54, the site of his first restaurant. A short time later, he opened Ivar's Salmon House at the north end of Lake Union. With its architecture and decor reflecting Coastal Salish culture, along with stunning Lake Union views, Ivar's Salmon House is a landmark for both Seattleites and visitors. Several quick-service restaurants featuring fish 'n' chip variations have also been added to the Ivar's group, including one at SeaTac airport where there is almost always a line.

With his string of six Duke's Chowder House restaurants, Duke Moscrip—who calls himself both a "food dude" and a "seafood sleuth"—began his food service career as an investor with pals who took over ownership of Ray's Boathouse in the 1970s. The lure of managing his own restaurant grew for the Seattle native, and in 1976 he opened the first Duke's as a Bar & Grill in the lower Queen Anne neighborhood. Ever astute and a trendsetter, Moscrip started serving wine varietals by the glass to guests, instead of the usual buy-a-bottle-to-drink sale requirement. He introduced his inherently practical—and income-generating—idea at the first Duke's, and it quickly became the standard for all restaurants. After winning the Seattle Chowder Cook-Off with his grandfather's recipe for three successive years in the 1980s, Duke's Bar & Grill changed its name to Duke's Chowder House. This change also heralded a renewed focus on seafood.

In fact, wild, sustainable Alaskan seafood is another passion point for Moscrip. He personally sources fish and shellfish for his restaurants, traveling far north to meet fishermen and develop premium fish processing standards. This effort ensures that Duke's executive chef, "Wild" Bill Ranniger, who supervises kitchen activities in all six restaurants, has top-quality seafood to prepare for diners' enjoyment. Moscrip earns credit as one of the first Seattle restaurateurs to feature Copper River salmon on Duke's menus. Sharing the business now with his son John Moscrip, the company also gives back to the community by supporting local charities and fish habitat rebuilding efforts. In 2019, the newest Duke's Chowder House will serve its sustainable seafood menu in a newly constructed building at Shilshole Marina showcasing unobstructed views of Puget Sound and the Olympics.

Jon Rowley (1943–2017) also stands tall on Seattle's seafood landscape as the instigator behind raising standards for fish served at Seattle's restaurants. Hailing from Astoria, Oregon, where his mom worked in a cannery, he arrived in Seattle in the 1960s, a decade he described in an interview as "a time when Canlis was serving oysters on the half shell and Emmett Watson's Oyster Bar was in full swing" in Pike Place Market. Aware of fish and fish processing, but a perfectionist when it came to food, Rowley had his own commercial fishing business for a time, supplying restaurants such as Ray's Boathouse with top-quality salmon. He also linked up with Bruce and Kathy Gore in Alaska, helping to perfect—and publicize to restaurants—the ideal method for flash-freezing wild-caught salmon within two hours of being caught to retain their flesh quality and flavor. A proselytizer for Copper River salmon beginning in the 1980s, Rowley is also credited with creating the buzz for its seasonal arrival each May. One bite and anyone will understand his obsession with this awesome fish.

Jon Rowley carrying a crate of peaches ready for Metropolitan Market's annual "Peach-O-Rama" sales event, starring the "sweetest, juiciest peaches around" as identified by his famous Brix refractometer test, a test he applied to peaches following the same Brix scale used for wine grapes but using the gadget to measure the percentage of sugar in the peach flesh. *Courtesy of Kai Raymond, photographer, and Jon Rowley's nephew.*

Equally passionate about oysters, Rowley studied their life cycle and processing steps in France. With his culinary knowledge and marketing smarts—he called himself "a professional dreamer"—he served as a longtime consultant for Taylor Shellfish at the south end of Puget Sound, the area's major shellfish producer, and he advised McCormick & Schmidt's about its oyster bar offerings, along with Wild Ginger Restaurant. He also managed the West Coast Oyster Wine competition for two decades. Other advisory engagements for Rowley included Metropolitan Markets and Frog Hollow Farms (peach growers in California). He was honored in 2007 with the first Angelo Pellegrini Award (named after the acclaimed UW professor who promoted eating locally) and received the Who's Who in America award from the James Beard Foundation.

Through their collective efforts in the realm of seafood—as well as other food areas—these individuals have enormously enriched Seattle's food universe.

THE 1970s—BOEING BUSTS WHILE RESTAURANTS BOOM

Seattle's food history can't be completely disconnected from social and business events happening in the region, or those occurring in the greater United States. The 1970s saw the Vietnam War spilling over into other parts of Southeast Asia, the launch of President Johnson's Great Society programs, an energy crisis affecting the giant rise in oil use over the past decade as Middle Eastern oil producers cut production to protest US support for Israel, and soaring consumer prices (up 12 percent in 1974 alone). Seattle was hugely affected by these events, as well as the cascading economic recession when Boeing's supersonic transport (SST) program funding was cut. As the major Puget Sound employer, layoffs at Boeing had a ripple-down effect and hard times overwhelmed the area. In 1971 a billboard with the satirical message "Will the last person leaving Seattle turn out the lights?" made headlines. It took fifteen years for the regional economy to recover. Ironically, while the *Seattle Times*'s Dorothy Neighbors department offered readers ideas for "cheap, starchy main dishes and chili made with buffalo" on the Women's Page, restaurants in this decade experienced a major boom. Perhaps this was because people needed an escape from doom and gloom and food was a delicious diversion?

Emmett Watson, the *Seattle Post-Intelligencer*'s restaurant columnist, in the foreword of Lott and Umbach's *Dining in Seattle: Past & Present*, describes Seattle's food scene in the 1970s as a "gastronomic explosion" and notes that it is now much more difficult to dine out than when he began his column in 1956:

> It is harder to make a choice of where to go . . . in those days there were none. Yellow page listings were a breeze in 1956; today your fingers get tired walking through twenty-three pages of listings.

A combination of factors no doubt influenced the restaurant community's and Seattleites' cravings for new food experiences. Without a doubt the observations of John Hinterberger, restaurant critic and columnist writing in Seattle's second daily newspaper, the *Seattle Times*, had a huge impact. When "Hint," as he was fondly known, described his latest eating adventure in the days before instant online social media reviews, a city-wide audience read every word—and listened too, as Hinterberger also spoke on air, both radio and (for a short while) TV. For twenty-five years, his quips and insights guided diners and influenced Seattle's dining boom.

Along with press reviews, increased European travel experiences for many residents, plus exposure to international cuisines at the 1962 World's Fair, all increased interest in ethnic dishes and flavors. The World's Fair also showcased the riches of local food choices, from seafood to ethnic flavors, making them even more desirable to visitors as well as local chefs and their clientele.

To enhance its Depression-era theme, the Bread Line & Soup Kitchen in Pioneer Square featured "1929 prices" and old-time posters, which made it stand out as the exception among the restaurants of this decade. Instead, most notable restaurants of the era featured international cuisines and classic dishes, while one new restaurant north of downtown Seattle anticipated the sustainable, local produce movement.

Riding the wave of popularity for French cuisine (Julia Child's TV shows about French cooking were a big hit in the 1970s), two restaurants with French themes were enormously popular in this decade. One was Rosellini's Other Place at 319 Union Street, opened in 1974 by Robert Rosellini (son of Seattle's premier restaurateur, Victor Rosellini). Its menu featured classic French dishes and was a refuge for downtown diners. The second popular French-focused restaurant, Brasserie Pittsbourg, opened in 1969, and it was owned and managed by Julia and Francoise Kissel. Chef Francoise Kissel, classically trained in France, converted a run-down soup kitchen, half-basement space in Pioneer Square, into an oasis of French cooking. Using fresh and dried herbs, spices, fragrant sauces, and serious cuts of meat such as leg of lamb, Chef Kissel established an enthusiastic following. He built on his Pioneer Square success by opening the City Loan Pavillion and Maximilien, both featuring traditional French dishes. Pavillion has since closed, but Maximilien remains a popular hide-away in Pike Place Market, continuing under new owners and remaining true to its original French roots.

To introduce flavors from Eastern Europe, Peter Cipra, an immigrant from Czechoslovakia, first opened the Prague, also in Pioneer Square. In the mid-1970s, Chef Cipra moved the restaurant to First Avenue near Pike Place Market and renamed it Labuznik (the Czech word for "gourmet"), where he was chef and owner until retiring in 1998. A total hands-on, old-school chef passionate about food, he made all his dishes from scratch, even down to the pastries and butchering.

Modern Asian food also made its debut in this decade when, in 1970, Maneki opened Seattle's first sushi bar. The star chef was Shiro Kashiba, direct from Tokyo. Kashiba's next stop in 1972 was his own sushi bar, Nikko, which moved to the Westin Hotel but closed there in 2003. Since then, he has established Shiro's Sushi Restaurant in Belltown.

With their traditional culinary focus and classically trained chefs, these restaurants from the 1970s set the stage for the next decade, when chefs exploded in new directions.

THE 1980s—MODERN CUISINE ARRIVES

Describing Seattle in the 1980s would mean describing a city and its residents betwixt and between. The economy was recovering from the Boeing downturn, and change was in the air, wafted by tech start-ups and the grunge music scene, indelibly identified with the Pacific Northwest. Seattle-based companies such as Nordstrom, Costco, Starbucks, and REI (Recreational Equipment, Inc.) were all expanding. Chinatown was turning into Little Saigon as the Vietnamese boat people arrived in the early 1980s, along with Hmong, Mien, and Khmer refugees. Other immigrants also arrived during this decade from East Africa, Central America, Myanmar, and parts of the Soviet Union, all impacting local culture and cuisine. Most significant, but not yet recognized, was the contract Bill Gates and Paul Allen had signed to create an operating system for IBM working from their software company's headquarters in Bellevue. In 1986, Microsoft went public.

On the restaurant scene, modern dining appeared, more sophisticated than home-style cafés and overlapping white-tablecloth restaurants of the 1960s and 1970s, but modern in the sense of finessed food presentations and chefs pushing the ground rules. Food became about more than nourishment or culinary traditions and now often reflected a chef's egocentric and creative personality. Add the impact of Alice Waters in California promoting seasonal and local, and Seattle's restaurant scene had another source of validation to celebrate its indigenous foods. When top food press, publishers, cookbook authors, and culinary stars such as Julia Child, Anne Willan, and Marion Cunningham came to Seattle in 1985 to attend the annual conference of the International Association of Culinary Professionals (IACP), the city quickly earned national attention for its thriving food scene.

With respect to international cuisines, France and Italy remained popular, with restaurants such as Le Tastevin in the lower Queen Anne neighborhood, Campagne at Pike Place Market across from the Inn at the Market, and Settebello leading the pack. Le Tastevin was housed in a mid-century modern building designed by Roland Terry, the architect who designed Canlis restaurant, and gained attention for its upscale "truffle-studded, wine-centric dinners," as described by Ronald Holden in his January 29, 2015, article in *Eater Seattle*, titled with the same words. Campagne welcomed diners through a serene courtyard a half block from the Market and delighted them with classic French dishes and wines. And while Capitol Hill's Settebello is gone, its chef, Luciano Bardinelli, raised the standard for Italian cuisine with his sophisticated dishes, as well as training future chefs such as Raffaele Calise (Salute) and Scott Carsberg (Lampreia).

Similar to the influence Seattle's early hotels had on residents' dining decisions, contemporary hotels in the 1980s were noted for their star chefs and sophisticated menus. Chef Kathy Casey started her career as a wunderkind chef at Fullers Restaurant in the Sheraton Seattle Hotel, breaking smoothly into a male-dominated profession. In 1985, *Food & Wine Magazine* recognized her as one of America's Hot New Chefs. She has since moved on to run her own food consulting business, specializing in cocktail trends. Along with Chef Casey, Fullers stood out as a venue promoting a succession of superstar women chefs, including Caprial Pence and Monique Barbeau, who also achieved star status and helped earn acclaim for Pacific Northwest cuisine.

Seasonal, farm-fresh, foraged, and regional cuisine also found their first acolytes in 1980s Seattle with chefs Bruce and Sara Naftaly. Considered pioneers of the farm-to-table movement (in a time when "imported" had more appeal), as well as being in sync with traditional French cooking, they opened Le Gourmand in 1985 in the Ballard neighborhood. Their focus was certainly a legacy of Chef Naftaly's apprenticeship to Chef Dominique Place at Robert Rosellini's Other Place, and his own stint there as head chef from 1977 to 1979. Right next door to their restaurant was their Parisien-style cocktail bar, Sambar. Intimate and welcoming while being high-end, Le Gourmand earned consistent applause for its impressive and innovative menus.

Although Le Gourmand closed in 2012, the Naftalys have kept their restaurant world connections. As they say on their website, www.marmiteseattle.com, "Cooking is like breathing; besides being necessary and life sustaining, it's the right thing to do." No surprise, then, that in 2016 Sara Naftaly opened Amandine Bakeshop in Capitol Hill's Chophouse Row building. Together they opened Marmite next door, naming the restaurant after the classy French baking dish. More casual than Le Gourmand, the space includes a cocktail bar called "Spirit in the Bottle" tucked into the back of the dining area.

Seasonal and local ingredients also define the Herbfarm's philosophy since its founding in 1986, spoken in shorthand as "sustainable." About an hour east of Seattle, the farm-to-table restaurant—the area's first—has played a significant role in helping to define Seattle's culinary standards and expectations, both at the chef-owner level and among guests. Co-owners Ron Zimmerman and his wife Carrie Van Dyke were and are the guiding force and inspiration behind the set

menus featuring seasonal themes, which can highlight heritage fruits and vegetables, wild mushrooms, locally produced cheeses, and more, with enlightened
wine pairings.

Originally housed in a building on a corner of Ron's parents' farm in Fall City,
tucked into the Snoqualmie River Valley, the Herbfarm's beginnings were 1980s
casual. In 1990, Chef Jerry Traunfeld, who had been executive chef at Seattle's
Alexis Hotel restaurant and trained with Jeremiah Tower in San Francisco, joined
as executive chef. He was with the Herbfarm until 2007, a duration when he proved
his superstar skills. After a fire forced a move in 1997, the Herbfarm reopened in
2001 in Woodinville, closer to its five-acre farm and kitchen garden, and advanced
into a special occasion, elegant dining experience. Today the restaurant features
themed, nine-course feasts that change every three weeks and are presented as
pageantry. Each successive course is paired with a companion wine selected from
a lavish wine cellar holding more than twenty-five thousand bottles. With the culinary aplomb of Chef Chris Weber, who moved into the top spot in 2007, guests
are guaranteed that their palates will be awakened and enchanted.

THE 1990s TO 2000s—PACIFIC NORTHWEST
CUISINE COMES OF AGE

As the decade when technology companies blossomed—Microsoft was the solo
tech power in Seattle until the late 1990s—the dining landscape grew more confi-
dent about celebrating Pacific Northwest cuisine with all its traditional ingredients,
plus the infusion of ethnic flavors. At the same time, a new generation of chefs
jumped on stage and grabbed the spotlight. Some had been here for some time,
working in restaurants belonging to others, but then grabbed their knife sets and
established their own spots. Others arrived, attracted by Seattle's culinary diversity
and the chance to find their own place in a welcoming city. While each decade has
its own discussion of who is the "founder" of Seattle's version of Pacific Northwest
cuisine, several standouts are always mentioned for their significant contributions
from the 1990s into the 2000s.

The nominations are notable for Seattle's interpretation of Pacific Northwest
cuisine because everyone is exceptional. Top names stretch from Scott Carsberg
and Bruce Naftaly to Tom Douglas, Jerry Traunfeld, Greg Atkinson, Renee Erickson, Kathy Casey, Maria Hines, Christine Keff, Matt Dillon, Ethan Stowell, John
Sundstrom, and several more. All things considered for dining out adventures, the
diversity and range of these stellar chefs make Seattle a food city like few others.
The fact that several chefs own and manage more than one restaurant in town—
some as many as seven or eight—also makes them stand out.

At the start of the modern era, Scott Carsberg, with his wife, Hyun Joo Paek, cooked and graciously hosted guests at Lampreia—an elegant, fine-dining Belltown restaurant on the corner of First Avenue and Battery Street—which they opened in 1992. The classically trained Carsberg prepared a changing menu of Northern Italian dishes using seasonal Pacific Northwest ingredients, receiving consistent accolades. Restaurant critic for the *Seattle Times* Nancy Leson called Lampreia "my castle of gastronomy, my stairway to heaven, my special-occasion treat and my answer to Seattle's four-star-restaurant question," in her article titled "Leson's List: Our Critic Picks Her Personal Best." Carsberg's beautifully presented plates created memorable dining moments for many guests. When Carsberg and his wife decided to switch from formal dining to a more relaxed format, they opened Bisato in 2010. In 2012, Carsberg decided to move on from the day-to-day cooking business and closed Bisato.

When one chef leaves the public stage, it doesn't take long for another to arrive. Few conversations about who's who in Seattle's restaurant world miss mentioning Tom Douglas. Born and raised in Maryland, Chef Douglas arrived in Seattle and started working in 1984 at Café Sport, a Seattle icon noted for its fine-dining menu and setting. At Café Sport, however, Chef Douglas changed the rules—for example, serving burgers on homemade rolls with house-made red onion jam.

In 1989, Douglas opened his first solo, full-service restaurant, Dahlia Lounge, downtown on Fourth Avenue, its signage a colorful neon fish flipping a lively tail. With its focus on Northwest ingredients from wild salmon, shrimp, and halibut to seasonal fruits and produce, Dahlia was an immediate hit and a "must-go" restaurant. What also set Dahlia Lounge apart was Douglas's style of adding Asian flavors to Northwest ingredients, along with his openness to training and elevating his chefs. Many moved on to open their own places, which enormously improved the overall quality of Seattle's dining landscape.

Since Dahlia Lounge, Douglas's restaurant list has grown, with each new restaurant revolving around a different concept. He's also collected numerous accolades. In 1994, he was awarded Best Northwest Chef by the James Beard Foundation. The decade was a busy one because he and his wife Jackie opened Etta's Seafood Restaurant in 1995, naming it after their daughter, and followed it with the Palace Kitchen in 1996, which was nominated for a James Beard Award in the same year for Best New Restaurant in the United States.

Not one to stand still, in the 2000s, Douglas went on a roll with restaurant openings. From downtown openings—Serious Pie, Lola, Dahlia Bakery, Carlile Room—his group restaurant company also moved into the South Lake Union neighborhood, opening Brave Horse Tavern, Serious Pie and Biscuits, and Tanaka-San. Along with his multiple restaurants, Tom Douglas Company launched a "Rub with Love" line of dry spice rubs for salmon and other seafood, meats, and poultry. Douglas also published four cookbooks during this decade.

Ethan Stowell, a Seattle native with parents who were artistic directors of the Pacific Northwest Ballet Company (1977 to 2005), with his wife and business partner Angela Dunleavy Stowell, opened his first restaurant, Union, in 2003, appropriately named for its street location in downtown Seattle. Although the timing was bad for Union, forcing its closure when the economy tanked in 2008, Stowell has gone on to open six more restaurants in all neighborhoods around town. The current list includes Tavolàta, How to Cook a Wolf, Anchovies and Olives, Staples and Fancy, Ballard Pizza Company, and Rione XIII.

Stowell was also the instigator behind updating—upgrading, in the eyes of many—the food offerings at the Pen in Safeco Field Ballpark, home of the Seattle Mariners. From hamburgers and crêpes to chicken wings and "Dirty Tater Tots" (tater tots topped with roasted pork belly, Beecher's cheese, and pickled peppers), his changing offerings mean food is now something to look forward to at a Mariners home game.

The chefs that follow might perhaps be considered runners-up for the title of most influential in defining Seattle cuisine; that's hardly a demotion since almost every chef in the city follows his or her own true path—or paths—in the kitchen. The result is an eclectic, exciting mix of dining options. Without exception, these chefs also all have a hand in making Seattle's food scene as vibrant as it is today.

Among those deserving—and earning—applause is another award winner, Chef John Sundstrom, who created a stir in 2003 with marvelous mix-and-match small plates at Lark when he opened his cozy restaurant on Twelfth Avenue East on Capitol Hill. Chef Sundstrom worked alongside Tom Douglas and opened the former Earth & Ocean Restaurant at W Hotel. His cooking is notable for imaginative combinations that often fuse Northwest ingredients with inventive seasonings. Lark moved to larger surroundings in late 2014 and became a full-service establishment, converting the original spot into a new pizzeria called Southpaw.

Greg Atkinson must also be included on the roster. A talented, thoughtful writer as well as an inspired chef, Atkinson first made his name at Canlis as executive chef from 1997 to 2002. A master of technique, with a fierce interest and training in French culinary techniques, his first cooking stint was in Friday Harbor in the San Juan Islands before moving to Seattle. Atkinson left Canlis to run the food and beverage division of IslandWood, an outdoor learning center on Bainbridge Island, and then taught at Seattle Central Community College. In 2012, he opened his own restaurant on Bainbridge Island named Restaurant Marché, a cozy setting serving dishes honoring Northwest ingredients and prepared with his undisputable skill.

Along with Atkinson, the French culinary thread connects several top Seattle chefs. Notable is Chef Bruce Naftaly, who, as described earlier, earned his stellar reputation at his restaurant Le Gourmand. In fact, he was called "the father of Northwest cuisine" in the 1980s and is giving it a new twist at Marmite, the restaurant he opened with his wife Sara on Capitol Hill. The French connection is also the reason Le Pitchet, an idyllic transplanted French bistro on First Avenue near Pike Place Market, has held its magic since 2000 under owners and managers Jim Drohman and Joanne Herron. The link is also there for Chef Thierry Rautureau, who arrived with six years of classical French culinary training and has the link, more intensely perhaps, because of being a French native.

Chef Rautureau, who is known by the name "The Chef in the Hat" due to his natty identifying fedora, arrived in Seattle and, from 1987 to 2013, was the magician managing the kitchen and menu creations at the elegant Rover's Restaurant in Madison Park. Another James Beard Award–winning chef for the Pacific Northwest, Rautureau opened Luc in 2010 in Madison Valley, a casual French American bar and café serving seasonal, sustainable food. In 2013, he opened Loulay Kitchen & Bar, adjoining the downtown Sheraton Hotel, where down-to-earth French cuisine shares the menu with favorites from the Pacific Northwest—wild salmon, seared albacore tuna, plus juicy burgers.

While Chef Jerry Traunfeld first achieved fame and glory at the Herbfarm showcasing local Northwest ingredients, he has since opened two of his own restaurants on Capitol Hill—Poppy (2008) and Lionhead (2015)—setting a new stage for himself with a new focus on Asian cuisine. At Poppy, Traunfeld serves an Indian "thali" menu of spiced and seasoned small dishes served Indian-style on one tray, while at Lionhead, he interprets traditional Szechuan ingredients, seasonings, and dishes with their anticipated temperature and chili-instigated spicy heat. A clue to his success: Lionhead's forty-seven seats are rarely empty.

A Pacific Northwest native, Chef Matt Dillon is another enthusiastic, award-winning chef and restaurateur. He is also a forager and farmer on five acres on Vashon Island. Pursuing his career after completing culinary school, he worked under Jerry Traunfeld at the Herbfarm. His dining sites include Sitka & Spruce, two Bar Ferd'nands (both on Capitol Hill), the Corson Building (Georgetown), Ciudad (Georgetown), plus the London Plane and the Little London Plane (both in Pioneer Square). Each spot showcases his passion for Northwest ingredients in creative, novel ways.

A celebration of chefs on Seattle's modern restaurant scene would be shortsighted if it didn't acknowledge the numerous women chefs who have been and are successful here. The number may be due to the Seattle restaurant world's welcoming climate, a historic spirit of camaraderie without boundaries and with support. In Seattle's atypical egalitarian culinary environment, all chefs are generally considered peers given their experience and culinary creativity, unlike the traditional hierarchical restaurant world. Several standouts in this group—Kathy Casey, Christine Keff, Caprial Pence, and Monique Barbeau—have been mentioned for their individual contributions; other stars include Reneé Erickson, Rachel Yang, and Maria Hines. All have played sizable roles enriching Seattle's dining experience with their adventurous visions of food.

Reflecting Seattle's appetite for international cuisines, especially the Asian fusion genre, anyone hungry for a taste of Korean barbecue or spicy noodles knows to head for Chef Rachel Yang's innovative restaurants: Joule and Revel in Fremont, and Trove on Capitol Hill. (The fourth restaurant, Revelry, is in Portland, also owned and operated by the Relay Restaurant Group, the company owned by Chef Yang and her husband.)

Chef Yang and her equally talented chef husband, Seif Chirchi, opened their first restaurant, Joule, in 2007, earning mega amounts of applause. Intrigued by nontraditional cuts of beef, they reimagined Joule's menu in 2013 and re-created the restaurant as a contemporary Korean steakhouse. It's also a delicious destination for enjoying a themed brunch buffet and winemakers' dinners. In 2010, the couple opened Revel, also in Fremont. Both Capitol Hill restaurants in their group have proven hugely popular, with Trove providing tabletop grills for cooking meats Korean-style.

Also inventive and another award-winning chef is Maria Hines. Her first claim to fame is as one of Seattle's most sustainably minded chefs, a pioneer in the movement to use locally sourced certified organic ingredients. When Tilth opened in 2006, tucked into a small Craftsman-style frame house in the Wallingford neighborhood, its seasonal, organic menu earned praise, which hasn't diminished at all over time. Chef Hines has since opened a Sicilian-style Italian restaurant named Agrodolce in Fremont. She went mainstream in late 2016 and opened Young American Ale House in Ballard. Conceived as a neighborhood pub, the casual restaurant offers soup, salads, and sandwiches along with pizzas at dinnertime.

From seafood to steak, Chef Renee Erickson has earned awards, numerous Hot 10 listings, and a faithful following with her inventive restaurant endeavors and Northwest- and French-focused dishes. Since launching solo at the Boat Street Café & Kitchen (2001–2015), her restaurant fleet has expanded to six nautically themed spots serving mainly maritime fare—the Walrus & the Carpenter in Ballard, the Whale Wins in Fremont, Barnacle Bar in Ballard, Bar Melusine on Capitol Hill, and General Porpoise, a take-away coffee and yeast doughnut emporium—plus Bateau, a steakhouse on Capitol Hill. It's appropriate her company is named Eat Sea Creatures. From seafood fare to "grandma-style" dishes and an aperitif bar featuring Italian-themed drinks, Chef Erickson is a culinary innovator.

The press effect was also significant in this dining era. Keeping tabs on all things culinary, the *Seattle Times* restaurant critic Nancy Leson added luster to many chefs' reputations with her comprehensive and entertaining reviews over a fifteen-year span. Award-winning food writer Rebekah Denn, with the *Seattle Post-Intelligencer*, also praised new restaurants and tracked happenings on the culinary landscape. (Denn now writes for the *Seattle Times* covering a range of food-related topics, while Providence Cicero reviews dining experiences throughout King County.) With everything stirred together, Seattle's recent dining decades have been indisputably delicious.

THE FUSS ABOUT FUSION

One additional factor defining Seattle restaurants that cannot be overstated is the impact of ethnic food—the ingredients, the recipes, and the techniques. How various immigrant cuisines and flavors have been woven into local dishes is only part of the story. The evolution of "Pan Asian" or fusion cooking also evolved here, sometimes with Asian ingredients linked to Pacific Northwest ingredients, and sometimes simply through creative combinations invented by a chef, with or without actual Asian ingredients and using contemporary cooking techniques. Think of "Cajun chicken sushi sliders or wasabi mac 'n' cheese," suggests Angela Garbes in her April 1, 2015, article for *The Stranger*. The aim in either case was to expand palates. As Garbes continues, "Chefs aren't 'fusing' anything, they're just being themselves."

However, back in 1981 when "fusion" was new and didn't require analysis, Annie Agostini and Robert Eickhof opened their restaurant, Annie et Robert, a small, elegant bistro. By combining Japanese and French techniques, ingredients, and presentation, it was one of the first to present "nouvelle cuisine" to Pacific Northwest diners.

Wild Ginger, opened by Americans Rick and Ann Yoder in 1989 after their trip through Southeast Asia, is often considered Seattle's first modern, fine-dining "fusion" restaurant. Rather than the norm of inexpensive traditional ethnic dishes, the Yoders served what they considered new, exciting flavors in satays and curries. Presenting these flavors in a Western setting made the experience of eating them more approachable to a curious audience. The Wild Ginger menu roamed across the cuisines of Southeast Asia, presenting various dishes such as seafood Thai noodles, a signature Sichuan duck dish, and a Vietnamese-style squash and sweet potato stew, along with a version of bouillabaisse using typical Malaysian ingredients such as coconut milk, garlic, and lemongrass in the seafood stew. In 2000, Wild Ginger expanded its audience by moving from its original location on Western Avenue below Pike Place Market to Fourth Avenue, a block from Benaroya Hall. In 2013, Wild Ginger opened a second location on the Eastside, first in Bellevue's Bravern Mall, and then, in 2017, at Bellevue's Lincoln Square.

As noted earlier, wife-and-husband chefs Rachel Yang and Seif Chirchi are also inventive participants in their own style of fusion cuisine, initiated in 2007 when they opened their first restaurant, Joule.

By giving Asian fusion cuisine a secondary role in their kitchen, Eric and Sophie Banh, brother and sister from Vietnam, stayed true to their ethnic cuisine instead of focusing on fusion adaptations. They first earned attention for traditional Vietnamese recipes at their sleek and sophisticated Monsoon restaurant on Capitol Hill (and later in Bellevue). Ba Bar at South Lake Union and at U-Village Shopping Center also uses Pacific Northwest ingredients for its Vietnamese street food menu. The siblings' most recent opening, Seven Beef Steak Shop in the Central District, features various cuts of Northwest beef along with a traditional *bò 7 món* tasting menu, meaning "seven courses of beef" in Vietnamese. By choosing mainstream locations instead of staying within Little Saigon, the couple exposed a wider audience to Vietnamese and fusion dishes.

The concept of "fusion" is not only for high-end dining. The menu at Marination Station, which started as a food truck in 1990 and by 2017 had four restaurants throughout the city, embodies the culinary globalization trend with dishes such as miso ginger chicken tacos, kimchi quesadillas, salt-cured salmon poke with serrano chilies and cilantro, and fried oysters with a *shiso* and kimchi tartar sauce.

Overall, eager diners flock to these places to engage their palates with new taste adventures. It's an innovative and successful blending of cuisines that keeps Seattle on the restaurant map.

FOOD TRUCKS ROLL IN

A sideline to Seattle's restaurant scene, the modern food truck phenomenon is thriving in the city. While some smile at this recent trend, recalling Uwajimaya's food trucks being first on the scene in the 1920s by delivering homemade fish cakes to Japanese loggers working around Tacoma—the first business enterprise of the Asian grocery's founder—Seattle's food truck culture took a while to emerge due to the city's health department street food regulations. Despite the slow start, especially when compared with Portland's impressive food truck wheel count from the early 2000s onward, Seattle's fast-moving posse of trucks, enough to form roundups at various sites around town at lunchtime, at neighborhood food fests, and at farmers' markets, has only evolved in the past six years. It happened after the city council passed a law in July 2011 allowing mobile food vending on city streets. Allison Int-hout interviewed food truck vendors for her article "A Year after New City Law, Seattle Food-Truck Industry Gaining Speed" (August 24, 2012, *Puget Sound Business Journal*) and estimated that eighty new food trucks rolled onto the streets the first year after the law changed.

Along with the city's legal changes, it's possible the Great Recession in 2008 jump-started food truck entrepreneurs in Seattle, a reasonable conclusion when the cost of outfitting a truck is weighed against the cost of opening a brick-and-mortar restaurant. Add expanding tastes for ethnic foods, plus Seattle's sizable population of foreign-born residents, and multiple factors have prompted the surge of food trucks. Christopher Werner calls it "curb cuisine" and described the motivation for food trucks in his article "Food Trucks 2012: The Wheel Reinvented" (April 30, 2012, *SeattleMet*): "The city's appetite for culinary adventure paved the way for a rolling revolution."

Painted in various colors and patterns with food items ranging from ethnic specialties to tried-and-true burgers, food trucks now appear every day throughout Seattle. A string of trucks will line sidewalks in the South Lake Union neighborhood around Amazon's headquarters, at Westlake Park in the downtown core, and at neighborhood farmers' markets such as the Fremont Sunday Market. Fragrances of food are guaranteed to attract hungry humans to these mobile lunch spots offering both familiar all-American and ethnic dishes according to the interests of each truck's cooks.

Add the efforts of the Mobile Food Rodeo, a local group that initiated truck pods at the year-round Fremont Sunday Market, at seasonal markets at Magnusson Park, and at the Saturday Market at South Lake Union, plus various street food and neighborhood fairs. The presence of food trucks in these places solidified their status as appealing food resources. In fact, at the Fifth Annual Seattle Street Food Festival in July 2017, more than 150 food trucks registered to join the event in South Lake Union, touted as Seattle's largest summer curbside gathering.

Standouts among Seattle's food truck community include several that were pioneers in the food truck evolution. Among them, Skillet's roaming food truck, a favorite in the SoDo neighborhood, earned early attention. Its founder, Chef Josh Henderson, seized the opportunity in 2007 when he saw the food trend emerging. As it happens, Skillet's silver food trucks helped launch its brick-and-mortar restaurant sites by determining the most popular dishes for sit-down menus. Marination also followed the food truck path before establishing its land sites. Many food truck operators see food trucks as a low-cost way to become involved in the food world with a miniature restaurant on wheels, movable to high-traffic areas where the crowds are, from clusters in Westlake Park at lunchtime to pods at neighborhood street festivals. The sophisticated offerings have traveled delicious light years from the days when gritty food trucks were dubbed "roach coaches."

Seattle's themed food trucks offer a universe of grab-and-go fast-food dishes. A quick list includes Asian noodles, Thai and New Orleans favorites, classic fish-and-chips, doughnuts, mac 'n' cheese to go, hot dogs, Middle Eastern specialties, tacos, curries, falafel, Northwest-style barbecue, ice cream and dessert, and burgers cooked to order, of course.

There are the big names on the food truck scene, ranging from Snout & Co., Cheese Wizards, and Sam Choy's Poke to the Max, Off the Rez for Native American specialties, and many more. One of the most original is the huge mobile silver piggy of Maximus Minimus, complete with a curly metal tail, where hungry folks can order pulled pork or veggie sandwiches with or without a topping of Beecher's Flagship cheese.

In 2011, a website and app named SeattleFoodTruck.com started keeping track of who's on the road and where. Some trucks stake out a consistent location, while others travel to different spots. The enjoyment for many lunchtime diners is discovering who is parked and dishing up in their front yard.

FARESTART—SEATTLE'S NATIONALLY ACCLAIMED FOOD SERVICE TRAINING PROGRAM

A recap of Seattle's restaurant history wouldn't be complete without ending on a humanitarian note and mentioning FareStart. Founded in 1987 by Chef David Lee as Common Meals, this nonprofit was originally established to serve meals at Seattle's homeless shelters, schools, and day-care centers. In a few years, it became apparent that teaching disadvantaged persons who relied on these services the skills to help them find food service employment would be a win on both sides. FareStart now provides life skills learning with a focus on front- and back-of-the-house food service training from resident chef Wayne Johnson. The restaurant, a few steps away from Seattle's downtown core, serves lunch daily and also showcases guest chefs who prepare and serve Thursday night fundraising dinners with student participation. Since the program started in 1992, more than 8,000 adults and youths have graduated from FareStart's programs, according to a February 16, 2017, article in the *Seattle Times*, achieving a 90 percent employment rate, according to the organization's website, www.farestart.org. With a FareStart diploma, almost all graduates who have faced past barriers to employment—from drug addiction to homelessness—have opportunities to find stable work situations. Many have been able to find a permanent solution to their work challenges in the high-demand restaurant and hospitality industry.

A measure of the program's success and a response to demand, FareStart started the Catalyst Kitchens network to expand its concept across the country and around the world. Now with sixty-five members, the alliance is a resource for communities seeking to establish FareStart-style food service training programs to help the homeless and those struggling in their own communities.

The FareStart story is also expanding in Seattle. As another measure of FareStart's success, Seattle's online powerhouse Amazon.com is donating space and equipment, plus funding an apprenticeship program, enabling the nonprofit to open five new restaurants in the South Lake Union neighborhood. This expansion will also allow FareStart to double the number of students in its training program.

Moving from specifics to a conclusion, exploring the diversity and dimensions of Seattle's restaurant universe over the decades since the city's founding in 1852 reaffirms the connections between the Pacific Northwest's bountiful natural resources, adventurers, immigrants, chefs, restaurateurs, and residents. For everyone in each time period, food cooked, served, and shared in a restaurant or café setting was not incidental or taken for granted. Instead, it was—and is—a form of expression, a celebration of the region's abundant indigenous resources, and of community. Of course, restaurants are also outlets for culinary and entrepreneurial passions. Underlying every food-related enterprise in Seattle is an adventurous, progressive spirit.

As William Speidel pointed out in 1955 in the introduction for *You Can't Eat Mount Rainier!*, mid-century Seattleites suffered from a needless inferiority complex about their city's restaurants. What they didn't realize, Speidel noted, is that "national restaurant experts rate Seattle up in the top 10 best restaurant cities," and "our restaurant industry—for the most part—is young, robust, progressive, competitive." It's an observation he could still make today, along with being thrilled by the diversity and accessibility of restaurants here. From all perspectives, it's a treasured ethos certain to remain the foundation of Seattle's thriving restaurant world.

8

❖ ❖

Raise a Glass!

A Toast to Seattle's Bounty of Beverages

Driving north or south on Interstate 5, the large, curvaceous, red neon "R" atop an industrial building looming beside the freeway is hard to miss. It's a Seattle landmark, one with a legacy on the city's brewing landscape. Translated, the "R" is the symbol for Rainier Beer, the most popular beer brewed in town in the last century, and it stands over the building that was once home to the Rainier Brewing Company. A symbol of Seattle's flourishing entrepreneurial breweries of the past, the "R"—first installed in 1954, removed, and then replaced in 2013—also signals today's craft brewery renaissance.

Along with libations from breweries, in a city where an enormous amount of liquid falls from the sky and also surrounds human habitat, substances for drinking come in many forms. Beer may be foremost, and certainly was in Seattle's early days, but wine, coffee, and distilled beverages such as whiskey, aquavit, hard cider, and bourbon also fill glasses. Investigating Seattle's liquid history reveals how social and political issues stirred into Washington State's Prohibition and Prohibition-repeal experiences emptied and filled the city's glasses during the past two centuries. While alcohol was often a source of pleasure, controlling access to it was also contentious and instigated change.

"Spruce beer" was most likely the first beer in the Pacific Northwest. Records indicate Captain George Vancouver brewed spruce beer, made from a boiled and fermented mixture of the green tips of spruce trees, hops, ginger, and molasses, as a tonic to prevent scurvy among his sailors in 1792 while sailing around Vancouver Island. The mixture was reputed to be a healthful drink throughout the 1800s.

When British fur trappers and traders first arrived in the greater Puget Sound area, alcohol was introduced as a type of currency. Mostly in the form of rum, it was traded with Native Americans for valuable fur pelts—with disastrous results for natives unused to alcohol's intoxicating effects. Aware of the negative cultural side effects, the Hudson's Bay Company, which dominated fur trade commerce and served as the de facto government in the region during the decades before 1849 (the year when the Oregon Territory and international boundary were established), eventually withdrew alcohol as a payment method. However, American ship merchants and traders continued to provide alcohol as a gift to Native Americans, which made enforcing this directive and practicing abstinence nearly impossible. Additionally, saloons were still licensed and numerous, offering an accessible source of alcohol for sailors and Native Americans alike.

Although the Denny Party consisted of teetotalers when it landed in 1851 at Alki Point, Henry Yesler followed a different path when he arrived in Seattle in 1852. As more settlers, including many immigrants hailing from beer-drinking cultures, arrived in the Seattle area and the logging and fishing industries expanded with myriad thirsty workers, everyday alcohol consumption became commonplace. It was also a reliable source of liquid when clean water wasn't always available for drinking. Steilacoom, south of Tacoma on Puget Sound, earned its place in history in 1858 as the site of the first brewery in Washington Territory. Started by German-born Martin Schmieg, the Steilacoom brewery used imported raw materials (hops from New York State, malt and yeast from Oregon) and then transported the finished brews in barrels to Seattle.

The cultivation of hops plants (*Humulus lupulus*) was another "first" for early settlers, and it supported beer endeavors in Steilacoom and eventually throughout the Pacific Northwest. In 1852, Jacob R. Meeker, a pioneer from Ohio who came to the region by way of the Oregon Trail, stopped briefly with his family in Portland, and then moved to the Puget Sound region. Settling in the Puyallup Valley in 1865, he planted the first hop rootstock grown in Washington State. As noted by Michael F. Rizzo in his detailed history titled *Washington Beer*, following Meeker's death in 1869, his son Ezra took over the family hop farm and, in subsequent decades, expanded the farm's hop-growing land to five hundred acres. At its peak, the farm produced four hundred tons of hops annually. Hops harvesting in this early period was undertaken by hand, primarily carried out by Native Americans. Prized for flavor, aroma, and quality, Meeker's hops were used by brewers in both Portland and Seattle. This small beginning turned out to be a prelude to the lucrative hops farming industry that spread to the Yakima Valley region of eastern Washington. By 1900, Washington State reigned as the largest hops producer in the country (a rank still held today).

A group photo of hops pickers in the early 1900s, near Auburn, Washington, which includes children, Asian immigrants, and Native Americans. *Courtesy of MOHAI, [Seattle Historical Society Collection], [shs6026].*

In 1863, five years after the Steilacoom brewery's founding, Seattle's first home-grown commercial brewery started operations. Built by entrepreneur and saloon owner (who also held various civic positions) Antonio B. Rabbeson, and named Washington Brewery, the facility provided residents with porter, beer, and ale. Although Rabbeson sold his brewery a year later, he is credited with successfully launching the city's brewing tradition for future brew masters and businessmen. In Steilacoom, Martin Schmieg and Joseph Butterfield, his business partner, witnessing Seattle's rapid growth, expanded their operations northward in 1865 and launched the North Pacific Brewery. Housed in a tidy, two-story, white clapboard building on First Avenue at Columbia Street—the Pioneer Square neighborhood—the brewery turned out barrels of porter, ale, and lager beer.

Other "big picture" factors influenced the development of Seattle's early brewing industry. The completion of the Northern Pacific and Great Northern transcontinental railroads, the Yukon Gold Rush, and later, mining in Utah with many transient workers passing through town, all increased the local ready-and-able-to-drink population. Add in refrigerated rail cars, plus the invention of the "crown" bottle cap (easily removable with a bottle key) in the late 1880s; both enabled shipping barrels of beer to towns and cities beyond a brewing location. In no time, brewing beer looked like a lucrative local business model. It didn't take long for Seattle's pioneer businessmen to recognize this and capitalize on the opportunity.

Chapter 8

SEATTLE'S EARLY BREWERIES
AND THE HEMRICH FAMILY LEGACY

Seattle's early brewing history takes many convoluted twists and turns with many players and financiers. Companies merge, consolidate, and reorganize, founding owners sell (or disappear, as Martin Schmieg did on a return trip to Germany in the 1870s), and brewery names change, sometimes overlap, and then change again. Unraveling the history takes perseverance—and a cold craft brew in hand doesn't hurt. To begin, several early breweries like the North Pacific opened in buildings along the Duwamish tidal flats (land later filled in to become today's SoDo neighborhood), while others started production near Pioneer Square and then moved to South Lake Union. The Great Seattle Fire in 1889 in the Pioneer Square business area compelled many breweries to relocate to other parts of the city.

Backstepping to 1886, a few years before the Great Seattle Fire, there were four noteworthy breweries operating: North Pacific, Seattle Brewery, Bay View Brewery, and the Puget Sound Brewery. Along with Martin Schmieg and his manager August Mehlhorn, who took over at North Pacific Brewery, one of the first brewmasters was Andrew Slorah, who ran what was initially called the Slorah Brewery. Renamed the Seattle Brewery, and one of the first in town to bottle its brew, it was acquired in 1897 by Alvin Hemrich, who came from a German American family of brewers in Wisconsin.

As it happened, Alvin helped establish the legacy of the Hemrich family in Seattle's brewing history. In his first business deal, he was following in the footsteps of his older brother Andrew, who had arrived in Seattle in 1883 after managing breweries in Wisconsin, Montana, and Vancouver. That year, partnering with John Kopp, Andrew had launched a small steam beer company, the Kopp & Hemrich Company, in the Beacon Hill neighborhood, taking advantage of a freshwater spring located there. Hugely successful, the Kopp & Hemrich Company started out with a "steam beer" product and later added a lager-style beer. In its first year of operation, the young brewery produced more than 2,600 barrels of beer.

In 1884, 1885, and 1890, three new breweries opened in Seattle environs, setting the stage for the next brewing episode. Edward F. Sweeney and William J. Rule founded the first in 1884 in Georgetown, a working neighborhood just south of Seattle's city limits. (Georgetown became part of Seattle in 1910.) Sweeney soon took over the business and, in 1889, turned it into the Claussen-Sweeney Brewing Company. The new name included Hans J. Claussen who served as the company's secretary-treasurer. The brewery, based in the Interbay neighborhood, became so successful it produced upward of twenty-five thousand gallons of beer annually, shipping barrels to Alaska, Russia, and even the Philippines. In the interim, the Bay View Brewery opened in 1885 with operating officers including John Hemrich, father of the Hemrich brothers, and his son Andrew Hemrich. A few years later, in 1890, Albert Braun founded the Albert Braun Brewing Association, establishing his new brewery on the southern edge of the city.

THE FIRST REIGN OF RAINIER

The year 1893 turned out to be a milestone in Seattle beer history. Formed that year through a merger of the Clause-Sweeney, Hemrich, and Braun breweries, the Seattle Brewing & Malting Company launched a new era of Seattle beer making. The new company included savvy management officials from all three original companies under Andrew Hemrich as president. Records indicate the new company was capitalized with $1 million and, with its three combined facilities, could produce 150,000 barrels annually. The first beer kegged by the Seattle Brewing & Malting Company was named Rainier Beer, in tribute to the lofty snow-covered peak looming south of Seattle. One early advertisement in 1907 claimed that "it makes the mountain smile." In almost no time the Rainier brand captivated beer drinkers up and down the West Coast and easily earned "most popular" status in the Pacific Northwest.

In 1903, the Seattle Brewing & Malting Company opened a new brewing facility in Georgetown (now incorporated as an official town)—complete with storage and malt rooms, plus adjacent carpentry and cooperage shops for constructing beer barrels—increasing its annual production capacity to more than six hundred thousand barrels. The company was now the largest brewery in the West (except for breweries in St. Louis, Missouri). According to Peter Blecha's *HistoryLink* article, by 1912 it was the largest industry in Washington State and was considered the sixth-largest brewing company in the world.

The company also owned its own glassworks factory (set up in the former Bay View plant) to produce beer bottles and complete bottle labeling. Due to demand, by 1905, the company was buying twelve thousand glass bottles per day from the Star Glassworks Company in Renton.

As Kurt Stream notes in his detailed photographic history, *Brewing in Seattle*, in 1906, the Seattle Brewing & Malting Company added a Pale Ale version of Rainier beer to its lineup for bottling purposes and, in 1908, expanded its product line with Bohemian and Pale Ale–style beers. The company also produced malt extracts and tonics, touted for their supposed health attributes, in a product line that included Malt Rainier. However, lurking in the background of the company's huge success was the specter of Prohibition.

A vintage 1907 print advertisement for Rainier Beer, launched in 1893, which
quickly became the star brand of the Seattle Brewing & Malting Company.
Courtesy of MOHAI, [Museum of History & Industry Collection], [2016.3.12].

STATEWIDE PROHIBITION CONSTERNATIONS

It may come as a surprise, but Prohibition became law in Washington State in January 1916, four years before retail sales of alcohol ended nationally after the US Congress ratified the Eighteenth Amendment. Setting the stage for an eventual statewide ban, the issue of controlling alcohol sales surfaced several times in Washington Territory before the region became a state. Driven by both national temperance organizations and movements to gain voting rights for women (who typically supported Prohibition), the issue was divisive on multiple levels. (Women gained an uncontested right to vote in Washington State in 1910.) In 1879, territorial legislators voted to prevent alcohol sales near construction sites of the Northern Pacific Railroad in an attempt to restrict excessive drinking by workers. In 1886, legislators passed a "local option law" allowing individual townships to hold local elections to determine each community's licensing practices for liquor sales. Although rejected in 1888 by the territorial Supreme Court, the law existed in a modified version until 1909, making some towns completely dry and others, such as Seattle, open for liquor sales at numerous saloons, hotels, and pubs.

As required by US law, in 1889, as part of Washington's bid to become a state, voters needed to approve a state constitution. Included in the constitution's framework were referendums on whether women could vote, whether Prohibition would be statewide, and where the state capital would be located. When all the votes were counted—all placed by men—the state capital was established in Olympia and the other two issues were rejected.

However, the issue of statewide Prohibition did not disappear. In 1909, voters again passed "local option" legislation, allowing individual towns the right to license—or not—local saloons. Various temperance and women's organizations campaigned heavily to pass the measure. In 1914, Prohibition again resurfaced for a statewide vote. With women now able to vote, Initiative Measure Number 3 passed, restricting the manufacture and sale of liquor anywhere in the state, despite its rejection by Seattle voters and voters in other sizable cities. While the initiative ended local alcohol production and sales—brewers and saloons across the state had to shut down by December 31, 1915—it did not make importing or drinking liquor illegal. As described by Paula Becker in her *HistoryLink* essay outlining Prohibition in Washington State:

> The only legal drinking from this point was via imported liquor that had been manufactured out of state—the law allowed individuals with permits to import up to two quarts of hard liquor or 12 quarts of beer every 20 days. Among those without permits (or those who lacked the means to prepay and ship alcohol), illegal drinking surged, largely via illegal sales at soft drink stands and restaurants. Drug stores, where prescription liquor could be obtained, boomed.

By January 1, 1916, faced with such devastating market changes and thinking an out-of-state move would protect the business, Louis Hemrich, then president of the Seattle Brewing & Malting Company, set about transferring beer production to San Francisco, building a new brewery there from the ground up. The company's downsized production facility in Georgetown switched to making nonalcoholic beverages such as syrups and cereal beverages. The Hemrich family did its best to ensure cash flow by opening a fish packing company in Aberdeen, Washington, and a cannery in Alaska. By April 1916, every brewery in Seattle, as well as throughout the rest of Washington State, had closed.

Subsequent attempts in 1916 to modify the complete statewide shutdown of liquor manufacturing and retail sales by allowing beer manufacturers to offer direct sales and direct sales in hotels failed in voter initiatives. The temperance advocates had won hands down. Restrictions tightened further in 1917 when the US Congress added measures to existing laws forbidding shipment of alcoholic liquors into states with "bone-dry" laws and preventing designated food products from being used in alcohol production, ostensibly in response to World War I food shortages. Washington State had adopted its own "bone-dry" directive in early 1917.

NATIONAL PROHIBITION EMPTIES GLASSES

In December 1918, Congress ratified the Eighteenth Amendment to the US Constitution declaring the manufacture, sale, and import/export of all alcoholic beverages illegal. Note that the Eighteenth Amendment did not make drinking alcohol illegal, only the manufacture, selling, and shipping of alcohol. Approved by Washington State lawmakers in January 1919, the amendment was ratified by three-quarters of US states in a record thirteen months and the national Prohibition law went into effect in January 1920. In tandem with this amendment, the Volstead Act, formally called the National Prohibition Act, was also passed by Congress to enforce regulations outlined in the Eighteenth Amendment. According to the Volstead Act definition, any liquor containing more than 0.5 percent alcohol was considered intoxicating and banned from manufacture, sale, or possession. This included light beer and wine. Only medicines, alcohol purchased before Prohibition started, and cider or wine fermented for personal home consumption could contain alcohol. Although vetoed by President Woodrow Wilson, in October 1919 Congress easily overrode his veto, and national Prohibition regulations started in January 1920. Commonly referred to as "The Noble Experiment," the new regulations took effect nationwide, piggybacking onto any state regulations already passed.

Even with strict Prohibition laws, options for obtaining alcohol in the Pacific Northwest were exploited. A primary smuggling channel was via boats sailing on Puget Sound between Washington State and British Columbia. With limited Coast Guard supervision, it was relatively easy to establish bootlegging routes for imported alcohol. Roy Olmstead, once a Seattle police lieutenant, was renowned as the area's most successful bootlegger, along with Peter Marinoff, who operated from Tacoma. To deter illegal alcohol sales, in Seattle a "Dry Squad" roved the city searching for bootleg barrels of beer and whiskey. In 1932, Alvin Hemrich, his son Elmer, and several colleagues associated with the Hemrich Brothers Brewing Company were arrested for selling home-brewing supplies. To survive financially, other brewers switched to producing "near beers" (beverages with the taste of beer but with low or no alcohol content) and sodas: Columbia Brewing Company produced a near beer named Columbia Brew, and in 1925, the Pacific Brewing & Malting Company (in Tacoma) introduced a soda named Orange Kist.

Fortuitously for brewers, social attitudes toward alcohol gradually changed. In the thirteen-plus years of Prohibition, drinking alcohol was no longer considered the dark path to surefire ruin it once had been. All things considered, the economic and social damage of Prohibition, in many ways, turned out to be worse than idealistic teetotalers cared to acknowledge. As Jennifer Latson notes in her article "A Toast to the End of Prohibition," the attempt to enforce temperance and sobriety on a national scale was unsuccessful: bootlegging was rampant; crime rates rose while law enforcement costs increased; the number of deaths and related illnesses caused by drinking bootleg liquor soared, "sparking a public health crisis"; and sales of non-alcoholic substitutes fizzled. Add the government's lost excise tax revenue, corruption among officials running bootleg operations, and economic malaise across the country due to the Great Depression, and Prohibition was doomed for both practical and economic reasons. Incoming president Franklin D. Roosevelt ran on a platform in 1932 calling for the end of Prohibition, a position setting the stage for change.

TAPS TURN ON AND GLASSES ARE REFILLED

Perhaps in reaction to the financial devastation of the Great Depression, Washington State was ahead of the curve when it came to repealing Prohibition, much to the relief of Seattle's brewers and brewery workers seeking income and employment. After seventeen years of Prohibition, in November 1932, the electorate passed Initiative Measure Number 61, which repealed all of Washington's liquor laws. Beginning in April 1933, brewing and selling beer with an alcohol content up to 3.2 percent was once again legal. Seattle's brewers celebrated and took up the charge of brewing beer for the city's thirsty populace.

Prohibition also soon ended at the federal level. It took a few interim steps—Congress first modified the National Prohibition Act, also known as the Volstead

Act, to allow sales of beer with up to 3.2 percent alcohol—and then, in December 1933, officially passed the Twenty-First Amendment, which repealed the Eighteenth Amendment. The new amendment ended all regulations relating to alcohol except those restricting liquor sales to minors. The spigot was now turned on for a new era of brewing.

Although restrictive Prohibition ended, various laws and modifications affecting alcohol sales and consumption in Washington State continued over the next decades. For starters, in 1934, Governor Clarence Martin signed the Steele Liquor Act, establishing the Washington State Liquor Control Board (WSLCB), and designating state-owned liquor stores as the only place hard liquor and wine could be purchased. The law also outlined strict restrictions prescribing how much alcohol could be sold—and consumed.

In 1935, the Steele Liquor Act was altered to allow private distributors the option of selling Washington wines. Under the modified law, beer and wine could be sold by the glass at restaurants and hotels but were subject to licensing regulations, including a ratio of food to beverage sales. Taverns could also sell beer and wine by the glass. Originally taverns were limited to beer, but wine was quickly added to discourage taverns from adding food to their menus in order to become "restaurants" and thus compete with the restaurant industry. Grocery stores could sell bottled beer and wine.

Hard liquor was only available for purchase at state liquor stores; it could not be purchased by the glass at bars or restaurants. The only exception was private clubs, which could serve drinks if the liquor was provided by members. However, during World War II, the number of these clubs increased greatly, and enforcement became a problem, with numerous raids and arrests.

Catching up with the times, and due to an effort by restaurant owners and hoteliers, in 1948, an initiative was put to the voters, and passed, allowing the WSLCB to license hotels, restaurants, clubs, trains, and boats (any place where serving full meals was a main business) to sell hard liquor. There was significant pressure from these establishments to continue to keep hard liquor out of taverns. In 1960, voters rejected a measure allowing liquor by the glass in taverns. Although framed as a moral issue, it likely failed thanks to significant lobbying from the hospitality industry, which didn't want the competition.

As the 1960s wound down, Washington State's Blue Laws were finally disbanded in 1966, sanctioning Sunday liquor sales. In 1969, the Steele Liquor Act was modified once again, giving distributors the right to sell *all* wines regardless of their source. Change was again in the air in 1972, although once more delayed. That year, State Initiative 261, which proposed to privatize liquor sales and close the network of state-owned liquor stores, came close to passing.

In 2010, the same proposal to privatize liquor sales and end state-owned retail outlets resurfaced as State Initiatives 1100 and 1105—and was again defeated. Barely a year later, in 2011, legislative changes significantly altered the liquor landscape in Washington State. Voters ended Washington State's monopoly over hard liquor sales, passing State Initiative 1183 by a 60 percent margin. Beginning in June 2012, consumers could buy all forms of alcohol almost anywhere, including at stores ranging from grocery and warehouse stores, such as Costco (a major backer of the initiative), to drugstores and corner markets. A negative side effect was that approximately 160 state liquor stores were closed, but, on the positive side, consumers could now buy directly from small distilleries without going through a distributor. The state's role in restricting the sales and drinking of alcoholic beverages had officially ended.

SEATTLE'S BREWERIES POST-PROHIBITION

Back to the historical story. In Seattle, the ending of statewide and then national Prohibition again inspired businessmen who had established the city's first breweries to launch a new chapter of brewing. For starters, in 1933, Alvin Hemrich continued in his family's footsteps and opened the Hemrich Brewing Company to operate two breweries in Seattle's SoDo neighborhood. Ever the entrepreneur, in 1934, he sold the rights to the Hemrich name and brand, along with his interest in one of the companies. Hemrich then renamed his remaining SoDo brewery the Apex Brewing Company and launched a new brand of beer under this name.

Another new brewery was started in 1933 by George F. Horluck. Formerly the owner of a creamery and chain of ice cream parlors in town, Horluck started the George F. Horluck Brewery on the corner of Westlake Avenue and Mercer Street. The brewery specialized in Vienna-style draught beer and eventually was named the Horluck Brewing Company. Also, not wanting to be left out and recognizing a legacy sales opportunity, the Rainier Brewing Company of San Francisco moved quickly and revved up production of Rainier Beer, shipping it north by rail, where it again earned first place for sales. (Both Hemrich and Horluck's breweries were eventually acquired by Emil Sick, a newcomer to Seattle's beer scene.) Seattle's thirsty and grateful beer fans were pleased by these developments—and more were to come.

SEATTLE'S BEER BARON
AND THE RENAISSANCE OF RAINIER BEER

Enter Emil Sick. A legend in Seattle's brewing history, Emil Sick arrived from Canada as Prohibition ended. Although born in Tacoma, Washington, Sick had moved to Lethbridge in Alberta, Canada, as a child. This is where he and his father,

Fritz Sick, originally a cooper from Germany skilled at making wooden beer casks, had founded a successful brewing business: the Lethbridge Brewing and Malting Company. Their brewery empire stretched across Canada, with sites in Lethbridge, Prince Edward, and Edmonton in Alberta and in Vancouver, British Columbia, plus sites in the United States in Montana and Spokane, Washington, eventually growing to include eleven breweries with its headquarters in Calgary, Alberta. (Sick was also cofounder in 1934 with several others of the Great Western Malting Company in Vancouver, Washington, a company still thriving today using the state's barley crops to produce malt extract, an essential ingredient for commercial beer making.)

Recognizing the lucrative potential of the Seattle market, Sick set his sights on the city, first investigating leasing the name "Rainier" from the San Francisco–based Rainier Brewing Company. He was turned down. Instead, in 1933, he leased the former Bay View Brewery building and launched the Century Brewing Association. The new brewery's first beer, named "Rheinlander, the Beer of the Century," was released a year later (and produced until the early 1980s). It was the beginning of Sick's impressive business acumen and his company's dominance over Seattle's brewing scene.

Not one to give up on a guaranteed business win, Emil Sick continued to pursue regional rights to using the name "Rainier Beer." He met success in April 1935, when he negotiated a royalty per barrel sold with the Rainier Brewing Company in San Francisco. In July 1935, after a twenty-plus-year hiatus, Rainier Beer was again brewed in Seattle. To mark the milestone, Sick also changed the name of his company from Century Brewing Association to Seattle Brewing & Malting Company, the identical name of the brewery that originally produced Rainier-branded beer before Prohibition.

The numbers prove Sick's persistence was worth it. In the first year of Seattle production, $2 million worth of Rainier Beer was sold in Washington and Oregon. By 1950, sales had climbed to $16 million. Sick expanded his brewery's lineup by producing the robustly flavored Rainier Old Stock Ale, Rainier Extra Pale, Sick's Select, Brew 66, and Emil Sick's Boss' Ale, among others. In 1957, Rainier Diamond Draft was released to commemorate the company's seventy-five years of brewing beer. Other beers were introduced over the years, including "light" versions, evolving in flavor and taste to reflect consumer beverage trends.

Another milestone for Sick: in 1938, his company was the first to sell canned beer in the Pacific Northwest. (The "official" birthday of beer cans is January 24, 1935.) Cans were produced locally by the Seattle Continental Can Company, which had opened a plant here in 1927. As noted by Kurt Stream in his photographic history book *Brewing in Seattle*, "in 1934, nearly 75 percent of all sales were draft beer from kegs, while 25 percent was packaged in bottles and cans. By 1949, these percentages were nearly reversed with 71 percent of all beer being packaged."

A view of Rainier Brewery in 1939, with rooftop signage reading "Sick's," "In the West It's Rainier Beer," and "Seattle Brewing & Malting Co. Since 1878." *Courtesy of MOHAI, [PEMCO Webster & Stevens Collection], [1983.10.13345].*

In 1953, Sick's long-standing desire came true. Following World War II, the Rainier Brewing Company of San Francisco hit competition and hard times. The business downturn made it possible for Sick to officially buy the company. Interested only in the name, he soon sold the brewery in San Francisco to the Theo Hamm Brewing Company. The Seattle Brewing & Malting Company was renamed Sick's Rainier Brewing Company, a name it held until 1970, when it was renamed again to Rainier Brewing Company.

Success in Seattle continued for Emil Sick. By 1957, the brewery produced more than 127 million units of packaged beer and built a modern packing facility on Airport Way South across from the brewery building. The brewery also featured a taproom named the Rainier Mountain Room, which was open to the public after brewery tours as well as to employees.

Anyone thinking that the brewery business stops when the foam reaches the top of the pint glass could take a lesson from Sick's multiple civic engagements. He served as president of the Seattle Chamber of Commerce and the Seattle Historical Society, built King County's first blood bank, raised funds to save St. Mark's Cathedral, and also bought the struggling Seattle Indians baseball team of the Pacific

Coast League, renaming it the Seattle Rainiers and building an official outdoor ballpark for the team. His tenure with the Seattle Historical Society inspired the founding of the Museum of History and Industry (MOHAI). Overall, Emil Sick gave back to Seattle as much as or more than he earned from its beer-loving residents.

CONSOLIDATION CHANGES THE PLAYING FIELD

By 1971, Rainier Brewing Company ranked twenty-fifth among US breweries and produced 835,000 barrels of beer annually. By 1977, the company was the fourteenth largest brewery with fully automated production, but it fell behind another local, the Olympia Brewing Company. Add the consolidation factor, and sales challenges were further aggravated. This business direction was rapidly becoming the style of the game in the mass-production commercial brewing industry amid a shrinking overall market as national brands moved into the market and took over sales by acquiring local brands. (In the broader beverage history of the 1970s, Americans were discovering wine, and national brands were aggressive marketers compared with regional brewers.)

In the 1970s, Canada-based Molson Breweries also acquired a majority share of Rainier's stock. In 1977, Rainier Brewing Company was sold to the G. Heileman Brewing Company based in Wisconsin. In 1996, Rainier Brewing Company was again sold, this time to Stroh Brewing Company. Only three years later, Stroh hit a ditch, and in 1999 it sold its brands to the giants Pabst Brewing Company and Miller Brewing Company. Production of Rainier Beer ceased in Seattle and moved to the Olympia Brewery in Tumwater, Washington, where it was brewed under contract until the plant closed in 2003 and production moved to Irwindale, California, its current brewing location. For the faithful, the Rainier brand still exists and can be poured regularly. Its brewery complex beside I-5 later became the home of Tully's Coffee and roasting facilities and is today a hub of artists' studios and recording studio rehearsal spaces.

The story of the Rainier Brewing Company is an inspiring chapter in the history of American brewing. The company was caught in the crossfire of a changing industry as craft brews grew in popularity when consumers discovered and grew to prefer flavorful artisan brews over mass-produced light lagers. Statistics shared by Kurt Stream in *Brewing in Seattle* also capture the trend of the 1980s. In 1981, there were fewer than ninety operating breweries in the United States. Stream goes on to say, "By 1983, there were only 51 brewing concerns operating a total of 80 breweries, a low watermark for the industry in the 20th century." To put this number in perspective, the Brewers Association lists the first historic high for breweries as the year 1873, when there were 4,131 breweries throughout the United States.

SEATTLE'S CRAFT BEER UPRISING

The renaissance or modern era of Seattle's brewing history overflows with a diverse group of creative entrepreneurs who combined their business smarts and eclectic backgrounds with a lust for lagers, pale ales, and IPAs to open a plethora of microbreweries. Some were founded by home-brewing hobbyists, environmental scientists, or chemical engineers; others opened in converted garages, and many started in the affordable, semi-industrial warehouses of the Ballard-Fremont neighborhoods with brewpubs sharing the same space. These "Northwest-style" craft brews, reflecting their brewmasters' passion, are often described as India Pale Ale–style (or IPAs), each abundantly hopped with complex and robust flavor. Flavor, with all its potential diversities, is the distinguishing element of this new beer-brewing era.

Building on surging consumer interest since the mid-1980s, the number of craft and artisanal breweries in Seattle has soared from a handful back then to ninety-five active licensed breweries in 2016, ranking fourth in the country, according to data from a Cushman & Wakefield report (the report excludes breweries owned by larger non-craft-beer companies). The Cushman & Wakefield report also notes the number of active US craft breweries has more than tripled over the past decade, rising to 5,234 in 2016 from 1,409 in 2006.

For enthusiasts of Seattle's artisanal beer history, 1982 was the landmark year that launched the craft-brewing movement. In April 1982, the first brewpub in the United States since the end of Prohibition opened with taps flowing in Yakima, Washington, under the inspired vision of Bert Grant, a Scottish American brewer. Named Grant's Brewery Pub, its inaugural beer, Grant's Scottish Ale, won second place at the 1984 American Beer Festival in the consumer's preference category. As Michael F. Rizzo observes in his in-depth history, *Washington Beer*, while large-scale breweries "were losing their appeal, Bert Grant was able to create something different and fresh, opening consumers' eyes to the flavor possibilities." Without realizing it at the time, Grant anticipated a movement and became a role model spawning a profusion of homegrown craft breweries in Seattle and elsewhere. Although Bert Grant passed on in 2001, and his pub closed in 2005, he continues to be cited as a legacy in Pacific Northwest artisanal brewing history.

REDHOOK, SEATTLE'S PIONEERING CRAFT BREWERY

Seattle's craft beer entrepreneurs shared Grant's vision. In April 1982, at the same time that Bert Grant opened Grant's Brewery Pub in Yakima, Washington, the Redhook Brewing Company opened Seattle's first microbrewery. The new brewing company set up shop in Seattle's Fremont neighborhood in a garage that was once the site of an automotive transmission workshop, and held its first release party in August 1982. Twenty investors had pooled $500,000 each to form the Independent Ale Brewing Company, soon renamed Redhook Ale Brewing Company, under the leadership of Paul Shipman and Gordon Bowker, with brewmaster Charles McElevey, who had worked at the Rainier Brewing Company. (In 1991, McElevey founded the West Seattle Brewing Company, a brewpub in the West Seattle neighborhood eventually named the California & Alaska Street Brewery, which he ran until 1996.) Shipman was a marketing and sales manager as well as a former wine salesman. He is credited with discovering the strain of Belgian yeast used in Independent Ale's first English-style brews.

Bowker, who knew Shipman from working with him on the Chateau Ste. Michelle Winery account, is recognized as the "idea man" behind the new brewery. This role overlapped with his creative position at the Bowker-Heckler advertising agency, which was applauded for its clever landmark ads for Rainier Beer in the 1970s. (Out of the limelight, mostly by choice and style, Bowker also launched *Seattle Weekly*, was cofounder with friends of Starbucks Coffee, and owned Peet's Coffee for a time.)

One of the new brewery's first batches was named Redhook Original Ale, and a second was dubbed Blackhook Bitter in 1983, a top seller until Redhook ESB (Extra Special Bitter) came on the market in 1990, which is still the flagship product. Other notable brands included Winterhook and Ballard Bitter IPA.

Redhook's launch was aligned for success. Along with evolving consumer taste trends for beer, changes were made in 1982 at the state level expanding sales channels for alcohol. As outlined by Kurt Stream in *Brewing in Seattle*, Washington legislators modified rules governing how and where beer could be sold. Before the change, distribution to restaurants and taverns of any malt beverage with more than 4 percent alcohol was only possible through the Washington State Liquor Control Board (WSLCB) and could only be sold at WSLCB retail stores. The 1982 legal change dropped this requirement and allowed Redhook's beer, with its 5 percent alcohol rating, to be sold everywhere in the region.

By 1989, the brewery was so successful that it moved to larger facilities in Seattle's Fremont neighborhood, taking over a former trolley barn once used by the Seattle Electric Railway, along with an old machine shop across the street. In 1994, Redhook expanded again, this time to a new, larger building in Woodinville east of Seattle, and, in 1996, it expanded across the country to set up a brewing facility in Portsmouth, New Hampshire. Sales in 1997 were reported at $40 million. The company's stellar growth and desire to expand further prompted an alliance in 2008 with Widmer Brothers Brewery in Portland to form the Craft Brew Alliance, which added Hawaii-based Kona Brewing Company in 2010. However, things changed when the group approved approximately one-third ownership by Anheuser-Busch InBev, the parent company of Budweiser based in Belgium. With a behemoth player in the mix, participating breweries in the Alliance are no longer considered craft breweries. Redhook's Woodinville facility closed in 2017, and all operations moved to Portland.

In an attempt to keep a local connection, in August 2017, Redhook opened a new brewpub called Redhook Brewlab in the trendy Capitol Hill neighborhood. Along with a seasonal bar food menu designed to complement the beers available, the brewpub's mission is to serve one hundred different small-batch beers annually. With many brews featuring local ingredients, the goal is to solicit customer feedback and guide the brewery's seasonal beer offering.

IN THE BEGINNING OF CRAFT BREWERIES

Along with Redhook, a range of microbreweries and brewpubs started in Seattle in the 1980s. Standouts on the craft brewery list deserving legend status are Charles and Rose Ann Finkel. Together they helped popularize homegrown craft beers with Seattle residents through their seasonal releases at the Pike Brewing Company— the city's third craft brewery to open—while promoting favorites such as ales and stouts.

The Finkels came to their beer business by way of the wine world. In their first shared enterprise, the dynamic duo founded Bon-Vin in 1969, which offered "boutique wines" from small, independent, and typically family-owned wineries in Europe, California, and Washington State, including Ste. Michelle (later named Chateau Ste. Michelle). This connection prompted the couple's move to Seattle in 1974 when Ste. Michelle acquired Bon-Vin and where Charles moved into the role of vice president of sales and marketing at the winery. (In Seattle, Rose Ann put her culinary skills to work in the Laurelhurst neighborhood and opened Truffles, a specialty food store and delicatessen, and, with two partners, the Gourmet Grocery.)

Equally passionate about beer as they were about wine, Charles and Rose Ann Finkel started Merchant du Vin in 1978 to import craft beers from around the world. With this business—today, the world's largest craft beer importer—they were first in the United States to import beers from Belgium, promote fruit-based beers, and revive many traditional brewing styles. Rose Ann developed menus and drink lists to help clients market imported beers to customers.

In 1989, the couple's beer-related activities revved into fifth gear. They established Pike Brewing (the original business name was the Pike Place Brewery) in Pike Place Market after purchasing Liberty Malt Supply, a supply store for home brewers founded in 1921, one of the oldest in the country. On a lower level of Pike

Place Market, they constructed their new brewery, which featured a four-barrel copper kettle for the beer fermenting process. The brewmaster of Pike Brewing was Jason Parker and Pike Pale Beer was its first beer, followed by XXXXX Stout. In 1996, the independent brewery expanded its footprint in Pike Place Market in order to be able to brew thirty barrels using a sophisticated gravity-flow, steam-powered brewing system. The brewery's expanded footprint also included a public house with a menu of classic pub fare chosen for beer pairings. The Finkels took a break from the brewing business in 1997 when they sold Pike Brewing. For the next nine years, until mid-2006, the Finkels pursued personal interests. In May 2006, remaining infatuated with the brewing business, Charles and Rose Ann reacquired Pike Brewery and the Pike Pub.

Along with its dozen-plus seasonal brews, Pike Brewing offers a year-round roster of award-wining favorites ranging from classic IPAs and pale ales to an extra stout version. Charles's innate wit and whimsy are evident in the beers' names, from Pike Naughty Nellie (named after the madam who ran a bawdy house in the La Salle Hotel once located above Pike Brewing's space), Pike Monk's Uncle, and Pike Kilt Lifter, while his award-winning design sense shines through in the bottle and can labels. Several brewmasters from Pike Brewery have gone on to establish their own breweries or assist other microbreweries.

Also a graphic designer, writer, and historian, Charles Finkel amassed a fountain of knowledge about the brewing industry, both around the world and in the United States. His fascination led him to establish the Microbrewery Museum, a special room within Pike Pub to showcase his personal collection of beer industry memorabilia. Ranging from historic photos to tankards, advertising posters, distinctive bottles, labels, and more, all spanning nine thousand years of human brewing history, every item has a significant story. In summer 2017, Pike Brewery added to Pike Place Market's dining and drinking choices by opening Tankard & Tun restaurant on the ground level. Of course, the new restaurant's menu showcases beer and seafood from the Pacific Northwest.

Other brewing activists in this time period include Richard Wrigley, who established Pacific Northwest Brewing Company in 1989 in Pioneer Square. Spinnaker's Brewpub in Victoria, British Columbia, came to Seattle in 1988 to open two Noggins Brewpubs, one at Westlake Center and another in the U-District, each serving classic English-style pub fare such as fish-and-chips and shepherd's pie. (Both locations closed in 1992.) In 1990, George and Jane Hancock founded Maritime Pacific Brewing Company in the Ballard neighborhood, which still operates in its original building and produces an outstanding line of craft beers.

Pioneering breweries were also founded outside of Seattle, many eventually moving into the city. The list is long, but notables include Hart Brewing, founded in 1984 by Tom Baune and Beth Hartwell in Kalama, Washington. In 1995, the company opened a large brewpub in its vintage brick headquarters building in the SoDo sports heartland, at the intersection of today's Safeco Field and Century Link Field. A name change occurred in 1996, when the company became Pyramid Breweries, a testament to its signature brews. Today, the company is owned by Florida Ice & Farm Co., but still officially headquartered in Seattle. It brews beer under the Pyramid brand in Seattle and Portland, operating brewpubs near both breweries, plus maintaining a small outlet at the Oakland International Airport in Oakland, California.

Other notable entrepreneurs in the 1980s and 1990s add even more color and personality to Seattle's beer story. Mike Hale is definitely worth calling out in the lineup of Seattle's early entrepreneurial brewers. Hale started Hale's Ales in Colville, Washington, in 1984, and operations subsequently moved to Kirkland on the east side of Lake Washington. In 1995, Hale's Ales completely changed locations, setting up production with a brewpub in Seattle's Fremont neighborhood. Across Elliott Bay on Bainbridge Island, Will Kemper, founder of the Thomas Kemper Brewery noted for producing German-style lagers, also earned raves for inaugurating Oktoberfest in 1989 in Poulsbo, Washington, just a ferry ride away from Seattle. (Kemper also developed a handcrafted root beer that became a huge hit and initiated the Thomas Kemper Soda Company in 1992. Both his brewery and his soda company were bought by Hart Brewing, and they are now part of Pyramid Breweries, Inc.) In Redmond in 1993, Malcolm Rankin and Jack Schropp founded Mac & Jack's. While selling only growlers and kegs until 2015, their brewery earned fame and glory in 2010 for producing the top-selling beer in the state.

This group of exceptional independent breweries pioneered Seattle's craft-brewing renaissance, which has inspired a plethora of neighborhood breweries of all sizes.

TOP BREWERY NEIGHBORHOODS

North and south, east and west—almost every Seattle neighborhood now has a microbrewery or three. Sizes range from nanobrewery-scale to established and thriving artisanal breweries with companion brewpubs. It's a trend that inspired Ian Roberts and partners to organize Seattle Beer Week in 2008, the city's biggest annual beer event—spanning eleven days—showcasing a plethora of worldwide beverages and including fun, wacky competitions such as a tin can sculpture contest and the loudest beer promo. And where does one find authentic, local craft brews the rest of the year? A recap of the most popularly regarded neighborhood breweries follows with call-outs based on a variety of sources.

Along with the SoDo district and Georgetown, one neighborhood stands out for beer lovers: the Ballard Brewing District, also called Ballard, once Seattle's Scandinavian neighborhood. Located north of the Ship Canal and west of Fremont, Ballard's semi-industrial blocks south of the Market Street thoroughfare have operated as an industrial zone since the city was founded in 1853 and were annexed in 1907 into Seattle proper. Today, craft breweries sit between traditional repair and machine shops, auto repair shops, architects, and boat restorers. Without question, it's a top destination for beer-loving residents. At least eight breweries are within walking distance of each other. New start-ups may brew one-of-a-kind ales or focus on seasonal flavors, the end result reflecting their brewmasters' passions.

Among the noteworthy is Stoup Brewing. Founded in 2013 by Brad Benson and Lara Zahaba, a husband-and-wife duo long smitten with craft beers, the pair teamed with Robyn Schumacher—who earned the distinction of becoming Washington's first female *Cicerone*—to honor the art and science behind craft brewing with small batches of Hefeweizen, IPA, and Porter brews. Peddler Brewing Company (its name is a clue to its founders' second passion) is both a microbrewery and a tasting room with an indoor bike rack and a bike workstation. NW Peaks Brewery is also a Ballard original. Started by an avid mountaineer, the "pint-size" (its own description) nanobrewery builds small batches featured a block away at the Bergschrund taproom, along with a few other limited release standouts. Then there is the Ballard Beer Company with a shop that's both pub and bottle shop, offering fifteen lagers, stouts, and IPAs on tap from neighborhood breweries. With this group as its core, more breweries come into being almost every month.

While the Fremont "Center of the Universe" neighborhood doesn't have Ballard's quantity of breweries, its prime brewery is a Seattle standout. Matt Lincecum, a passionate home brewer, made a bold move by launching the Fremont Brewing Company in 2009 during the Great Recession. It's a move that has paid off. Known for small-batch regular brews, plus seasonal offerings such as Summer Ale and Interurban IPA, the sustainable, local ingredients characterize the brewery's inventive, entrepreneurial approach to beer making. The legions of merry fans sitting inside and outside the brewery while quaffing brews are also a vivid measure of the Fremont Brewing Company's success.

Once upon a time, Georgetown was flush with young breweries. Today, the story continues. In fact, it's had a recent renaissance. As the location of Seattle's many early and successful twentieth-century breweries, the semi-industrial neighborhood remains a center for microbrews. An independent town before being annexed into Seattle in 1910, its historic blue-collar profile makes the neighborhood receptive to breweries both past and present. Of the half-dozen-plus modern, small-batch brewing companies, several found homes by renting space in the former Rainier

Brewery building (crowned once again by its new owners with the iconic red "R"). These include Emerald City Beer (with its Beer Lab tasting room) and Machine House Brewery (featuring English-style ales). Nearby, Georgetown Brewing offers growlers and kegs for taking home Manny's Pale Ale; Epic Ales, noted for brewing with unconventional ingredients such as spruce tips and peppercorns, offers tastes, plus an innovative menu in its Gastropod brewpub. Schooner Exact Brewing offers both barrel-aged brews and food in its brewery, while Elysian Brewing (owned by Anheuser-Busch since 2015) occupies the largest warehouse brewery space in the neighborhood. Although they seem off the beaten path, these innovative micro-breweries make Georgetown a beer lover's "must-visit" destination.

Considering Seattle's vibrant brewing history that surmounted Prohibition and then not only recovered but also thrived, it's fitting that craft breweries are enjoying a lovefest in the modern city—and definitely a fact worth raising a glass for.

DISTILLERIES THEN AND NOW

In Seattle's pioneer days, the rough-and-tumble character of the early city experiencing a surge of prosperity led to an uncomplimentary identity overlapping with the beverages available to its first settlers: "Long known as the 'most wicked city on the coast,' the settlement had courted that dubious honor as far back as 1861, when the first brothel was established near Yesler's sawmill." Ursula Smith and Linda S. Peavy include this description in their book, *Women in Waiting in the Westward Movement*, in the chapter outlining Sarah Burgert Yesler's life in the booming seaport and lumber city that her husband was instrumental in establishing. Alcoholic beverages were part of this negative description. Easy-to-make, affordable, and accessible beer was the beverage of choice for the city's workers, but backyard distilleries were also present.

To combat this dark character, in the early 1880s, Seattle's Law & Order League protested Seattle's "two distilleries, eleven drinking establishments, one bawdy house . . . and gambling," as described by Clarence B. Bagley in his book *History of Seattle: From the Earliest Settlement to the Present Time*. In opposition to the League's support for regulating liquor "to improve the morals of the town," Bagley continues, was the Business Men's Ticket with Henry Yesler as its mayoral candidate. Yesler insisted regulation would damage the city's prosperity. (Yesler ran for mayor in 1870 and 1873, and he finally won in 1874. Sarah Yesler was a founding member of Seattle's chapter of the Female Suffrage Society.) As described earlier, the seesaw swing of alcohol restrictions in the state and city eventually became a statewide ban in 1916, and then a federal ban in 1919. All commercial distilleries quickly became history.

Although the end of Prohibition—in Washington State in 1932, and nationwide in 1933—had improved the landscape for breweries and wineries, craft distilleries were still restricted by state laws from offering samples or selling directly to customers—until 2008. That year, Don Poffenroth and Kent Fleischman, vodka and whiskey fans who were owners of Dry Fly Distillery in Spokane, cultivated support for legislative changes that would help craft distilleries by working with Washington State senator Chris Marr. Following Marr's proposal, Washington legislators passed a bill enabling craft distilleries to open tasting rooms and earn tax breaks when 51 percent of the ingredients they used were sourced and grown in Washington State and annual production was under twenty thousand gallons. As Tan Vinh recounts in his *Seattle Times* article, "The Boutique Booze Boom in Washington," describing the new wave of distilleries, "The 'drink local' and 'farm-to-table' angle gave the bill sex appeal," and it easily passed. Add Seattle's steady maritime climate, which mirrors Scotland's prime whiskey-making area, and a new chapter in Washington's distilling history opened.

Today, Seattle has more micro-distilleries than any other city in the United States. At last count, there were twenty-four. (Statewide, there are now 110 micro-distilleries, more than any other state.) Distilleries here are crafting everything from vodka to aquavit, gin and scotch to bourbon and whiskey. The push to create a single-malt scotch is strong given the Pacific Northwest's ideal growing and aging climate for profitable crops of barley and wheat. In 2015, just north of Seattle, the Skagit Valley Malting Company started using local barley to produce malt for local distillers and brewers. Even with the distribution challenges and costs of competing against big-name distillers, once the state approved privatized liquor retailing in 2012, craft distilleries with business-savvy owners flourished.

As the story of craft distilling reveals, there are now many distilleries throughout Washington State creating a range of high-quality spirits—with "high quality" a value all emphasize. As pioneers, Mike Sherlock and his wife Patty Bishop founded Fremont Mischief Distillery in 2009 to distill an award-winning rye, plus vodka, and gin made from local barley. Sound Spirits, founded in 2010 by Steven Stone, earned distinction for its use of locally grown malted barley to distill vodka, gin, and aquavit. In Seattle's historic Scandinavian neighborhood, since 2012, the Old Ballard Liquor Company has continued and expanded tradition with innovative and flavorful aquavit served at its tasting room, plus in its small café.

This short list of call-outs for Seattle's notable grain-to-glass craft distillers must also include 2Bar Spirits, founded by Nathan Kaiser and currently Washington State's only bourbon distillery. On Capitol Hill, Sun Liquor Distillery and bar owned by Erik Chapman and Michael Klebeck serves house-made gin and vodka, while OOLA Distillery, under Kirby Kallas-Lewis as founder and head distiller, makes a range of small-batch spirits including barrel-aged whiskeys. In the SoDo neighborhood, two inventive distillers stand out. Letterpress Distilling features small batches of Italian-style liqueurs such as *arancello* and *amaro*, and 3 Howls Distillery stars with its twelve award-winning, handcrafted spirits spanning various styles of gin, rum, vodka, and whiskey, plus several naturally flavored, vapor-infused vodkas.

Not far away in Woodinville is the Woodinville Whiskey Company. Launched under Orlin Sorensen and Brett Carlile—and in a move not unusual for innovative start-ups, but changing the landscape for everyone—the distillery was taken over in July 2017 by Moët Hennessy, the global French spirits company.

Anyone craving a variety of whiskey and/or bourbon tastes can head for Radiator Whiskey on the top floor of the Corner Building at Pike Place Market. Along with national and local brews plus offerings from micro-distillers across the country and seasonal cocktails, the bustling brewpub serves a robust menu to complement its wide-ranging drink list.

WINE ALSO FILLS SEATTLE'S GLASSES

While Seattle's beverage history is not directly connected with commercially grown wine grapes—Eastern Washington's climate and irrigation systems are much more hospitable—residents here love wine, particularly varietals produced in-state. Without doubt, the city's culinary traditions wouldn't be what they are without Washington State wines. Exploring the state's wine history reveals that many settlers arriving in the Pacific Northwest in the 1840s and 1850s brought wine grape rootstock (along with apple cuttings) with them. Records indicate the first wine grapes were planted in 1827 in Ft. Vancouver, the Hudson's Bay Company outpost on the Columbia River. In later years, immigrants from wine-loving countries such as Italy, France, and Germany brought early varieties of wine grapes with them, and rootstock was also available at local nurseries for family gardens.

Railroads arriving in the Pacific Northwest were also a factor prompting wine agriculture by bringing both settlers and rootstock north from Oregon and California. Commercial vineyard production started in Yakima and Wenatchee Valleys in eastern Washington in the early 1900s as irrigation projects expanded and stimulated wine grape agriculture on inviting and diverse soils that make up the eastern terroir of the Cascade Range.

Although Washington State's initial Prohibition act in 1916 allowed drinking wine at home, a loophole encouraging many Seattle residents to grow grapes in backyard gardens and make their own wine, national Prohibition laws quickly changed this. Statewide, the wine industry shriveled. But once Prohibition was repealed in 1933, many new businesses filed to become commercial wineries.

Peter Blecha, in his *HistoryLink* article, calls out the St. Charles Winery, founded on Stretch Island (near Olympia) by Charles Somers and his son C. W. "Bill" Somers, as the first "bonded" winery in Washington State following the repeal of Prohibition.

Wine production in Washington State took off after Prohibition, and by 1935 it was commercially viable enough to launch the Washington Wine Producers Association. In 1937, there were twenty-eight wineries; by 1938, there were forty-two. In 1938, the Producers' Association was renamed the Washington Wine Council, an organization hugely active today, as Washington stands only behind California in wine production.

With terroir similar to wine regions in France and Italy, Washington State Wine Commission materials and the US Treasury Department (Bureau of Alcohol, Tobacco, and Firearms) report that the state is home to thirteen officially recognized "appellations" or AVAs (American Viticultural Areas). Many credit Professor Walter J. Clore of Washington State University (WSU was founded in 1890 as a land grant college) with laying the foundation for Washington State's modern wine industry based on his forty years of dedicated research to identify the ideal European vinifera wine grapes for this region. A key figure at WSU's Irrigated Agricultural Research Extension Center in Prosser from the 1930s to the 1970s, Professor Clore established the Riesling, Chenin Blanc, Gewurztraminer, Semillon, Cabernet Sauvignon, and Merlot varieties for Central Washington wine growers. In 2003, the Washington State Legislature officially recognized Dr. Clore as the "Father of the Washington State Wine Industry," as John Vitale recounts in his profile of the wine grape pioneer for *Washington Tasting Room Magazine.*

Over the years, wine grape production in the state expanded as wine palates became more sophisticated and individual wine enthusiasts entered the business. The 1950s saw a surge of new commercial wineries, and another bump occurred during the 1970s as smaller boutique-style wineries started. As of 2017, despite market fluctuations and severe weather ups and downs over the decades, there were more than 850 wineries in the state, growing varietals ranging from Concord to Pinot Noir, Pinot Gris, Riesling, Cabernet, and Chardonnay on an estimated forty-three thousand acres. The largest commercial wineries are Columbia Crest, based in the south-central town of Paterson, Washington, and Chateau Ste. Michelle, based in Woodinville.

For Seattle residents, Pacific Northwest wine explorations became accessible in 1975. That year, Ron Irvine and his partner, Jack Bagdade, opened the Pike & Western Wine Shop across from Pike Place Market. Considered a bold move in an era touting European wines, the shop thrives today under Michael Teer, who took ownership in 1991, and still showcases wines from the Pacific Northwest. Irvine, credited with planting the first Pinot Noir in King County on Vashon Island, where he owns the Vashon Winery, is also a historian at heart. Expanding his passion for all things wine, he went on in 1997 to write *The Wine Project: Washington State's Winemaking History* with Dr. Walter J. Clore. Adding to discovery options for Seattle wine fans, many wineries of all sizes from Central Washington and elsewhere have tasting rooms in Woodinville, a short drive east of the city.

COFFEE CAPITAL OF THE WORLD

Seattle is a coffee town, and some call it the coffee capital of the United States. Confirmation of this claim is the Starbucks mermaid atop the tower of the company's SoDo headquarters. Either a Starbucks or another independent coffee shop or drive-by coffee bar is visible in every neighborhood; in downtown Seattle one can be found on almost every block. It's certainly conceivable that Starbucks, founded here in 1971, first brought the culinary traditions of the city and the Pacific Northwest into the national food scene's spotlight. For Seattle, like many American frontier cities founded by settlers and immigrants, drinking coffee was a custom transplanted to make their new homes in an unfamiliar place both welcoming and a source of camaraderie. Stating the obvious, Seattle's inclement weather may also have fostered coffee culture.

Looking backward, in the mid-1800s, early settlers brought coffee beans, coffee grinders, and coffee pots with them on their overland journeys. But their coffee bean stashes never lasted long enough. Once used, they relied on ship captains to replenish supplies and, eventually, shipments arriving by railroad and stocked by merchants in general stores in forty- to fifty-pound burlap sacks.

Without a regular supply of coffee beans, improvising by necessity was the rule for home cooks. As Jacqueline B. Williams outlines in *The Way We Ate*, letters and diaries from women settlers describe substituting roasted grains and legumes such as rye, barley, bran, or peas in place of coffee beans—with little enthusiasm. When mocha, Java, Rio, or other whole coffee beans were available, most home cooks roasted and ground their own beans to brew coffee, savoring both the aroma and the hot beverage.

Williams also shares another footnote from American coffee history impacting coffee rituals for Seattle's pioneers: pre-roasted beans were not available until 1869, when Arbuckle Brothers, a company in Pittsburgh, Pennsylvania, patented a method to successfully seal in flavors during the roasting process. As other measures of progress—or the advent of mass production—in 1878, Caleb Chase and James Sanborn of Chase & Sanborn Coffee fame introduced the first ground coffee packaged in a tin can, and, in 1898, their company started packing coffee in vacuum cans.

As Seattle expanded with new arrivals and Yukon Gold Rush prospectors, hotels and immigrant-owned bakeries offered companion coffee shops as social centers. In the early 1900s, there were eleven Scandinavian bakery-cafés in the city—full-service bakeries with adjoining coffee shops. All were gathering places for new and established Nordic immigrants—a natural occurrence, considering how "coffee culture" also pervades Nordic countries. In Rainier Valley, Italian, Jewish, Filipino, and French immigrants in the 1900s brought their coffee traditions to their new country. Italians are credited with introducing espresso to their new countrymen. (This tradition continues today with recent Ethiopian and Vietnamese immigrants in Rainier Valley, who are introducing their Seattle neighbors to coffee practices from their homelands.)

Coffee is a cherished beverage in a soggy city where inhabitants crave a mood boost on gray, wet days. Coffee, after all, is a sensory experience as much as a physical one. Underscoring the value of coffee, in 1938 *The American Woman's Cookbook*, a nationally available cookbook, gave detailed instructions on how to brew coffee correctly, a measure of the beverage's importance for home cooks' daily routines. A little historical stirring reveals several local coffee roasters and retailers in Seattle dating to the early part of the twentieth century.

The Schwabacher Brothers, owners of a large general store (the first brick building in Seattle) in Pioneer Square and nearby pier in Elliott Bay, were both coffee retailers and wholesalers, with roots dating to Seattle's pioneer days. Acting as the savvy entrepreneurs they were, the brothers roasted and sold Gold Shield Coffee from 1869 into the 1950s. The coffee brand was eventually sold to Crescent Manufacturing Company, a Seattle-based spice importer and manufacturer, but disappeared in the 1970s.

Long before Starbucks was a gleam in someone's eye, there was Manning's Coffee. Founded in 1908, Manning's is often mentioned as Seattle's first commercial coffee purveyor. Roasting and selling coffee beans in bulk, both wholesale and retail, and pouring coffee by the cup—prices then were twenty to thirty-three cents per pound for beans, and two cents for a small cup of coffee or four cents for a large cup—Manning's quickly became successful. In 1923, Manning's expanded to San Francisco and Palo Alto. Over time, the company established forty cafeterias and restaurants in nine Western states, along with food service operations in hospitals and businesses. The original Pike Place Market storefront was razed in 1957, and Lowell's Restaurant took over the location. The Manning's coffee brand was sold in local grocery stores into the 1970s, but, as business slowed, Manning's was sold twice: first to LaBatt of Canada, and then to Del Monte.

Several other names belong in this early group of local brands. The Commercial Importing Company roasted Corona Coffee from 1900 into the 1940s. Reliance Coffee—sold with the tagline "Better 7 Ways"—was also a roasted-in-Seattle brand packed into distinctive green cans (occasionally found in collectible shops) and sold to independent grocery stores from the 1930s into the 1950s. Bargreen's Coffee, although based a bit north in Everett, Washington, is one survivor from this era. Founded in 1898 by Sam Bargreen, who relocated from Chicago, the company is run today by his grandson, Howie Bargreen, and sells to independent grocery stores and a few coffee stands.

In the 1950s, most coffee drinking happened at home, the result of mass-produced coffee options, making the morning ritual extra easy. (Remember Chase & Sanborn? Add Folger's, Nestlé, and instant coffee to the home kitchen landscape.) But the landscape changed in the 1960s and 1970s when coffee roasters and coffeehouses appeared, specializing in freshly roasted coffee beans from a variety of countries. As things developed, Seattle was an ideal habitat for seducing customers with batch-roasted, direct-trade coffee beans from Central and South America and the resulting luscious, steaming caffeinated beverages.

STARBUCKS MAKES COFFEE AN EVERYDAY LUXURY

As it happened, 1971 turned out to be "the year" for pioneers in Seattle's coffee world. Jim Stewart opened the Wet Whisker coffee roastery and ice cream shop on Pier 70, a business that expanded into Stewart Brothers Coffee, and eventually Seattle's Best Coffee, also shortened to SBC, with a local chain of Seattle's Best Coffee cafés in Seattle, plus a few shops in San Francisco. Stewart roasted his beans at the Vashon Island Coffee Roasterie, another heirloom establishment from this era. The same year, not far away on Post Alley, Joe Kittay opened the Good Coffee Company, selling hand-roasted beans to appreciative coffee drinkers. And then stars aligned and the birth of Starbucks came to pass.

The original Starbucks confluence was due mainly to one man: Seattle native and food explorer, Gordon Bowker. A food nomad in Italy during his college years (and in England, where he discovered craft beers), Bowker discovered cappuccinos and espressos brewed to order from freshly roasted beans. Back in Seattle, after fetching roasted coffee beans regularly from Murchie's Tea & Coffee by traveling to Vancouver, British Columbia, Bowker had a brainstorm: he could resurrect his Italian coffee experience by roasting his own beans. Enlisting his pals Jerry Baldwin and Zev Siegl, the trio opened their own coffee roastery in 1971 on the corner of Western and Virginia called Starbucks Coffee, Tea & Spices. (Sorry, tourists, but the Pike Place Market Starbucks you line up in front of thinking it's the first Starbucks was actually the second shop and didn't open until 1977.) The company was named after Mister Starbucks, the coffee-loving first mate aboard the *Pequod* (according to the film version of the novel *Moby-Dick*), who reported to Captain

Ahab during his quest to find Moby-Dick. The first shop sold batch-roasted coffee beans of various origins, spices, and teas. Their original "Full City" roast distinguished Starbucks' coffee from mass-market brands and quickly earned fans.

Over the next decade-plus, the trio opened six more Starbucks stores in Seattle. Selling individually prepared coffee drinks was not part of the business until a store opened at Fourth Avenue and Spring Street in downtown Seattle. Then it was the vision and instigation of Howard Schultz, who joined Starbucks in 1982 as its marketing leader, and who gained a controlling interest in 1987, that propelled the company into high-speed expansion mode. Starbucks grew rapidly in the 1980s, and seemingly overnight, the company had opened coffeehouses in several major US cities. These Starbucks cafés offered a menu featuring made-to-order lattes, Frappuccinos, a range of espresso-based drinks, and seasonal concoctions such as the Pumpkin Spice Latte. Schultz's concept was to create a community space where people would gravitate, mingle, and feel at home. Coffee was almost an

Starbucks' founding trio of entrepreneurs and coffee connoisseurs, Jerry Baldwin, Zev Siegl, and Gordon Bowker, in 1979, outside their second shop in Pike Place Market. (Note that the first Starbucks store was on the corner of Western and Virginia.) *Courtesy of MOHAI, [Museum of History & Industry Photograph Collection], [2002.46.3067].*

afterthought to this concept, initiating the idea of a "third place," between home and work. The idea created a cultural shift in urban areas, but a complementary one. Even with the move from "coffee shop to gathering place," roasted beans—Starbucks Pike Place Roast and seasonal Christmas blends, for example—are still sold in stores. Most stores also offer the option of grinding the beans "to go" on the spot.

In the 1990s, Starbucks took off. Opening on practically every corner of practically every city, airport, and train station in the United States, Starbucks made premium-quality coffee and espresso-based drinks mainstream. Coffee remained the flagship brew, but, in pursuit of new concepts, Starbucks expanded into the tea arena by purchasing Tazo and Teavana in 2012 (in 2018, Starbucks shut down all Teavana stores) and, also in 2012, added more upscale choices to bakery offerings by acquiring La Boulange, a California-based chain serving French-style pastries (all the bakery's retail outlets were closed in 2015). In 2011, Starbucks expanded its drink menu by acquiring Evolution Fresh, a brand offering fresh juices and smoothies. Evolution Fresh subsequently opened four stores between the Seattle area and San Francisco but closed all stores by 2017. Tazo and Teavana teas, plus ready-to-drink Evolution Fresh juices, continue to be produced and sold in grocery stores as well as Starbucks stores.

Reinventing itself and growing globally under the leadership of Howard Schultz, the company went public in 1992 and, in 2017, operated 25,085 stores worldwide in seventy countries. In a recent new direction, the first Reserve Roastery and Tasting Room opened in Seattle in 2014 with the purpose of presenting limited-supply, super-premium Reserve coffees. Prepared using unconventional methods, such as siphon brewing, the concept aims to take sophisticated coffee drinkers to the next level. Since 2016, Reserve coffee "bars" have opened in one thousand Starbucks cafés. Although Howard Schultz left his CEO position in spring 2017, turning the leadership of the company over to Kevin Johnson, he remains executive chairman, focused on developing Starbucks' premium businesses.

NEIGHBORHOOD COFFEE CULTURE

Starbucks may have grabbed the main stage spotlight with its national expansion, but throughout Seattle in the 1980s and into the 1990s, independent coffeehouses opened in every neighborhood. All had the mission—and passion—of sharing high quality, handcrafted coffees with their customers to raise taste levels and awareness of what outstanding coffee could really taste like.

In this mix, and tagged as the city's first espresso bar, Café Allegro opened in 1975 in the University District. Its founder, Dave Olsen, seized an opportunity to roast his own coffee beans and share the results with customers in a relaxed setting.

Olsen went on to become the head buyer and master roaster at Starbucks, selling the café in 1990 to Chris Peterson.

Overall, it didn't take long for independent artisanal roasters who were buying coffee directly from growers to establish Seattle as a mecca for single-origin, small-batch, fair-trade roasteries. It's a reputation still percolating in the city today. Among the first, Vivace Roasterie, founded by David Schomer and Geneva Sullican, opened in 1988, focusing exclusively on espresso-based beverages. Caffè Appassionato, opened in 1991 in the Magnolia neighborhood bordering Fishermen's Terminal, is noted for bold, full-flavored roasts sold and served in its spacious, comfortable café. Anyone can walk to the warehouse window to see roasters in action.

Tully's Coffee, namesake of founder Tom Tully O'Keefe, opened in 1992 and is still operating with its roastery in the old Rainier Brewery building and specializing in retail and wholesale accounts. Lighthouse Roasters, established in 1993 by owner-manager Ed Leebrick, was also acclaimed for its small-batch, artisanal roastings. Café Vita began roasting coffee in 1995 in its shop in the Lower Queen Anne neighborhood; over the years, it has expanded to eleven cafés in the Pacific Northwest, New York, and Los Angeles. Back on home turf, Jeff Babcock opened Zoka Coffee Roasting Company in 1997, tucked inside his Greenlake neighborhood coffee shop. Along with a thriving coffee-roasting business based on direct relationships with farmers, he established two additional cafés in Seattle, plus another in Kirkland. Victrola Coffee opened in 2000 in a small café on Capitol Hill, expanding in 2003 to add its own roasting facility. Finding success, today the company dark roasts and sells small batches of beans online and from three Capitol Hill shops.

Caffè Umbria adds more flavor to Seattle's coffee universe. It launched in Georgetown in 2002 as a wholesale coffee roaster under the ownership and roasting skills of Emanuele Bizzarri with partners Jesse Sweeney and Pasquale Madeddu. Their Northern Italian–style roasting method and elegant, old-school-style café in Pioneer Square set a high standard for Seattle's coffee scene.

Bizzarri, following in his father and grandfather's footsteps, is naturally endowed with a passion for coffee roasting. Arriving in Seattle from Italy in 1986, his father, Umberto Bizzarri, started Torrefazione Italia, growing the business into a chain of seventeen cafés. The company was purchased by Starbucks in 2003, and then closed in 2005. As a consequence, and to keep the family tradition of artisan coffee roasting alive, Emanuele Bizzarri opened his roastery and aimed for the food service market. Today, Caffè Umbria's signature blends are served in multiple hotels and restaurants across the country, as well as at its own line of cafés.

Along with specialty coffeehouses, funky, mobile drive-by pit stops or walk-up coffee carts such as Monorail Espresso—tagged in 1980 as the city's (and the world's) first coffee cart—were set up to give Seattle residents a choice of places to order their morning brew when they weren't making it at home. Drive-throughs offering lattes and espressos popped up in record numbers, enticing drivers to detour when headed to work.

After this recap of available beverage options, it's easy to understand why no one ever goes thirsty in Seattle. The beverages that became popular here over the decades reflect the city's underlying spirit of camaraderie, creative innovation, sense of adventure and goodwill, and—it must be said—weather. We'll raise a glass to that!

Bibliography

INTRODUCTION

Bruni, Frank. June 10, 2011. "Seattle, a Tasting Menu." *New York Times*. http://www.ny times.com/2011/06/12/travel/eating-in-and-around-seattle.html.

CHAPTER 1: THE MATERIAL RESOURCES

Alden, Peter, and Dennis Pulson, eds. 1998. *National Audubon Society Field Guide to the Pacific Northwest*. New York: Knopf.

Benedict, Audrey DeLella, and Joseph K. Gaydos. 2015. *The Salish Sea: Jewel of the Pacific Northwest*. Seattle: Sasquatch Books.

Brewer, Karen Gaudette. 2014. *Seafood Lover's Pacific Northwest: Restaurants, Markets, Recipes & Traditions*. Guilford, CT: Globe Pequot Press.

Brown, Michael P., and Richard L. Morrill. 2011. *Seattle Geographies*. Seattle: University of Washington Press.

Casey, Kathy, ed. 1993. *Pacific Northwest: The Beautiful Cookbook*. San Francisco: Collins Publishers.

Cervenka, Tom. n.d. "Wild Edible Plants of the Pacific Northwest." *Northern Bushcraft*. Accessed March 8, 2017. http://northernbushcraft.com/plants/index.htm.

Clement, Bethany Jean. July 8, 2015. "The Pacific Northwest's Better (and Native) Blackberry." *Seattle Times*. https://www.seattletimes.com/life/food-drink/the-pacific-northwests-better-and-native-blackberry/.

Cocoran, Penelope. February 13, 2003. "Northwest Oysters." *Seattle Post-Intelligencer.* http://www.seattlepi.com/news/article/Northwest-oysters-1107446.php.

Egan, Timothy. 2011. *The Good Rain: Across Time & Terrain in the Pacific Northwest.* New York: Knopf Doubleday.

Encyclopaedia Britannica Online. s.v. "Pangea." Accessed June 10, 2016. https://www.britannica.com/place/Pangea.

Grinell, Max. March 7, 2016. "Seven Monumental Moments in Seattle." *Seattle Times.*

Hinton, Marc. 2013. Pacific Northwest Cuisine: Mastodons to Molecular Gastronomy. Charleston, SC: History Press.

Jacobsen, Rowan. 2010. *American Terroir: Savoring the Flavors of Our Woods, Waters, and Fields.* New York: Bloomsbury USA.

Kruckeberg, Arthur R. 1991. *The Natural History of Puget Sound Country.* Seattle: University of Washington Press.

Laskin, David. 1997. *Rains All the Time: A Connoisseur's History of Weather in the Pacific Northwest.* Seattle: Sasquatch Books.

Nijhuis, Michelle. August 27, 2014. "World's Largest Dam Removal Unleashes U.S. River after Century of Electric Production." *National Geographic News.* http://news.nationalgeographic.com/news/2014/08/140826-elwha-river-dam-removal-salmon-science-olympic/.

Nims, Cynthia. 2016. *Crab: 50 Recipes with the Fresh Taste of the Sea from the Pacific, Atlantic & Gulf Coasts.* Seattle: Sasquatch Books.

———. 2016. *Oysters: Recipes That Bring Home a Taste of the Sea.* Seattle: Sasquatch Books.

NOAA Fisheries. May 26, 2016. "Chinook Salmon (Oncorhynchus Tshawytscha)." http://www.nmfs.noaa.gov/pr/species/fish/chinook-salmon.html#habitat.

North Pacific Anadromous Fish Commission. n.d. "Pacific Salmon Species." http://www.npafc.org/new/science_species.html.

O'Connell, Libby. 2014. *The American Plate: A Culinary History in 100 Bites.* Naperville, IL: Sourcebooks.

Slater Museum of Natural History, University of Puget Sound. n.d. "Pacific Herring." Accessed March 7, 2017. https://www.pugetsound.edu/academics/academic-resources/slater-museum/exhibits/marine-panel/pacific-herring/.

Tucker, David S. 2015. *Geology Underfoot in Western Washington.* Missoula, MT: Mountain Press.

Vermillion, Allecia. March 2016. "The Five Oysters You Meet in Washington." *Seattle Met.* https://www.seattlemet.com/articles/2016/3/1/the-five-oysters-you-meet-in-washington.

Washington Department of Fish & Wildlife, Fishing & Shellfishing. n.d. "Clams." http://wdfw.wa.gov/fishing/shellfish/clams/.

———. n.d. "Crab." http://wdfw.wa.gov/fishing/shellfish/crab/.

———. n.d. "Geoduck Clams." http://wdfw.wa.gov/fishing/shellfish/geoduck/.

———. n.d. "Oysters." http://wdfw.wa.gov/fishing/shellfish/oysters/.

———. n.d. "Razor Clams." http://wdfw.wa.gov/fishing/shellfish/razorclams/.

Williams, David B. 2015. *Too High & Too Steep: Reshaping Seattle's Topography.* Seattle: University of Washington Press.

Woody, Elizabeth, Edward C. Wolf, and Seth Zuckerman, eds. 1999. *Salmon Nation: People and Fish at the Edge.* Portland, OR: Ecotrust.

CHAPTER 2: THE INDIGENOUS PEOPLE OF THE PACIFIC NORTHWEST

Bohan, Heidi. 2009. *The People of Cascadia: Pacific Northwest Native American History.* Seattle: King County / 4Culture (Special Projects Grant).

Burke Museum of Natural History and Culture. Archeology Division. January 28 to June 10, 2012. "Salish Bounty: Traditional Native American Foods of Puget Sound." Burke Museum of Natural History and Culture. Archeology Division.

de la Harpe, Jackleen. 2012. "Salish Bounty: Tulalip Tribes Host Traveling Food History Exhibit to Illustrate Its Correlation to Indian Health." *Indian Country Today.* November 23. https://indiancountrymedianetwork.com/culture/health-wellness/salish-bounty -tulalip-tribes-host-traveling-food-history-exhibit-to-illustrate-its-correlation-to-indian -health/.

Deloria, Vine, Jr. 1977. *Indians of the Pacific Northwest: From the Coming of the White Man to the Present Day.* New York: Doubleday.

Kelly, Leslie. November 25, 2008. "On Dining: Casino's Blackfish Goes Native." *Seattle Post-Intelligencer.* http://www.seattlepi.com/lifestyle/food/article/On-Dining-Casino-s -Blackfish-goes-native-1292663.php.

Krohn, Elise, and Valerie Segrest. 2010. *Feeding the People, Feeding the Spirit: Revitalizing Northwest Coastal Indian Food Culture.* Seattle: Chatwin Books.

Liptak, Karen. 1991. *Indians of the Pacific Northwest.* First Americans Series. New York: Facts on File.

MacKinnon, J. B. n.d. "The Salvation Fish." Maptia.com. https://maptia.com/jbmackinnon /stories/the-salvation-fish.

Northwest Indian Fisheries Commission. n.d. "Northwest Indian Fisheries Commission." http://nwifc.org/about-us/.

Ott, Jennifer. March 28, 2011. "Northwest Indian Fisheries Commission." *HistoryLink,* Essay 9786. http://www.historylink.org/File/9786.

Ryser, Rudolph C., and Leslie Korn. March 2007. "A Salish Feast: Ancient Roots and Modern Applications." *Cultural Survival Quarterly Magazine.* https://www.cultural survival.org/publications/cultural-survival-quarterly/salish-feast-ancient-roots-and-modern -applications.

Smith, Andrew, ed. 2004. "Pacific Northwest Regional Cookery." In *Oxford Encyclopedia of Food and Drink in America.* New York: Oxford University Press.

Thrush, Coll. 2007. *Native Seattle: Histories from the Crossing-Over Place.* Seattle: University of Washington Press.

Watson, Kenneth Greg. 1999. "Native Americans of Puget Sound: A Brief History of the First People and Their Cultures." *HistoryLink*, Essay 1506. http://www.historylink.org /File/1506.

White, Sid, and S. E. Solberg, eds. 1989. *Peoples of Washington: Perspectives on Cultural Diversity*. Pullman: Washington State University Press.

Wolf, Edward C., and Seth Zuckerman, eds. 1999. *Salmon Nation: People and Fish at the Edge*. Portland, OR: Ecotrust.

Wright, Mary, ed. 2002. *More Voices, New Stories: King County, Washington's First 150 Years*. Seattle: Pacific Northwest Historians Guild.

CHAPTER 3: EARLY HISTORY

Anderson, Ross, and Sara Jean Green. May 27, 2001. "150 Years Seattle By and By: A Culture Slips Away." *Seattle Times*. http://old.seattletimes.com/news/local/seattle_history /articles/story1.html.

Bagley, Clarence B. 1916. *History of King County, Washington: From the Earliest Settlement to the Present Time*, vol. 1. Chicago: The S. J. Clarke Publishing Company. https:// archive.org/stream/historyofseattle01bagl/historyofseattle01bagl_djvu.txt.

Berner, Richard C., and Paul Dorpat. 1991. *Seattle 1900–1920: From Boomtown, Urban Turbulence, to Restoration*. Philadelphia: Charles Press. http://edge-archive.com/books /seattle_1900-1920.pdf.

Calbrick, John. 2014. "Yesler, Henry L. (1810?–1892)." *HistoryLink*, Essay 286. http:// www.historylink.org/File/286.

Denny, Arthur Armstrong, and Alice Harrington, ed. 1908 [1889]. *Pioneer Days on Puget Sound*. Seattle: Alice Harrington Co. https://archive.org/details/pioneerdaysonpug00denn.

Denny, Emily Inez. 1909. *Blazing the Way; Or, True Stories, Songs and Sketches of Puget Sound and Other Pioneers*. Seattle: Rainier Printing Company. http://archive.org/details /blazingwayortru00denngoog.

Dougherty, Phil. 2009. "Alaska-Yukon-Pacific Exposition (1909): Chinese Village." *History Link*, Essay 8964. http://www.historylink.org/File/8964.

Flood, Chuck. 2017. *Lost Restaurants of Seattle*. Charleston, SC: American Palate, a division of the History Press.

Fricken, Robert E., and Charles P. LeWarne. 1988. *Washington: A Centennial History*. Seattle: University of Washington Press.

Grant, James Frederic, ed. 1891. *History of Seattle, Washington*. New York: American Publishing and Engraving Company. https://archive.org/details/historyseattlew00grangoog.

Horrocks, Hattie Graham. n.d. *Restaurants of Seattle, 1853–1960*. Unpublished manuscript, Seattle Public Library Special Collections, http://cdm16118.contentdm.oclc.org/cdm/ref /collection/p15015coll6/id/2028.

Ketcherside, Rob. 2013. *Lost Seattle*. London: Pavilion Books.

Kruckenberg, Arthur. 1991. *The Natural History of Puget Sound Country*. Seattle: University of Washington Press.

Lange, Greg. n.d. "Charles Terry Opens First Store in Future King County No Later Than November 28, 1851." *HistoryLink*, Essay 5395. http://historylink.org/File/5395.

Lanier, Clint, and Derek Hembree. 2013. *Bucket List Bars: Historic Saloons, Pubs and Dives of America*. Austin, TX: Emerald Book Company.

Lee, Hilde Gabriel. 1992. *Taste of the States: A Food History of America*. Charlottesville, VA: Howell Press.

Morse, Kathryn. n.d. *The Klondike Gold Rush*. Center for the Study of the Pacific Northwest. University of Washington Department of History. http://www.washington.edu/uwired/out reach/cspn/Website/Classroom Materials/Curriculum Packets/Klondike/Klondike Main .html.

Mumford, Ester Hall. 1980. *Seattle's Black Victorians, 1852–1901*. Seattle: Ananse Press.

Nash, Linda. January 27, 2016. *Putting People in Their Place: Seattle's Environmental History*. Associate Professor, Director, Center for the Study of the Pacific Northwest. University of Washington lecture.

National Park Service. n.d. *Klondike Gold Rush—Seattle Unit*. https://www.nps.gov/klse /learn/historyculture/index.htm.

Newell, Gordon R. 1977. *Westward to Alki: The Story of David and Louisa Denny*. Seattle: Superior Publishing Company.

Occidental Hotel. 1888? Occidental Hotel Menu, Sunday Dec. 16, 1888. University of Washington Libraries Special Collections, MEN017. http://digitalcollections.lib.washington .edu/cdm/ref/collection/menus/id/441.

Sale, Roger. 1976. *Seattle, Past to Present: An Interpretation of the History of the Foremost City in the Pacific Northwest*. Seattle: University of Washington Press.

Smith, Ursula, and Linda S. Peavy. 1994. *Women in Waiting in the Westward Movement: Life on the Home Frontier*. Norman: University of Oklahoma Press.

Speidel, William. 1967. *Sons of the Profits: Or, There's No Business Like Grow Business: The Seattle Story, 1851–1901*. Seattle: Nettle Creek.

Stein, Alan, Paula Becker, and Jennifer Ott. 2008. "Alaska-Yukon-Pacific Exposition (1909)— A Tour of Selected Buildings." *HistoryLink*, Essay 8678. http://www.historylink.org/File/8678.

White, Sid, and S. E. Solberg, eds. 1989. *People of Washington: Perspectives on Cultural Diversity*. Pullman: Washington State University Press.

Williams, Jacqueline B. 1996. *The Way We Ate: Pacific Northwest Cooking, 1843–1900*. Pullman: Washington State University Press.

Wright, Mary C., ed. 2002. *More Voices, New Stories: King County, Washington's First 150 Years*. Seattle: Pacific Northwest Historians Guild.

CHAPTER 4: IMMIGRANT AND MIGRATION PATTERNS

Anima, Tina. January 8, 1997. "A Brenner Reopening? Maybe—Famed Bellevue Bakery-Deli Could Be Back in Spring If All Goes Well." *Seattle Times*. http://community.seattle times.nwsource.com/archive/?date=19970108&slug=2517719.

Barrett, Meredith. October 31, 2013. "Byen Bakeri Is Now Open on Nickerson." *Seattle Met*. https://www.seattlemet.com/articles/2013/10/31/byen-bakeri-is-now-open-on-nickerson -october-2013.

Belle, Rachel. June 25, 2015. "'A Taste of Home' Tells the Story of History, Food in Seattle's Chinatown" (audio recording). *Ron and Don Show*. KIRO Radio. Transcript and podcast audio, 3:07. http://mynorthwest.com/80398/a-taste-of-home-tells-the-story-of -history-food-in-seattles-chinatown/.

Bhatt, Amy, and Nalini Iyer. 2013. *Roots & Reflections: South Asians in the Pacific Northwest*. Seattle: University of Washington Press.

Bloom, Leora Y. January 12, 2016. "One Family Has Been Making Noodles at Tsue Chong for Nearly 100 Years." *Seattle Times*. http://www.seattletimes.com/pacific-nw-magazine /one-family-has-been-making-noodles-at-tsue-chong-for-nearly-100-years/.

Bradford, Harry. January 14, 2015. "Here Is the Most Disproportionately Popular Cuisine in Each State." *Huffington Post*. http://www.huffingtonpost.com/2015/01/14/most-popular -cuisine-state_n_6457252.html.

Caldbick, John. n.d. "1910 Census: The 13th Federal Census Shows Washington's Population Growing at Many Times the National Average; Every County but One Increases Population; Trend toward Urban Living Is Apparent." *HistoryLink*, Essay 9444. http:// www.historylink.org/File/9444.

Chan, Maxine. Personal interview with Deborah Ashin, October 2016.

Chin, Doug. 2001. *Seattle's International District: The Making of a Pan-Asian American Community*. Seattle: International Examiner Press.

Clement, Bethany Jean. July 13, 2016. "Stop Saying 'Food Porn': 9 Seattle Chefs Share Their Most-Hated Food Terms." *Seattle Times*. http://www.seattletimes.com/life/food-drink /stop-saying-food-porn-9-seattle-chefs-share-their-most-hated-food-terms/.

Cordova, Dorothy Laigo. 2009. *Filipinos in Puget Sound*. Charleston, SC: Arcadia.

Coughlin, Jovina. August 30, 2013. "Seattle's Italian Community." *Jovina Cooks*. https:// jovinacooksitalian.com/2013/08/30/seattles-italian-community/.

Damm, Jen, Annette Damm, and Stig Thornsohn, eds. 1986. *The Dream of America*. Højbjerg, Denmark: Moesgaard.

Diaz, Ed. 2002. "Reexamining the Past: A Different Perspective of Black Strikebreakers in King County's Coal Mining Industry." *More Voices, New Stories: King County, Washington's First 150 Years*. Edited by Mary C. Wright. Seattle: Pacific Northwest Historians Guild.

Dietrich, Heidi. December 11, 2005. "The Road from Cuautla: Remote Mexican Town Spawns 300 Washington Restaurants, and Paves a Path to Riches." *Puget Sound Business Journal*. http://www.bizjournals.com/seattle/stories/2005/12/12/story1.html.

fat pig in the market. January 17, 2014. "Mon Hei Chinese Bakery: Come Back to the ID." *Fat Pig in the Market Blog*. http://fatpiginthemarket.com/wordpress/mon-hei-bakery/.

Ferguson, Caroline. February 10, 2015. "A Place at the Table Opens at MOHAI." *Seattle Met*. https://www.seattlemet.com/articles/2015/2/10/a-place-at-the-table-is-now-open-at -mohai-february-2015.

Festa Italiana. n.d. "The Seattle Italian Story." Accessed April 8, 2017. https://www.festa seattle.com/seattle_italian_story.htm.

Fisher, Robert S. 2002. "Mirror of Taste: The Restaurant as a Reflection of the Changing Appetites of Seattle." In *More Voices, New Stories: King County, Washington's First 150 Years*. Edited by Mary C. Wright. Seattle: Pacific Northwest Historians Guild.

Garbes, Angela. April 1, 2015. "Seattle, It's Time to Retire the Phrase 'Asian Fusion.'" *The Stranger*. http://www.thestranger.com/food-and-drink/feature/2015/04/01/21961988 /seattle-its-time-to-retire-the-phrase-asian-fusion.

———. July 15, 2015. "The Long, Fascinating Road from Successful Pop-Up to Kraken Congee." *The Stranger*. http://www.thestranger.com/food-and-drink/feature /2015/07/15/22546194/the-long-fascinating-road-from-successful-pop-up-to-kraken -congee.

———. October 13, 2015. "Five of Seattle's Black Culinary Leaders Talk about Their Food, Their City, and Their Lives." *The Stranger*. http://www.thestranger.com /food-and-drink/feature/2015/10/14/23001246/five-of-seattles-black-culinary-leaders -talk-about-their-food-their-city-and-their-lives.

Gardner, Nancy. March 2, 2016. "A Century of Success at Tsue Chong: It's a Family Affair for the International District Noodle and Fortune Cookie Company." *The Voice, the Newspaper of Neighborhood House*. http://voice.seattlehousing.net/2016/03/02/tsue -chong-co/.

Giudici, Carey. May 31, 2001. "Korean Americans in King County." *HistoryLink*, Essay 3251. Accessed April 6, 2017. http://www.historylink.org/File/3251.

Guzman, Gonzalo. 2006. "Latino History of Washington State." *HistoryLink*, Essay 7901. http://historylink.org/File/7901.

Harris, Taryn. April 24, 2014. "Sephardic Jews in Washington." *HistoryLink*, Essay 10778. http://www.historylink.org/File/10778.

Hill, Megan. May 2016. "Boyos and Bagels." *Jewish in Seattle Magazine*. https://mag.jewish inseattle.org/articles/2016/4/1/boyos-and-bagels.

Hinchliff, Catherine. November 16, 2010. "Ethiopian and Eritrean Communities in Seattle." *HistoryLink*, Essay 9615. http://www.historylink.org/File/9615.

Hinterberger, John. December 18, 1991. "Hinterberger to Go: Some Reflections, Friends, as This Column Inches to a Close." *Seattle Times*. http://community.seattletimes.nwsource .com/archive/?date=19911218&slug=1323781#_ga=2.87417182.710489303.1495314807 -1718479102.1419642505.

Hugo, Kugiya. August 5, 2010. "Southcenter Has a Hit with Filipino, Asian Food." *Crosscut .com*. http://crosscut.com/2010/08/southcenter-has-hit-with-filipino-asian-food/.

Hullett, Alysa. August 22, 2015. "Mexican Town's Fruitful Link with Seattle Area." *Seattle Times*. http://www.seattletimes.com/business/international-trade/food-a-lasting-connection -for-seattle-mexican-town-mexican-towns-fruitful-link-with-seattle-area/.

Jones, Nicholas A. May 2, 2012. "The Asian Population in the United States: Results from the 2010 Census" (PDF). Asian Americans and Pacific Islanders. Social Security Administration. Retrieved November 13, 2014. https://www.ssa.gov/people/aapi/materials /pdfs/2010census-data.pdf.

Kauffman, Jonathan. August 14, 2007. "How Teriyaki Became Seattle's Own Fast-Food Phenomenon." *Seattle Weekly*. http://archive.seattleweekly.com/2007-08-15/food/how-teriyaki-became-seattle-s-own-fast-food-phenomenon/.

Kugiya, Hugo. January 11, 1998. "The Self-Made Man—Corporate America Does Not Have Much Room for Types Like Art Oberto, Candid in a Way That Frightens Most Managers. Then There's the Jerky Mobile." *Seattle Times*, http://community.seattletimes.nwsource.com/archive/?date=19980111&slug=2727969.

Leson, Nancy. June 13, 2007. "Pike Place Market Pioneers: It Was Our Life." *Seattle Times*. http://www.seattletimes.com/seattle-news/special-reports/pike-place-market-pioneers-it-was-our-life/.

Leson, Nancy, and Aaron Spencer. May 6, 2008. "Anybody Know This Guy?" *Seattle Times*. http://www.seattletimes.com/life/food-drink/anybody-know-this-guy/.

Lobos, Ignacio. April 3, 1994. "Life after Lutefisk: How One Mexican Village Spiced Up Seattle." *Seattle Times*. http://community.seattletimes.nwsource.com/archive/?date=19940403&slug=1903497.

Luna, Ruby de. October 22, 2004. "History of Washington through Food: Desegregation Through Food." Seattle: KUOW-FM. http://www2.kuow.org/program.php?id=7937.

McDermott, Kara. September 10, 2016. "Where Seattle's Refugees Come From and Other Things You Should Know." Seattle: KUOW-FM. http://kuow.org/post/where-seattles-refugees-come-and-other-things-you-should-know.

Mejia-Giudici, Cynthia. December 3, 1998. "Filipino Americans in Seattle." *HistoryLink*, Essay 409. http://www.historylink.org/File/409.

———. December 3, 1998. "Filipino Cannery Workers." *HistoryLink*, Essay 411. http://www.historylink.org/File/411.

Micklin, Lee. October 16, 1998. "Seattle Sephardim: Early Beginnings." *HistoryLink*, Essay 864. http://www.historylink.org/File/864.

Migration Policy Institute. "The Integration Outcomes of US Refugees: Success and Challenges." June 2015. https://www.migrationpolicy.org/research/integration-outcomes-us-refugees-successes-and-challenges.

Moskin, Julia. May 27, 2014. "The New Golden Age of Jewish-American Deli Food." *New York Times*. https://www.nytimes.com/2014/05/28/dining/everything-new-is-old-again.html.

Mudede, Charles. August 10, 2011. "Fat, Flavors, Family: Everything Is on the Table at Oriental Mart." *The Stranger*, Food & Drink. http://www.thestranger.com/seattle/fat-flavors-family/Content?oid=9433508.

Nguyen, Nhien T. 2002. "Building a Vietnamese Community from Scratch: The First Fifteen Years in King County." In *More Voices, New Stories: King County, Washington's First 150 Years*. Edited by Mary C. Wright. Seattle: Pacific Northwest Historians Guild.

Old Village Korean Bistro. 2017. "About Us." http://oldvillagekoreanbbq.com/about/.

Ott, Jennifer. November 19, 2010. "Somali Community in Seattle." *HistoryLink*, Essay 9634. http://www.historylink.org/File/9634.

Pho Bac. n.d. "About Pho Bac." Accessed April 7, 2017. http://www.thephobac.com/pb_about/.

Project Feast. n.d. "About Us." Report Submitted to Tolan Congressional Committee on National Defense Migration. Accessed April 8, 2017. http://projectfeast.org/about-us.html.

Quibuyen, Geo, and Chera Amlag. n.d. "About Food & Sh*t." Accessed April 7, 2017. http://www.foodandsh-t.com/about/.

Robinson, Kathryn. November 2008. "The Restaurants That Changed the Way We Eat." *Seattle Met.* https://www.seattlemet.com/articles/2008/12/17/1108-feat-restchange.

Sadis, Stephen. 2001. *The Sephardic Jews and the Pike Place Market.* Sadis & Vaughn: Perpetual Motion Pictures.

Salas, Elizabeth. 2002. "Mexican-American Women Politicians in Seattle." *More Voices, New Stories: King County, Washington's First 150 Years.* Seattle, Washington: Landmarks & Heritage Commission.

———. December 30, 2003. "Mexican American Women in Washington." *HistoryLink*, Essay 5629. http://historylink.org/File/5629.

Sanders, Eli. December 21, 2006. "The Jewish Problem: My Family, My City, My Religion." *The Stranger.* http://www.thestranger.com/seattle/the-jewish-problem /Content?oid=122431.

Scheff, Allison Austin. February 2015. "A Filipino Food Movement Is Rising in Seattle." *Seattle Magazine.* http://seattlemag.com/article/filipino-food-movement-rising-seattle.

Scott, Joseph W., and Solomon Addis Getahun. 2013. *Little Ethiopia of the Pacific Northwest.* Piscataway, NJ: Transaction.

Sherman, Elizabeth. May 15, 2014. "America's Best Delis." *Food & Wine.* http://www .foodandwine.com/slideshows/americas-best-delis.

Sommer, Erika. December 23, 2014. "Seattle Restaurant Program to Address Immigrant, Minority Needs." *Seattle Globalist.* http://www.seattleglobalist.com/2014/12/23/attaining -the-american-dream-is-made-easier-with-the-new-restaurant-success-initiative/31158.

Sprinkle, Nicole. March 4, 2014. "Lahi Pop-Up: Where Filipino Food Finally Gets Its Due." *Seattle Weekly.* http://archive.seattleweekly.com/food/951462-129/lahi-pop-up-where -filipino-food-finally.

———. January 26, 2016. "Discovering a New Cuisine and Community at a Local Somali Restaurant." *Seattle Weekly.* http://archive.seattleweekly.com/food/962797 -129/discovering-a-new-cuisine-and-community.

Stuteville, Sarah. January 16, 2015. "Old-World Jewish Food Gets a New Seattle Spin." *Seattle Globalist.* http://www.seattleglobalist.com/2015/01/16/jewish-ashkenazi-food -revival-gefilte-fish/32310.

———. January 26, 2016. "Discovering a New Cuisine and Community at a Local Somali Restaurant." *Seattle Weekly.* http://archive.seattleweekly.com/food/962797-129/discovering -a-new-cuisine-and-community.

Taylor, Quintard. 1994. *The Foraging of a Black Community: Seattle's Central District from 1870 through the Civil Rights Era.* Seattle: University of Washington Press.

———. March 29, 2016. "A History of Blacks in Seattle." Lecture: Museum of History and Industry.

Tomky, Naomi. May 31, 2015. "The Last Jews of Pike Place." *The Forward.* http://forward .com/culture/longform/308592/the-last-jews-of-pike-place/.

Tsue Chong Company. n.d. "Tsue Chong Company History." *Tsue Chong Company.* Accessed April 6, 2017. http://tsuechong.com/about-us/about-tsue-chong.

Turnbull, Lornet. February 17, 2010. "Seattle Fortune Cookies Hold Census Message." *Seattle Times.* http://www.seattletimes.com/seattle-news/seattle-fortune-cookies-hold -census-message/.

United States Census Bureau. n.d. "Thirteenth Census of the United States: 1910." Vol. 42–46 (Supplement of Washington). http://www2.census.gov/prod2/decennial /documents/41033935v42-46ch6.pdf.

Va'ad HaRabanim of Greater Seattle. n.d. "Seattle Va'ad." Accessed April 8, 2017. http:// seattlevaad.org/.

Veirs, Kristina, ed. 1982. *Nordic Heritage Northwest.* Seattle: Writing Works.

Vermillion, Allecia. February 2016. "The Best New Asian Restaurants in Seattle." *Seattle Met.* https://www.seattlemet.com/articles/2016/1/29/best-asian-restaurants.

Warren, Joseph. January 14, 2013. "Seattle-Style Teriyaki." *Inquisitive Eater Blog.* http:// inquisitiveeater.com/2013/01/14/seattle-style-teriyaki/.

Washington State Jewish Historical Society. 2011. *Yesterday's Mavens, Today's Foodies: Traditions in Northwest Jewish Kitchens.* Seattle: Peanut Butter Publishing.

Wayne, Julia. September 2014. "The Best Korean Restaurants in Seattle." *Seattle Magazine.* http://www.seattlemag.com/article/best-korean-restaurants-seattle.

White, Sid, and S. E. Solberg, eds. 1989. *Peoples of Washington: Perspectives on Cultural Diversity.* Pullman: Washington State University Press.

Woodward, Mikala. 2003. *The Rainier Valley Food Stories Cookbook: A Culinary History of the Rainier Valley Going Back 100 Years with Recipes and Stories from Our Multicultural Community.* Seattle: Rainier Valley Historical Society.

Wright, Mary C., ed. 2002. *More Voices, New Stories: King County, Washington's First 150 Years.* Seattle: Pacific Northwest Historians Guild.

Yadegaran, Jessica. October 2015. "Seattle's Surge in Soul Food Restaurants." *Seattle Magazine.* http://www.seattlemag.com/article/seattles-surge-soul-food-restaurants.

CHAPTER 5: GROWING AND SHARING THE BOUNTY

Bloom, Leora. 2012. *Washington Food Artisans: Farm Stories and Chef Recipes.* Seattle: Sasquatch Books.

Cho, Janet H. August 7, 2014. "J. M. Smucker Buys Sahale Snacks Brand Nut and Fruit Mixes of Seattle." Cleveland.com. http://www.cleveland.com/business/index .ssf/2014/08/jm_smucker_buys_sahale_snacks.html.

Clifton, Denise. October 2, 2012. "Market's Three Girls Bakery 100 Years Old." *Seattle Times.* http://www.seattletimes.com/life/food-drink/markets-three-girls-bakery -100-years-old/.

Dammeier, Kurt Beecher, and Laura Holmes Haddad. 2009. *Pure Flavor: 125 Fresh All-American Recipes from the Pacific Northwest.* New York: Clarkson Potter.

Decoster, Dotty. September 7, 2009. "A Piggly Wiggly History of Chain Stores on 15th Ave." *Capitol Hill Seattle Blog*. http://www.capitolhillseattle.com/2009/09/a-piggly -wiggly-history-of-chain-stores-on-15th-ave/.

Dietrich, William. June 3, 2007. "A Century at the Pike Place Market." *Seattle Times*. http:// www.seattletimes.com/seattle-news/special-reports/a-century-at-the-pike-place-market/.

Etherington, Darrell. March 28, 2017. "Amazon Debuts AmazonFresh Pickup, Drive-up Groceries Delivered to Your Trunk." TechCrunch.com. https://techcrunch.com/2017/03/28 /amazon-debuts-amazonfresh-pickup-drive-up-groceries-delivered-to-your-trunk/.

Frey, Christine. April 30, 2003. "Gourmet Thriftways Change Name to Metropolitan Market." SeattlePI.com. http://www.seattlepi.com/business/article/Gourmet-Thriftways -change-name-to-Metropolitan-1113643.php.

Gallen-Kimmel, Cornelia, and Cordula Drossel-Brown. 2015. *Seattle Chocolatiers*. Charleston, SC: Arcadia.

Gardener, James Ross. May 20, 2011. "The Day Pike Place Market Almost Died (Again)." *Seattle Met*. https://www.seattlemet.com/articles/2011/5/20/pike-place-market-history -june-2011.

Godden, Jean. July 10, 2017. "This City Has a Soul." WestsideSeattle.com. https://www .westsideseattle.com/2017/07/10/city-has-soul.

Gonzalez, Angel. July 8, 2015. "PCC Natural Markets to Open Bothell Store in 2016." *Seattle Times*. http://www.seattletimes.com/business/retail/pcc-natural-markets-to-open -bothell-store-in-2016/.

Guzman, Monica. August 10, 2009. "Why Is a Seattle Community Garden Called a 'P-Patch'?" SeattlePI.com. http://blog.seattlepi.com/thebigblog/2009/08/10/why-is-a-seattle -community-garden-called-a-p-patch/.

Hadley, Jan. November 5, 2016. "Remembering Queen Anne's Neighborhood Grocery Stores: S&M Market." Queen Anne Historical Society. http://qahistory.org/remembering -queen-annes-neighborhood-grocery-stores-sm-market/.

———. January 5, 2017. "Remembering Queen Anne's Neighborhood Grocery Stores." Queen Anne Historical Society. http://qahistory.org/grocer05/.

Harris, Craig. August 31, 2006. "Changes on the Way at this Larry's." SeattlePI.com. http:// www.seattlepi.com/business/article/Changes-on-the-way-at-this-Larry-s-1213299.php.

Hinton, Marc, and Pamela Hinton, eds. 2013. *A History of Pacific Northwest Cuisine, Mastodons to Molecular Gastronomy*. Charleston, SC: American Palate, a division of the History Press.

Holden, Dominic. July 22, 2010. "Fifty Bucks in Little Saigon: The Amazing Stuff You Can Afford at Your New Favorite Grocery Store." *The Stranger*. http://www.thestranger.com /seattle/fifty-bucks-in-little-saigon/Content?oid=4497395.

Holden, Ronald. 2014. *Homegrown Seattle: 101 True Tales of Local Food & Drink*. Seattle: Ronald Holden.

———. 2016. *Forking Seattle: Tales of Local Food and Drink, from Farm to Table to Landfill*. Seattle: Ronald Holden.

Hucka, Judy. n.d. "Part 1: 1973–1983, Picardo, Passion and People: 30 Years of P-Patching." Seattle.gov. https://www.seattle.gov/neighborhoods/programs-and-services/p -patch-community-gardening/about-the-p-patch-program/history.

Humphrey, Clark. 2006. *Vanishing Seattle*. Charleston, SC: Arcadia.

Kauffman, Jonathan. February 12, 2007. "Honoring Jon Rowley." *Seattle Weekly.* http:// archive.seattleweekly.com/2006-10-18/food/honoring-jon-rowley.

Ketcherside, Rob. July 11, 2014. "Groceteria—A Tradewell Grocery Story." ba-kground .com. http://ba-kground.com/seattle-groceteria-tradewell-pt-3/.

———. September 25, 2014. "Anderson, United and Mutual Markets—A Tradewell Story." ba-kground.com. http://ba-kground.com/anderson-mutual-markets-tradewell -story-part-6/.

———. October 15, 2014. "Eba's Cut Rate Markets—A Tradewell Story." ba-kground .com. http://ba-kground.com/ebas-cut-rate-markets-tradewell-story-part-7/.

Lacitis, Eric. June 26, 2017. "Why the Pike Place Market Will Always Have a Place in Our Hearts." *Seattle Times.* http://www.seattletimes.com/seattle-news/why-pike-place -market-will-always-have-a-place-in-our-hearts/.

Lewis, Peter. March 15, 2008. "Jon Rowley Promotes the Tastes We Come to Crave." *Seattle Times.* http://www.seattletimes.com/pacific-nw-magazine/jon-rowley-promotes -the-tastes-we-come-to-crave/.

MacIntosh, Heather. 1999. "Victor Steinbrueck: Life and Ideas." *HistoryLink*, Essay 2126. http://www.historylink.org/File/2126.

Miller, Margaret. January 20, 1993. "Refugees Farm Project Gets Surprise Backing." *Seattle Times.* http://community.seattletimes.nwsource.com/archive/?date=19930120&s lug=1680983.

Musick, Mark. February 12, 2008. "The History of the Tilth Movement." Tilth Alliance. http://www.seattletilth.org/about/abriefhistoryoftilth.

Oldham, Pat. 2012. "Seattle's Fishermen's Terminal Is Dedicated on January 10, 2014." *HistoryLink*, Essay 10020. http://www.historylink.org/File/10020.

Parr, Tami. 2013. *Pacific Northwest Cheese: A History*. Corvallis: Oregon State University Press.

Payne, Patti. May 7, 2013. "The Man Behind the Copper River Salmon Frenzy as Season Fast Approaches." *Puget Sound Business Journal.* https://www.bizjournals.com/seattle /blog/2013/05/the-man-behind-copper-river-salmon.html.

Pike Place Market Foundation. September 20, 2016. "The Immigrant Farmer Who Built a Community at the Market." *Seattle Weekly.* http://www.seattleweekly.com/marketplace /the-immigrant-farmer-who-built-a-community-at-the-market/.

Pike Place Market Preservation & Development Authority. 2007. *Pike Place Market: 100 Years*. Seattle: Sasquatch Books.

Reilly, Aoife. May 6, 2015. "What's New at Seattle Farmers Markets This Season." *Seattle Met.* https://www.seattlemet.com/articles/2015/5/6/heres-whats-new-at-the-seattle-farm ers-markets-this-season-may-2015.

Robinson, Kathryn. May 4, 2015. "This Neighborhood Is about to Get a Farmers Market." *Seattle Met.* https://www.seattlemet.com/articles/2015/5/4/this-neighborhood-is-about -to-get-a-farmers-market-april-2015.

Sale, Roger. 1976. *Seattle, Past to Present*. Seattle: University of Washington Press.

Sanders, Jeffrey Craig. 2010. *Seattle & the Roots of Urban Sustainability: Inventing Ecotopia*. Pittsburgh, PA: University of Pittsburgh Press.

Scher, Steve. June 27, 2007. "Waking Up with the Pike Place Market." Crosscut.com. http://crosscut.com/2007/06/waking-up-with-pike-place-market/.

Schmid, Calvin F., and Stanton E. Schmid. 1969. *Growth of Cities and Towns, State of Washington*. Washington State Planning and Community Affairs Agency.

Shorett, Alice, and Murray Morgan. 2007. *Soul of the City: The Pike Place Public Market*. Seattle: Market Foundation in association with the University of Washington Press.

Tu, Janet I. September 17, 2016. "PCC's Challenge to Keep Its Brand Relevant, Yet Retain Its Core Values." *Seattle Times*. http://www.seattletimes.com/business/retail/pccs-challenge-to-keep-its-brand-relevant-yet-retain-its-core-values/.

———. April 5, 2017. "PCC Natural Markets Plans to Open Its 12th Store in Burien in Early 2018." *Seattle Times*. http://www.seattletimes.com/business/retail/pcc-will-expand-to-the-south-with-burien-location/.

———. September 13, 2017. "PCC Rebrands to Emphasize Its Local Roots." *Seattle Times*. http://www.seattletimes.com/business/retail/pcc-rebrands-to-emphasize-its-local-roots/.

Vinh, Tan. November 20, 2005. "Farmers Markets in Winter?" *Seattle Times*. http://www.seattletimes.com/seattle-news/farmers-markets-in-winter/.

Wright, Mary, ed. 2002. *More Voices, New Stories: King County, Washington's First 150 Years*. Seattle: Pacific Northwest Historians Guild.

CHAPTER 6: COOKING AT HOME, THE SEATTLE WAY

Atkinson, Greg. 1999. *Northwest Essentials Cookbook: Cooking with Ingredients That Define a Regional Cuisine*. Seattle: Sasquatch Books.

Becker, Paula. May 2, 2008. "Washington Equal Suffrage Association Publishes *Washington Women's Cook Book* in Seattle in Late 1908." *HistoryLink*, Essay 8552. http://www.historylink.org/File/8552.

———. March 20, 2015. "Seafair Cook Book." *Paula Becker*. http://paulabecker.org/seafair-cook-book/.

Beecher, Catharine Esther. 1846. *Miss Beecher's Domestic Receipt Book*. New York: Harper & Brothers. http://vintagecookbooks.healthyeatingandlifestyle.org/books/1846missbeecher.html.

Berolzheimer, Ruth, ed. 1943. *The Victory Binding of the American Woman's Cook Book, Wartime Edition*. Chicago: Consolidated Book Publishers.

Casey, Kathy, ed. 1993. *Pacific Northwest: The Beautiful Cookbook*. San Francisco: Collins Publishers.

Chou, Hsiao-Ching. August 24, 2005. "Rediscovering Pellegrini: His Seminal Book Set the Table for Foodies." *Seattle Post-Intelligencer*. http://www.webcitation.org/65bu3qR1X?url=http://o.seattlepi.com/food/237681_pelle24.html.

Denn, Rebekah. May 16, 2013. "Venerable City Kitchens Closes Shop." Food & Wine, *Seattle Times*. http://blogs.seattletimes.com/allyoucaneat/2013/05/16/venerable-city-kitchens-closes-shop/.

————. August 28, 2017. "Seattleites Swamp Hands-On Cooking Classes." *Seattle Times.* http://www.seattletimes.com/pacific-nw-magazine/seattleites-swamp-hands-on-cooking-classes/.

Douglas, Tom, Duskie Estes, and Denis Kelly. 2000. *Tom Douglas' Seattle Kitchen: A Food Lover's Cookbook and Guide.* New York: HarperCollins.

Engel, KariLynn. 2013. "Fannie Farmer, the Mother of Level Measurements." *Amazing Women in History: Inspiring Stories of 20 Women the History Books Left Out.* http://www.amazingwomeninhistory.com/fannie-farmer/.

Fexy Media Press Release. July 26, 2015. "Fexy Media Debuts as a Top Lifestyle-Food Media Company on comScore." Cision, PR Newswire. https://www.prnewswire.com/news-releases/fexy-media-debuts-as-a-top-lifestyle-food-media-company-on-comscore-300304090.html.

Geise, Judie. 1978. *The Northwest Kitchen: A Seasonal Cookbook.* B. Wright & Company.

Gordinier, Jeff. June 8, 2015. "Serious Eats and Roadfood Are Sold to Fexy Media." *New York Times.* https://www.nytimes.com/2015/06/02/dining/serious-eats-roadfood-websites-sold-to-fexy-media.html?_r=0.

Harmon Jenkins, Nancy. August 9, 1989. "A Man of the Earth Reaps the Good Life." Home & Garden. *New York Times,* http://www.nytimes.com/1989/08/09/garden/a-man-of-the-earth-reaps-the-good-life.html?pagewanted=all.

Holden, Ronald. 2016. *Forking Seattle: Tales of Local Food and Drink, from Farm to Table to Landfill.* Seattle: Ronald Holden.

————. October 28, 2017. "You've Never Heard of Fexy, Amazon Prime's Newest Food Partner." Food & Agriculture, *Forbes.* https://www.forbes.com/sites/ronaldholden/2017/10/28/youve-never-heard-of-fexy-amazon-primes-newest-food-partner/#621a3e0e5043.

Ingle, Schuyler, and Sharon Kramis. 1988. *Northwest Bounty: The Extraordinary Foods and Wonderful Cooking of the Pacific Northwest.* New York: Simon & Schuster.

Kuglin, Jenny. June 26, 2014. "5 of Seattle's Best Seafood Markets." SeattleRefined.com. http://seattlerefined.com/eat-drink/5-of-seattles-best-seafood-markets.

Myhrvold, Nathan, and Francisco Migiya. 2017. *Modernist Bread: The Art and Science.* Bellevue, WA: Cooking Lab.

Myhrvold, Nathan, Chris Young, and Maxime Biletand. 2011. *Modernist Cuisine: The Art and Science of Cooking.* Bellevue, WA: Cooking Lab.

————. 2012. *Modernist Cuisine at Home.* Bellevue, WA: Cooking Lab.

Pellegrini, Angelo. 1948. *The Unprejudiced Palate: Classic Thoughts on Food and the Good Life.* New York: Macmillan Books.

Reichl, Ruth. April 13, 2010. "Ruth Reichl on Angelo Pellegrini, a Slow-Food Voice in a Fast-Food Nation." *Seattle Weekly.* http://archive.seattleweekly.com/2010-04-14/food/ruth-reichl-on-angelo-pellegrini-a-slow-food-voice-in-a-fast-food-nation/.

Rex-Johnson, Braiden. 1992. *Pike Place Market Cookbook: Recipes, Anecdotes, and Personalities from Seattle's Renowned Public Market.* Seattle: Sasquatch Books.

Schumm, Laura. May 29, 2014. "History Stories: America's Patriotic Victory Gardens." History.com. http://www.history.com/news/hungry-history/americas-patriotic-victory-gardens.

Sokol, Chad. July 16, 2017. "The World of Wheat: Growing Grain in Washington." *Spokesman Review.* http://www.spokesman.com/stories/2017/jul/16/the-world-of-wheat/#/0.

Sundstrom, John. 2012. *Lark: Cooking against the Grain.* Seattle: Community Supported Cookbooks.

Traunfeld, Jerry. 2000. *The Herbfarm Cookbook.* New York: Scribner.

Union Advertising Company. 1911. *The Seattle Brides Cook Book.* Seattle: Union Advertising Company. http://cdm15015.contentdm.oclc.org/cdm/ref/collection/p15015coll6/id/1903.

Vermillion, Allecia, and Kathryn Robinson. July 9, 2015. "The A to Z Food Lover's Guide to Seattle." *Seattle Met.* https://www.seattlemet.com/articles/2015/7/9/the-a-z-food-lover-s-guide-to-seattle.

Wells, Jeff. October 25, 2017. "Amazon Prime Now Partners with Recipe Sites." Food Dive.com. https://www.fooddive.com/news/grocery--amazon-prime-now-partners-with-recipe-sites/508115/.

Williams, Jacqueline B. 1996. *The Way We Ate: Pacific Northwest Cooking, 1843–1900.* Pullman: Washington State University Press.

Women's Guild of St. Mark's Church. 1896. *Clever Cooking.* Seattle: Metropolitan Printing & Binding Company. https://archive.org/details/clevercooking00seat.

Woodward, Mikala, ed. 2003. *The Rainier Valley Food Stories Cookbook: A Culinary History Going Back 100 Years with Recipes and Stories from Our Multicultural Community.* Seattle: Rainier Valley Historical Society.

Yuasa, Mark. September 30, 2015. "Harry Yoshimura, Owner of Mutual Fish Market in Seattle, Has a Tasty Baked Salmon Recipe to Wow Your Guests at the Dining Table." *Seattle Times.* http://www.seattletimes.com/sports/harry-yoshimura-owner-of-mutual-fish-market-in-seattle-has-a-tasty-baked-salmon-recipe-to-wow-your-guests-at-dining-table/.

CHAPTER 7: DINING OUT

Atkinson, Greg. May 2, 2003. "Hooked on Fish: With Fresh Thinking, Ray's Boathouse Sets a Seafood Standard." *Seattle Times.* http://community.seattletimes.nwsource.com/archive/?date=20030502&slug=ptaste04.

Bagley, Clarence. 1916. *History of Seattle.* Vol. 1, Chapter 23, "Seattle's Great Fire." Chicago: S. J. Clarke Publishing Co.

Becker, Paula. November 20, 2010. "Prohibition in Washington State." *HistoryLink*, Essay 9630. http://www.historylink.org/File/9630.

Berger, Knute. February 2012. "Back to the Future: Why Seattle's World's Fair Mattered." *Seattle Magazine.* http://www.seattlemag.com/article/back-future-why-seattles-worlds-fair-mattered.

———. April 12, 2012. "World's Fair Expanded Seattle's Taste for International Food." *Crosscut.* http://crosscut.com/2012/04/worlds-fair-expanded-seattles-taste-for-internatio/.

Boswell, Sharon, and Lorraine McConaghy. June 2, 1996. "Homeward Bound." *Seattle Times*. http://old.seattletimes.com/special/centennial/june/homeward.html.

———. November 3, 1996. "Lights Out, Seattle." *Seattle Times*. http://old.seattletimes.com/special/centennial/november/lights_out.html.

Buerge, David. 1986. *Seattle in the 1880s*. Seattle: Historical Society of Seattle and King County.

Cicero, Providence. January 12, 2017. "Maria Hines Goes Mainstream with Young American Ale House." *Seattle Times*. http://www.seattletimes.com/life/food-drink/maria-hines-goes-mainstream-with-young-american-ale-house/.

Clement, Bethany Jean. October 28, 2015. "How Trove's Rachel Yang Put a More Diverse Seattle on the Culinary Map." *Seattle Times*, Food & Drink. http://www.seattletimes.com/life/food-drink/rachel-yangs-food-is-great-just-dont-call-it-fusion/.

———. November 11, 2015. "On Vashon, Matt Dillon's Happy Pigs, Vocal Sheep and Food Philosophy." *Seattle Times*, Food & Drink.

———. January 12, 2016. "Dick Spady, Co-Founder and Namesake of Dick's Drive-In, Dies at 92." *Seattle Times*. http://www.seattletimes.com/seattle-news/obituaries/dick-spady-co-founder-and-namesake-of-dicks-drive-in-dies-at-91/.

Crowley, Walt. December 15, 2000. "Twin T-Ps Restaurant, Early Roadside Attraction, Opens on March 13, 1937." *HistoryLink*, Essay 2890. http://www.historylink.org/File/2890.

Denn, Rebekah. September 5, 2012. "Pioneering Le Gourmand Chef Has Plenty of Plans." *Seattle Times.* http://www.seattletimes.com/life/food-drink/pioneering-le-gourmand-chef-has-plenty-of-plans/.

———. October 10, 2012. "After 20 Years, 'Chef-Genius' Scott Carsberg Closes His Restaurant." *Seattle Times*, Food & Drink. http://www.seattletimes.com/life/food-drink/after-20-years-chef-genius-scott-carsberg-closes-his-restaurant/.

———. 2016. *Edible City*. Seattle: Museum of History & Industry.

Dorpat, Paul. September 5, 2009. *Seattle Now & Then: All Roads Lead to the Dog House*. https://pauldorpat.com/2009/09/05/seattle-now-then-all-roads-lead-to-the-dog-house/.

———. September 13, 2009. "The Dog House Restaurant Served Comfort on the Edge of Seattle's Aurora Avenue." *Pacific Northwest Magazine* (*Seattle Times*). http://www.seattletimes.com/pacific-nw-magazine/the-dog-house-restaurant-served-comfort-on-the-edge-of-seattles-aurora-avenue/.

———. June 11, 2011. "Dag's Served Seattle Food Fast and Fun." *Pacific Northwest Magazine* (*Seattle Times*). http://www.seattletimes.com/pacific-nw-magazine/dags-served-seattle-food-fast-and-fun/.

———. June 11, 2011. *Seattle Now & Then: Where's the Beef?* https://pauldorpat.com/2011/06/11/seattle-now-then-wheres-the-beef/.

———. February 25, 2012. *Seattle Now & Then: The Jolly Roger on Lake City Way*. https://pauldorpat.com/2012/02/25/seattle-now-then-the-jolly-roger-on-lake-city-way/.

———. May 24, 2013. *Seattle Now & Then: The Four Winds*. https://pauldorpat.com/2013/05/24/seattle-now-then-the-four-winds/.

Drosendahl, Glenn. November 4, 2014. "Chef John Howie to Close Seattle Restaurant." *Puget Sound Business Journal*. http://www.bizjournals.com/seattle/blog/2014/11/chef-john-howie-to-close-seattle-seastar.html.

Duncan, Don. June 23, 1990. "Walter Clark, 93, Longtime Leader of Seattle Restaurant Industry." *Seattle Times*. http://community.seattletimes.nwsource.com/archive/?date=19 900623&slug=1078578.

Eskenazi, Stuart. January 6, 2005. "Don't Call It Frango in Seattle." *Seattle Times*. http:// community.seattletimes.nwsource.com/archive/?date=20050106&slug=frango06m.

Flood, Chuck. 2017. *Lost Restaurants of Seattle*. Charleston, SC: American Palate, a division of the History Press.

Fisher, Robert S. 2002. "Mirror of Taste: the Restaurant as a Reflection of the Changing Appetites of Seattle." *More Voices, New Stories: King County, Washington's First 150 Years*. Edited by Mary C. Wright. Seattle: King County Landmarks & Heritage Commission.

Garbes, Angela. April 1, 2015. "Seattle, It's Time to Retire the Phrase 'Asian Fusion': Chefs Aren't 'Fusing' Anything, They're Just Being Themselves." *The Stranger*. http://www.the stranger.com/food-and-drink/feature/2015/04/01/21961988/seattle-its-time-to-retire-the -phrase-asian-fusion.

———. October 14, 2015. "When Five Restaurateurs Own 40 Restaurants, What Does That Mean for Seattle's Dining Scene?" *The Stranger*. http://www.thestranger.com /food-and-drink/feature/2015/10/14/22981981/when-five-restaurateurs-own-40-restaurants -what-does-that-mean-for-seattles-dining-scene.

Gaudette Brewer, Karen. 2014. *Seafood Lovers Pacific Northwest: Restaurants, Markets, Recipes & Traditions*. Guilford, CT: Globe Pequot.

Godden, Jean. March 16, 1998. "Manca's Next Life: Starbucks." *Seattle Times*. http://com munity.seattletimes.nwsource.com/archive/?date=19980316&slug=2739961.

Gonzales, Angel. February 16, 2017. "Amazon Donates Space, Equipment for Five New FareStart Eateries." *Seattle Times*. http://www.seattletimes.com/business/amazon/amazon -donates-space-equipment-for-five-new-farestart-eateries/.

Griffith, Stephen. February 1, 2013. "Acres of Clams." FolksongIndex.com. http://www .stephengriffith.com/folksongindex/acres-of-clams-2/.

Guanco, Frank. August 1, 2014. "The Evolving Ethan Stowell." *Seattle Refined*. http://seattle refined.com/eat-drink/the-evolving-ethan-stowell.

Hanford, C. H. 1924. *Seattle and Environs, 1852–1924*. Chicago: Pioneer Historical Pub.

Hardy, Quentin. June 11, 2014. "Seattle, the New Center of a Tech Boom." *New York Times*. https://bits.blogs.nytimes.com/2014/06/11/seattle-the-new-center-of-a-tech-boom/?_r=0.

Hill, Megan. August 18, 2016. "John Sundstrom Plans Casual Pizza Spot on Capitol Hill: Southpaw Is Coming This Fall." *Eater Seattle*. https://seattle.eater.com/2016 /8/18/12522164/southpaw-pizza-john-sundstrom-lark.

———. May 12, 2017. "Duke's Chowder House Will Have Sweeping Views at Shilshole Marina—But Not Until 2019." *Eater Seattle*. https://seattle.eater.com/2017/5/12/156305 42/dukes-chowder-house-shilshole-marina-expansion.

Ho, Vanessa. January 22, 2014. "Remember These Seattle Restaurants?" SeattlePI.com. http://blog.seattlepi.com/thebigblog/2014/01/22/remember-these-seattle-restaurants/.

Holden, Ronald. January 29, 2015. "Brasserie Pittsbourg Brought French Food to a Former Soup Kitchen: Remembering Great Restaurants from Seattle's Past." *Eater Seattle*, Power Hour. https://seattle.eater.com/2015/1/29/7947027/brasserie-pittsbourg-brought-french -food-to-a-former-soup-kitchen.

————. January 29, 2015. "Le Tastevin's Splashy, Truffle-Studded Wine Dinners." *Eater Seattle*. https://seattle.eater.com/2015/1/29/7947163/le-tastevins-splashy-truffle-studded -wine-dinners.

————. 2016. *Forking Seattle: Tales of Local Food and Drink, from Farm to Table to Landfill*. Seattle: Ronald Holden.

Hood, Michael. July 26, 2002. "Rosellini, Victor (1915–2003), Restaurateur and Epicure." *HistoryLink*, Essay 3902. http://www.historylink.org/File/3902.

Horrocks, Hattie Graham. n.d. *Restaurants of Seattle, 1853–1960*. Unpublished manuscript, Seattle Public Library Special Collections, http://cdm16118.contentdm.oclc.org/cdm/ref /collection/p15015coll6/id/2028.

Ingle, Schuyler, and Sharon Kramis. 1988. *Northwest Bounty: The Extraordinary Foods and Wonderful Cooking of the Pacific Northwest*. New York: Simon and Schuster.

Int-Hout, Allison. August 24, 2012. "A Year after New City Law, Seattle Food-Truck Indus-try Gaining Speed" (slide show). *Puget Sound Business Journal*. https://www.bizjournals .com/seattle/news/2012/08/24/1-year-after-new-city-law-food-trucks.html.

Jones, Nard. 1972. *Seattle*. Chapter 10, "The Big Fire." Garden City, NY: Doubleday.

Kahn, Howie. August 24, 2012. "At Canlis, Dinner with a Side of Camaraderie." *New York Times, TMagazine*. http://tmagazine.blogs.nytimes.com/2012/08/24/at-canlis-dinner-with -a-side-of-camaraderie/?_r=0.

Kelly, Leslie. May 22, 2008. "The Trick at Dick's Hold the Cheese on a Deluxe Burger." *Seattle Post-Intelligencer*. http://www.seattlepi.com/lifestyle/food/article/The-trick-at -Dick-s-Hold-the-cheese-on-a-deluxe-1274148.php.

Knauf, Ana Sofia. October 21, 2016. "Good News Seattle Foodies: Chefs behind Le Gour-mand to Open New Restaurant on Capitol Hill." *The Stranger*. http://www.thestranger .com/slog/2016/10/21/24644967/good-news-seattle-foodies-chefs-behind-le-gourmand -to-open-new-restaurant-in-capitol-hill.

Knowlton, Andrew. April 27, 2016. "Why Seattle Is One of the Most Exciting Places to Eat in the Country." *Bon Appetit*. http://www.bonappetit.com/restaurants-travel/article /seattle-renee-erickson.

Lanier, Clint, and Derk Hembree. 2013. *Bucket List Bars: Historic Saloons, Pubs & Dives of America*. Austin, TX: Emerald Book Company.

Leson, Nancy. November 17, 2002. "Leson's List: Our Critic Picks Her Personal Best." *Seattle Times*. http://community.seattletimes.nwsource.com/archive/?date=20021117&s lug=pdineout17#_ga=2.187184299.2092809767.1494815420-1718479102.1419642505.

Leson, Nancy, and Monica Soto Ouchi. March 28, 2007. "Buyout Firm Purchases Res-taurants Unlimited." *Seattle Times*. http://www.seattletimes.com/business/buyout-firm -purchases-restaurants-unlimited/.

Lott, Andrea, and Andrea Umbach. 2010. *Dining in Seattle: Past & Present*. Seattle: Peanut Butter Publishing.

Morgan, Murray. 1951. *Skid Road: An Informal Portrait of Seattle*. Seattle and London: University of Washington Press.

Moscrip, Duke, and Bill Ranniger. 2016. *As Wild as It Gets: Duke's Secret Sustainable Seafood Recipes*. New York: Aviva.

Patterson, Lisa. March 16, 2016. "Interview: Duke Moscrip—The Gourmet." *425 Magazine*.

"Red Robin Gourmet Burgers, Inc. History." *Funding Universe.* http://www.fundinguniverse
.com/company-histories/red-robin-gourmet-burgers-inc-history/.

Reichl, Ruth. December 1, 1985. "The Sun Shines on Seattle." *Los Angeles Times.* http://
articles.latimes.com/1985-12-01/entertainment/ca-5403_1_restaurants/2.

Robinson, Kathryn. November 28, 2012. "Tom Douglas vs. Ethan Stowell: Battle of Seattle Restaurant Titans." *Seattle Met*, Eat & Drink. https://www.seattlemet.com/articles
/2012/11/28/tom-douglas-vs-ethan-stowell-december-2012.

Roth, Catherine. 2009. "The Coon Chicken Inn: North Seattle's Beacon of Bigotry." Seattle
Civil Rights & Labor History Project. http://depts.washington.edu/civilr/coon_chicken
.htm.

Saez, Rosin. May 1, 2017. "Canlis Takes Home Its First James Beard Award." *Seattle Met.*
http://tmagazine.blogs.nytimes.com/2012/08/24/at-canlis-dinner-with-a-side-of-camara
derie/?_r=0.

Sale, Roger. 1976. *Seattle, Past to Present: An Interpretation of the History of the Foremost
City in the Pacific Northwest.* Seattle: University of Washington Press.

Scheff, Allison Austin. January 2014. "The Best Oyster Bars and Raw Palaces in Seattle."
Seattle Magazine. http://www.seattlemag.com/article/best-oyster-palaces-and-raw-bars
-seattle.

Scigliano, Eric. March 30, 2016. "Seattle in the '80s: Big Tech and Boomtown Economics
Arrive." *Seattle Weekly.* http://archive.seattleweekly.com/news/963543-129/seattle-in-the
-80s-big-tech.

Searcey, Dionne. March 4, 1999. "Hard-Liquor Sales in Taverns Backed." *Seattle Times.*
http://community.seattletimes.nwsource.com/archive/?date=19990304&slug=2947474.

Shannon, Robin. 2008. *Seattle's Historic Restaurants.* Charleston, SC: Arcadia.

Spector, Robert. 1993. *The Legend of Frango Chocolate.* Kirkland, WA: Documentary
Book Publishers Corporation.

Speidel, William C., Jr. 1955. *You Can't Eat Mount Rainier! The Seattle Guide to Restaurants, Recipes and Food.* Portland, OR: Binfords & Mort, Publishers.

———. 1961. *You Still Can't Eat Mount Rainier!* Seattle: Nettle Creek Publishing.

Stein, Alain J. May 26, 1999. "Igloo—The Lost Landmark of Seattle's Auto-Tecture." *HistoryLink*, Essay 1162. http://www.historylink.org/File/1162.

———. September 23, 2004. "Igloo, Frederick & Nelson's Frozen Dessert (Later Mints)
Frango Is Named on June 1, 1918." *HistoryLink*, Essay 5771. http://www.historylink.org
/File/5771.

Tibbetts, P.E. 1990. *Mr. Restaurant: A Biography of Walter F. Clark.* Seattle: Murray
Publishing.

Turnbull, Lornet. December 22, 2011. "Labuznik Restaurant's Peter Cipra Dies at
68." *Seattle Times*, Food & Drink. https://www.seattletimes.com/seattle-news/labuznik
-restaurants-peter-cipra-dies-at-68/.

Vermillion, Allecia. October 17, 2016. "Bruce and Sara Naftaly Will Open a Restaurant in
Chophouse Row." *Seattle Met.* https://www.seattlemet.com/articles/2016/10/17/bruce-and
-sara-naftaly-will-open-a-restaurant-marmite-in-chophouse-row.

Warren, James. 1989. *The Day Seattle Burned.* Seattle: James Warren. http://www.pstos.org
/instruments/wa/seattle/rhodes.htm.

Werner, Christopher. April 30, 2012. "Food Trucks 2012: The Wheel Reinvented." *Seattle Met*. https://www.seattlemet.com/articles/2012/4/30/food-trucks-the-wheel-reinvented-may-2012.

———. May 2012. "Food Truck City." *Seattle Met*. https://www.seattlemet.com/features/seattles-best-food-trucks-2012.

Wright, Mary, ed. 2002. *More Voices, New Stories: King County, Washington's First 150 Years*. Seattle: Pacific Northwest Historians Guild.

CHAPTER 8: RAISE A GLASS!

Allison, Melissa. March 10, 2008. "Starbucks Co-Founder Talks about Early Days, Launching Redhook and Seattle Weekly, Too." *Seattle Times*. http://www.seattletimes.com/business/starbucks-co-founder-talks-about-early-days-launching-redhook-and-seattle-weekly-too/.

Bagley, Clarence B. 1916. *History of Seattle: From the Earliest Settlement to the Present Time*. Chicago: S. J. Clarke Publishing Company.

———. 2017. *History of Seattle: From the Earliest Settlement to the Present Time, Volume 2*. Classic Reprint Series, Forgotten Books. https://books.google.com/books?id=K4EUA AAAYAAJ&pg=PA625&dq=slorah+brewery&hl=en&ei=l-. HTToTTHsH48QPs6KnO BQ&sa=X&oi=book_result&ct=result&resnum=2&ved=0CDkQ6AEwAQ#v=onepage &q=slorah%20brewery&f=false.

Banel, Felix. April 26, 2017. "Not All Coffee Brands Took the Path of World Domination." MyNorthwest.com. http://mynorthwest.com/613270/seattle-coffee-world-domination/.

Becker, Pamela. November 20, 2010. "Prohibition in Washington State." *HistoryLink*, Essay 9630. http://www.historylink.org/File/9630.

Blecha, Peter. July 7, 2008; updated January 14, 2014. "Wine in Washington." *HistoryLink*, Essay 8658. http://www.historylink.org/File/8658.

———. August 26, 2009. "Rainier Beer—Seattle's Iconic Brewery." *HistoryLink*, Essay 9130. http://historylink.org/File/9130.

Borg, Shannon. October 2010. "Seattle Coffee Guide: Locally Roasted Beans." *Seattle Magazine*. http://www.seattlemag.com/article/seattle-coffee-guide-locally-roasted-beans.

Clark, Norman H. 1988. *The Dry Years: Prohibition & Social Change in Washington*. Revised edition. Seattle: University of Washington Press.

Crowley, Walt. March 31, 1999. "Seattle Neighborhoods: Ballard—Thumbnail History." *HistoryLink*, Essay 983. http://www.historylink.org/File/983.

Denn, Rebekah. 2016. *Edible City*. Seattle: Museum of History and Industry.

Dickerman, Sara. October 2010. "Seattle Coffee Guide: The Evolution of Coffee." *Seattle Magazine*. http://www.seattlemag.com/article/seattle-coffee-guide-evolution-coffee.

Grimm, Lisa. December 2011. "A Brief History of Beer in Seattle." *Serious Eats*. http://drinks.seriouseats.com/2011/12/print/history-of-beer-in-seattle-rainier-georgetown-brewing.html.

Grunbaum, Rami. August 11, 2016. "Seattle's Pioneering Redhook Beer Soon Won't Be Brewed in Woodinville." *Seattle Times.* http://www.seattletimes.com/business/redhook -beer-imported-from-oregon/.

————. May 3, 2017. "Redhook Owner Will Close and Sell Large Woodinville Brewery, Focus on Capitol Hill Brewpub." *Seattle Times.* www.seattletimes.com /business/retail/redhook-owner-will-close-and-sell-large-woodinville-brewery-focus-on -capitol-hill-brewpub/.

Harding, William B. 2017. *Best Seattle Breweries in 2017, by Neighborhood.* Basement Press.com. http://williambharding.com/basement/best-seattle-breweries-2017-by-neighbor hood/.

Hill, Megan. Spring 2017. "Tracking Seattle's Newest Breweries." *Eater Seattle.* https:// seattle.eater.com/maps/new-seattle-breweries-beer.

————. July 12, 2017. "Redhook Brewery Returns to Seattle Roots August 17." *Eater Seattle.* https://seattle.eater.com/2017/7/12/15952970/redhook-brewery-opening-capitol -hill.

Hirsh, Lou. June 15, 2017. "Report: San Diego Tops U.S. Markets for Number of Active Breweries." *San Diego Business Journal.* https://sdbj.com/news/2017/jun/15/report-san -diego-tops-us-markets-number-active-bre/.

Holden, Ronald. 2014. *Home Grown Seattle: 101 True Tales of Local Food & Drink.* Seattle: Ronald Holden.

————. 2016. *Forking Seattle: Tales of Local Food and Drink, from Farm to Table to Landfill.* Seattle: Ronald Holden.

Jones, Kendall. October 2013. "Local Brewery District: Georgetown/SoDo." *Seattle Maga- zine.* http://www.seattlemag.com/article/local-brewery-district-georgetownsodo.

Latson, Jennifer. December 5, 2014. "A Toast to the End of Prohibition." *Time.* http://time .com/3605609/a-toast-to-the-end-of-prohibition/.

Marshall, Colin. May 14, 2015. "The First Starbucks Coffee Shop, Seattle—a History of Cities in 50 Buildings, Day 36." *The Guardian.* https://www.theguardian.com/cities /2015/may/14/the-first-starbucks-coffee-shop-seattle-a-history-of-cities-in-50-buildings -day-36.

Nisbet, Jack, and Claire Nisbet. July 24, 2011. "Hudson's Bay Company." *HistoryLink,* Es- say 9881. http://www.historylink.org/File/9881.

Ouchi, Monica Soto. June 15, 2005. "Starbucks Shutting Its Torrefazione Coffee Bars." *Seattle Times.* http://old.seattletimes.com/html/businesstechnology/2002335093_coffee 14.html.

Rathbun, A. J. December 2011. "Explore Seattle's Distillery Boom." *Seattle Magazine.* http://www.seattlemag.com/article/explore-seattles-distillery-boom.

Rizzo, Michael F. 2016. *Washington Beer: A Heady History of Evergreen State Brewing.* Charleston, SC: American Palate, a division of the History Press.

Roth, Jean. Summer 1997. "Part 1: The Schwabacher Family of Washington State." Jewish Genealogical Society of Washington State. http://www.jgsws.org/schwabacher.php.

Seattle Coffee Scene. n.d. "Seattle's Oldest Coffee Shop: Caffe Allegro: A Little Seattle Coffee History." http://seattlecoffeescene.com/seattles-oldest-coffee-shop-cafe-allegro/.

Seattle Magazine. September 6, 2011. "The History of Beer in Seattle." *Seattle Magazine.* http://www.seattlemag.com/article/history-beer-seattle.

Smith, Ursula, and Linda S. Peavy. 1994. *Women in Waiting in the Westward Movement: Life on the Home Frontier.* Norman: University of Oklahoma Press.

Stream, Kurt. 2012. *Brewing in Seattle.* Charleston, SC: Arcadia.

Tu, Janet. February 24, 2017. "Starbucks Closes Last Two Evolution Fresh Stores." *Seattle Times.* http://www.seattletimes.com/business/starbucks/starbucks-closes-last-two-evolution-fresh-stores/.

———. March 18, 2017. "An Era Ends for Starbucks and Howard Schultz." *Seattle Times.* http://www.seattletimes.com/business/starbucks/an-era-ends-for-starbucks-and-howard-schultz/.

Vinh, Tan. September 18, 2013. "The Exciting Craft Beers at Reuben's Brews in Ballard." *Seattle Times.* http://www.seattletimes.com/entertainment/the-exciting-craft-beers-at-reubenrsquos-brews-in-ballard/.

———. April 29, 2015. "The Boutique Booze Boom in Washington." *Seattle Times.* http://www.seattletimes.com/entertainment/the-boutique-booze-boom-in-washington-3/.

———. May 11, 2016. "Seattle Beer Week 2016: These Are the Best Events on Tap." *Seattle Times.* http://www.seattletimes.com/life/food-drink/seattle-beer-week-2016-these-are-the-best-events-on-tap/.

———. July 13, 2017. "Moët Hennessy buys Woodinville Whiskey Company." *Seattle Times.* http://www.seattletimes.com/life/food-drink/moet-hennessy-buys-woodinville-whiskey-company/.

Vitale, John. n.d. "Walter Clore: Father of Washington Wine." *Washington Tasting Room Magazine.* http://www.washingtontastingroom.com/taste/walter-clore-the-father-of-washington-wine.

Williams, Jacqueline B. 1996. *The Way We Ate: Pacific Northwest Cooking, 1843–1900.* Pullman: Washington State University Press.

Wilma, David. February 10, 2001. "Seattle Neighborhoods: Georgetown—Thumbnail History." *HistoryLink,* Essay 2975. http://historylink.org/File/2975.

Wizenberg, Molly. April 2016. "Coffee's Third Wave (Finally) Washes Ashore in Seattle." *Serious Eats.* http://www.seriouseats.com/2016/04/best-coffee-in-seattle-new-roasters-third-wave.html.

Woodward, Mikala, ed. 2003. *Rainier Valley Food Stories Cookbook: A Culinary History of the Rainier Valley.* Seattle: Rainier Valley Historical Society.

ADDITIONAL RESOURCES

Abala, Ken. 2014. *The Food History Reader: Primary Sources.* London: Bloomsbury Academic.

Clore, Walter J. 1976. *Ten Years of Grape Variety Responses and Wine-Making Trials in Central Washington.* Pullman: Washington State University, College of Agriculture Research Center.

Elias, Megan J. 2017. *Food on the Page: Cookbooks and the American Culture*. Philadelphia: University of Pennsylvania Press.

Fox, Robin. 2014. "Food and Eating: An Anthropological Perspective." Social Issues Research Centre. http://www.sirc.org/publik/food_and_eating_0.html.

Irvine, Ron, Walter J. Clore, and Miriam Bulmer, eds. 1997. *The Wine Project: Washington State's Winemaking History*. Vashon, WA: Sketch Publications.

Lee, Hilde Gabriel. 1992. *Taste of the States: A Food History of America*. Charlottesville, VA: Howell Press.

Mariani, John. 1999. *The Encyclopedia of American Food & Drink*. New York: Lebhar-Friedman Books.

Scheuerman, Richard D., and Alexander C. McGregor. 2013. *Harvest Heritage: Agricultural Origins and Heirloom Crops of the Pacific Northwest*. Pullman: Washington State University Press.

Stewart, Katie. 1972. *The Joy of Eating: A Cook's Tour of History, Illustrated with a Cook's Section of the Great Recipes of Every Era*. Keene, NH: Stemmer House.

Weaver, William Woys. 1989. *America Eats: Forms of Edible Folk Art. Museum of American Folk Art*. New York: Harper & Row.

Index

About the Author

A published author with numerous cookbooks and national and regional articles to her credit, **Judith H. Dern** has pursued word wizardry and all things edible for her career, the outcome of cooking and collecting cookbooks since she was a teenager. Her most recent cookbook is *The Food and Cooking of Scandinavia: Sweden, Norway & Denmark* (2011). She moved to Seattle in 1994 after flying out of its airport on a sunny day when the islands, mountains, and sparkling sea reminded her of Scandinavia, where she had lived for a year. The city turned out to offer multiple delectable food resources, from Pike Place Market and neighborhood farmers' markets to Copper River salmon, plump cherries, and wild blackberries. In her day job, she serves as senior research insights manager at Meredith Corporation, having joined its leading digital site, Allrecipes.com (the world's largest digital food brand), in 2007. She is also on the board of directors for the International Association of Culinary Professionals (IACP) and is a member of Les Dames D'Escoffier.